How Did
I Do That?

A LIFE OF RISK AND REWARD

How Did
I Do That?

BILL DUTCHER

To my lovely and loving granddaughters,
Hanna and Millie

CONTENTS

INTRODUCTION

My *granddaughter Hanna* was an aspiring ballerina at age three. Watching her practice at home one day, I saw her do a graceful pirouette, then exclaim in amazement: "How did I do that?"

That's the same question I have asked myself, looking back, at age seventy-eight, on a life that has felt like a balancing act on a roller coaster. There are lots of books that prescribe a balanced life. This book shows what a balanced life looks like.

Like a mosaic, my book is composed of bits and pieces of memories dating back to the end of World War II. Each memory is associated with some heightened emotion, not just "the thrill of victory and the agony of defeat" experienced in sports and business, but also the love, laughter, joy, and pain shared with friends and family.

My mom once told me that when I was a baby, the Caney River flooded our hometown of Bartlesville, Oklahoma. When the high waters reached our home, she had to hand me off from our front porch to a man on a rowboat. This might have been an omen that I would lead an adventurous life.

From running my own neighborhood gang of "Little Rascals" to turning a journalism degree and a $500 investment into my own little oil-and-gas company, this book answers the question: "How did I do that?"

If life is a game, it is a game that can be won. As the famous television detective Monk would say when a case was solved: "Here's what happened."

— • — • —

PART ONE

"Glory days, well they'll pass you by
Glory days, in the wink of a young girl's eye."

— BRUCE SPRINGSTEEN

Mike Hewitt leads the way as I head for the end zone

CHAPTER ONE

A BARTLESVILLE BOYHOOD

"*The war is over!*" my dad called out to my mom as he bounded in the front door. I was playing with a toy truck in front of our living room fireplace. Dad's news sounded important, and I made what must have been my earliest mental note. Assuming this was VJ Day, which marked the end of World War II on August 14, 1945, I was about two and a half years old. At that age, I liked to welcome Dad home by sitting on his good shoes, wrapping my arms around his calves, and holding on tight while he lugged me around the house for a while. He didn't seem to mind when I untied his shoelaces. He was probably ready to slip on his house shoes anyway.

My dad, Harris, my mom, Louise, and my brother, Del, older than me by three and a half years, made up my family. We lived in a small, white, one-story, two-bedroom, ranch-style home at 1515 Jennings, about a mile south of downtown Bartlesville, Oklahoma. My hometown had sprung up in January 1897 in what was then Indian Territory. Three months later, the Territory's first commercial oil well, the Nellie Johnstone No. 1, was drilled on the banks of the nearby Caney River, touching off an era of oil exploration and development in the area. Bartlesville's population shot up from around seven hundred in 1900 to over six thousand in 1910, and the boom town eventually became the headquarters for two large oil companies, Phillips Petroleum Company and Cities Service.

With big brother Del at home on Jennings Street

Dad was a chemist who worked in the research-and-development department at Phillips. He was also the first clarinetist in the Phillips company orchestra. Mom was an indifferent housewife and dedicated club woman. If Dad joined the Lions Club, she would join the Lion Tamers. When Dad was a Toastmaster, she was a Toastmistress. On Tuesdays, she would go to her Tuesday Club. Mom often mentioned she had worked as a legal secretary in Tulsa "for a dollar a day" during the Depression. But, in post-World War II Bartlesville, it was considered an admission of failure if a man's wife had to work "outside the home."

My favorite early playmate was Dorothy Ann Bash, a girl my age who lived next door. She was a tomboy with long, black pigtails, always willing to go along with whatever mischief I could get us into. While I was a good boy who at times minded his mother, I often ignored her in search of adventure. Her default suggestion, "Just go outside and play," was easy to comply with, and subject to a wide range of interpretation. Operating under the twin theories that what my parents didn't know would not hurt them, and that it is better to seek forgiveness than permission, I could always find something fun to do.

Mom often asked, "What's going on?" If something was going on, she wanted to be part of it. I took her desire a step further. If nothing was going on, I wanted to make something happen.

Our gang, a real-life version of Hollywood's "Little Rascals," included Teddy and Johnny, each a year younger than Dorothy Ann and me. We had the run of the neighborhood, but usually played within an area defined by Dorothy Ann's house on the south, a row of six houses running north along Jennings Street, up to Teddy's house. The houses had small backyards and a large, undeveloped field that separated them from the Santa Fe Railroad track, which ran through the west side of town. On many nights as a boy, the last thing I heard before falling asleep was the sound of a whistle as a train pulled into town and approached the Bartlesville station.

The Iceman Cometh

Lacking many of the modern appliances we now take for granted, we kept our food in a wooden "icebox." An ice man would deliver a block of ice from time to time, just like the milk man, to a side door on our driveway. (To this day, I still call a refrigerator an icebox.)

In my pre-kindergarten days, there was a form of money in Oklahoma called mills. A mill was a small paper coin, worth one-tenth of a penny. But the big money was in pop bottles. Most soda pop was sold in glass bottles, and you could get a two-cent refund for each bottle returned to a store. Two cents would buy a piece of bubble gum. A Milky Way candy bar cost a nickel. An enterprising kid could buy a candy bar for two empty pop bottles and ten mills.

There was a little mom-and-pop grocery store on Armstrong, near the railroad tracks, a couple of blocks from our house. Our gang liked to take empty pop bottles to this store and cash them in for bubble gum or candy. One day I noticed that the store owner stored the bottles in crates behind the store. Sneaking behind the store, I took a couple of pop bottles, brought them back through the front door, and cashed them in for four pennies. Then I bought two pieces of bubble gum and walked out, my crime undetected. Either the store owner didn't realize the source of the pop bottles, or he just laughed and let it pass.

When my mom would have some sort of club meeting to attend, she would drop me off at a day care service run by a stern old lady named Mrs. Varco in her little house across the street from McKinley Grade School, about a block from our house.

A stay at Mrs. Varco's seemed like serving time for bad behavior. I passed the time digging around in a sand box, under a big oak tree, in her backyard, or playing with toys on the floor of her playroom. I couldn't sleep during nap time, which made my sentence there seem even longer.

My dad's parents lived in Guthrie, the original capital of Oklahoma, about twenty miles north of Oklahoma City. Grandfather Dutcher was seven years old in 1889 when the Rush to Guthrie brought ten thousand settlers there overnight. My folks had a little black two-seater coupe. On our earliest drives to Guthrie in the mid-1940s, Del would ride in the front seat with my parents, and I would lay on a little shelf behind them. Later, when we got a bigger car, Del and I would sit in the back seat, begging my dad to crank up the speed to fifty miles per hour. Dad, being conservative, would drive forty-five, but not any faster.

While in Guthrie, Del and I would watch Grandfather Dutcher walk out to the chicken pens in his backyard, select a chicken, and wring its neck. He would then bring the chicken into the kitchen and give it to Grandmother Dutcher, who would pluck it, cut it up, and fry it for our lunch. I usually got a drumstick. Not my favorite piece, but at least it was fresh.

When I was four, our family drove to the East Coast for a summer vacation. In Washington, DC, Del and I fed peanuts to the squirrels through a White House fence. In New York City, we strained our necks trying to see the top of the skyscrapers, becoming "rubber-necking tourists" before I ever heard that term. We also took an elevator ride, probably my first, to the top of the Empire State Building, where I bought a small metal replica of what was then the world's tallest building.

Later that summer, I attended a few sessions of Vacation Bible School at the First Methodist Church. I have a vague recollection of being expelled for misbehavior. I liked the David and Goliath story but didn't believe the one about Jonah and the Whale.

The Battle of the Belt

My mom was usually more of an appeaser than a disciplinarian, but one day before kindergarten we had a rare fight over what I would wear to school that day. I wanted to wear a belt, but she insisted that I wear suspenders, apparently in fear that I could not keep my pants up with just a belt. I thought the suspenders looked sissy and refused to put them on. After a long power struggle, including more than a little shouting, screaming and tears, we reached a compromise. I wore the suspenders under my shirt, so that they would not show, and got to wear my belt as well. I don't think we ever fought again. My dad would be called in to provide discipline, as needed.

When I was five, Mom arranged for me to sing a song at a Republican presidential campaign event at the Moose Lodge just south of Bartlesville. Standing on a little stage and wearing my complete cowboy outfit (boots, spurs, chaps, vest, six shooters, and cowboy hat) I sang:

"I'm an old cowhand
From the Rio Grande
And my legs ain't bowed
And my cheeks ain't tan.
I'm a cowboy who never saw a cow
Never roped a steer, 'cause I don't know how
And I sure ain't fixing to start in now
Yippie Eye Oh Ki Ay"

When I finished my song, I tipped my cowboy hat to the audience and yelled:

"Vote for Dewey!" (Even though Dewey lost to Truman in the 1948 presidential election, he did carry Bartlesville by a large margin.)

My first basketball game was played against a kid named Rex, who had a backboard and goal attached to the garage behind his house on Keeler Street. I was about five, and he was a year older. Despite his home court advantage, I not only won the game, but set a personal record for blocked shots that stands today. The fact that he shot underhanded, like a Rick Barry free throw, may have had something to do with me blocking so many of his shots. At least I knew to launch my shots from my right shoulder.

I wasn't a mean or destructive kid, just an adventurous risk taker who was always looking for excitement in our quiet little company town. I got my first bicycle when I was about six. It was a little black Schwinn. I soon got into trouble when I rode it outside of our neighborhood, about a mile up Jennings Street, past my kindergarten school, and on to downtown. Fortunately, there wasn't much traffic in town between the hours of 8 am and 5 pm, when the oil company employees were ensconced in their office buildings and research labs. This may have been the first of many incidents in a misspent youth. It seems I was always testing boundaries, a living Dennis the Menace about two years before the cartoon character first appeared. (Was this a coincidence, or was I being watched?)

Kicking the Can Down the Driveway

We didn't have a television while we lived on Jennings. On most days, when I wasn't in school, I was left to my own devices. I would go next door, ask if Dorothy Ann could come out and play, and then we would round up Teddy and Johnny. We called one of our favorite games "Kick the Can." An empty tin can, most likely once filled with Campbell's tomato soup, was placed on our driveway. One of the kids was "it." The others would hide in the immediate area. The kid who was "it" would look for the other kids. When he saw one of them, he would race back and jump over the can, yelling, for example, "Over the can for Johnny!" If he beat Johnny to the can, Johnny was caught and had to sit out until he was freed. This occurred when another player would beat the "it" kid back to the can and kick it down the driveway, before the "it" kid could jump over the can and capture him. We would play this game for hours. To this day, the sound of "over the can for Johnny" brings back a wave of nostalgia for the days of unsupervised play. Whether the game was football, hopscotch, or piggyback fights, we made up our own rules, resolved our own disputes, and played until dark.

Given my adventurous nature, my boyhood was relatively injury free. My worst injury occurred when, sick with what was called the "croup," I fell out of bed and landed on a hot water vaporizer, severely burning my left thigh. My parents rushed me to the hospital. I still have the scar.

My little brother Phil was born in June 1949. I remember going to the hospital with my dad to bring Mom and him home. By then, as a recent kindergarten graduate, I was too independent to be jealous.

Our first-grade reading book featured Dick and Jane. They had a dog named Spot. The stories were simple, as were the sentences: "See Spot run." Our reading books seemed highly repetitive and learning to read seemed easy.

In the second grade, I had a little crush on a classmate named Dona Dalton. On Valentine's Day, after school, I rode my bike to her house, about a block down Jennings. I was sitting in her living room, waiting to give her a package of Life Savers, when I panicked and fled the scene. At school the next day, she walked by my desk and thanked me for the candy. I never went back.

The First Picture Show

That summer, I went to the aptly named Arrow Theater to see a movie called *Apache Drums*. A hostile tribe of Apaches had a group of settlers and a small contingent of soldiers trapped inside a fort. Tension built as the Apaches surrounded the fort and banged on their war drums as they prepared for battle. To begin their assault, the Indians set fire to the tips of their arrows and shot the flaming arrows into the fort, creating havoc inside.

As an impressionable eight year old, I thought this was a pretty cool strategy. So cool, in fact, that I wanted to try it as soon as I got home. I got out my bow and arrow set, then recruited Dorothy Ann to come watch. We went into my backyard and set up a target. I put a ball of newspaper on the tip of an arrow, lit it with a match, and shot it at the target. My aim was a little high. The flaming arrow whizzed over the target and landed on the top of old Smokey's doghouse, which backed up to our garage. Since the doghouse had a tar paper roof, it immediately burst into flames.

Once again, I panicked, but I didn't flee the scene. My first thought was to smother the fire with a big rock. But the rock was too heavy for me to lift. At that point, with flames shooting up the back wall of our garage, my ability to reason broke down entirely, and I started throwing small rocks at the fire. Luckily, a cooler head prevailed. Dorothy Ann ran next door and got her older brother,

David, who calmly hooked up our garden hose and put out the fire. The back wall of our garage was scorched, but at least it came out better than the fort in the movie. My folks took the incident in stride, falling back on their "boys will be boys" attitude, one of the many reasons I loved them so much.

It must have been about that time in my life when another movie almost got me killed. I went to the Osage Theater to see a show about a little boy named Skyler. If his parents asked him to do something he didn't want to do, he would put a paper bag over his head and say, "Skyler doesn't want to." Somehow, this odd behavior gave me the idea to try to walk home with a paper bag over my head. Starting out a few homes up the block, I put a grocery sack over my head and headed home. I got about halfway there when I heard car brakes screeching. Nearby. I took the bag off my head, turned around, and was surprised to find myself in the middle of the street, with a car stopped a few feet away. The woman who was driving the car got out to make sure I was okay, then went on her way. I may have neglected to mention this near miss to anyone for several decades.

Movies continued to put bad ideas into my impressionable head. I had seen a cowboy movie in which Roy Rogers (or possibly Gene Autry or Tom Mix) grabbed a tree branch and pulled himself up into the tree while his horse galloped on without him. So, one day while riding my bike, I decided to try this maneuver myself. I rode around our neighborhood, looking for a tree limb at about the right height. When I found one, I circled back. Peddling my bike at full speed, I raced under the limb, grabbed it with both hands, and pulled myself up into the tree, just as planned. Unfortunately, my bike, lacking in horse sense, careened into a car parked in the tree owner's driveway. My bike was unhurt, but it may have put a little scratch on the back door of the car. I didn't really look. I swung down from the tree, retrieved my bike, and got out of there as fast as possible.

The Dutcher boys

The Easter Bummer

Another neighborhood adventure during the early 1950s era occurred a few weeks after Easter. My folks had given me a pet bunny for Easter, but later decided that the care and feeding of a bunny was more trouble than it was worth, so they gave it to a neighbor. I missed the little guy. One day I went to visit the neighbor's house to see the bunny, who was being kept with some other bunnies in a pen in their backyard. (In our neighborhood, most of the backyards were unfenced.) My dog Smokey, a black cocker spaniel, followed me on this jaunt. I don't know how the bunny got out of its cage, but when it saw Smokey it took off running. Smokey took off in pursuit, and I chased after them. The three of us raced across Fifteenth Street and across three backyards, with Smokey gaining on the bunny, and me sprinting as fast as I could but falling farther behind. When the bunny reached our backyard, he turned up the driveway, made another left turn, and headed up Jennings, across the front yard of our next-door neighbor. By the time I got there, all I found was some furry evidence that this was where Smokey had caught the bunny. I never saw the bunny again, and Smokey eventually came home.

In the summer of 1952, we took a family vacation in Colorado. We attended a formal presidential campaign event, held in a Denver office building for Dwight D. Eisenhower and Richard Nixon. We were ushered into a long greeting line, with Dad carrying

Phil likes Ike

my three-year-old brother Phil. I watched as Dad and Phil met the candidates. Phil extended his hand to Ike's chin as the press photographers' cameras flashed away. The next morning, a photo of Dad, Phil, and Ike appeared on the front pages of newspapers around the nation. According to the photo caption, Phil told the future President: "You're a nice man." (I suspect some public relations man made up that quote. Phil doesn't remember saying it.)

Our third-grade teacher, Mrs. Dorsett, asked the kids in her class to write an autobiography. Mine told about our trip to Washington, DC, and New York City, which was apparently the highlight of my life to that point. Perhaps overdramatically, I called my story "What I've Lived Through."

One experience I lived through, but didn't write about, occurred each summer. A city truck would drive slowly through our neighborhood to spray DDT for mosquito control, and all the kids would joyfully follow behind, on foot or on bikes, inhaling the toxic mist. It didn't kill us, so it must have made us stronger.

My folks gave me a small record player when I was ten. My favorite song, by comedian Red Buttons, was "Strange Things are Happening." Being a mischievous boy, my favorite verse was:

I once had a teacher
Who flunked me in History
She asked, "Who shot Lincoln?"
I answered, "Don't blame me."

When playing outside with my friends, a little touch of danger always seemed to add to our fun. Behind my home on Jennings, there was a field of tall grass, then a small creek running along an elevated railroad track. We liked to put pennies on the rails for the trains to flatten into the size of a nickel as they roared by. The creek turned west and ran through a large drainage pipe. A kid could walk through the pipe to the other side of the track, but we didn't do that very often because on the other side of the track was an abandoned oil field. The oily sand would ruin your shoes, and water in the ponds shined orange and purple in the sun.

The Fourth of July was my second favorite holiday, right after Halloween. Each June, Del and I would look at the classified ads in *Boys' Life* magazine for firecracker assortments. We would try to convince Dad to order a large arsenal of fireworks. He would order one box. My favorites were cherry bombs and Roman candles.

For a private Fourth of July celebration, I made an armada of little rafts out of toothpicks and rubber bands, then added a small paper sail to each craft, leaving enough room on the deck for one cherry bomb. I snuck down to the creek by the railroad track with my rafts, placed a cherry bomb on one, lit it, and launched the raft onto the creek. As hoped, after a brief journey down the creek, the raft was blown to smithereens. The rest of my little fleet met the same fate. There were no witnesses, and I was the only survivor.

That summer, I suggested it would be a good idea for the neighborhood kids to organize ourselves like an army. We had a race to determine who would be the general. Unexpectedly, Dorothy Ann won. After a day of playing second-in-command, I decided maybe this wasn't such a good idea after all.

There was one boy in our neighborhood I could never get along with. He was my age and a would-be bully to my younger friends. He must have come by his bad temper naturally. After one of our frequent confrontations, his dad came down the street to our house, all red-faced and steaming, wanting to fight my dad. My dad kept his cool. To him, the idea of fighting one of our neighbors must have seemed bizarre. The riled-up dad eventually calmed down.

Another time, the kid's mother jumped out of a bedroom window, onto their driveway, to break up an impending fight between her son and me. I was surprised by her sudden appearance, but it was probably just as well that she came between us. Her son was holding a board, while I was empty handed. I wasn't scared. I must have thought I could take the board away from him.

Liberating the Goldfish

One summer afternoon, during our ongoing neighborhood feud, our gang played a practical joke on our nemesis. I borrowed a wire coat hanger and an old pair of nylon stockings from my mother's bedroom closet and used them to make a fish net. We took a bucket, filled it with water, and snuck into enemy territory, our unpleasant neighbor's backyard. After hiding in some bushes to make sure the coast was clear, we crept up to their shallow goldfish pond and, using our homemade net, caught several goldfish and put them into our water bucket. As we fled the scene, I felt like the leader of a small liberation army. We didn't steal their goldfish. We freed them. We took the goldfish to the creek by the railroad and set them free. If our daring daylight raid was ever detected, we never heard about it.

Another prank I got away with involved a rather grumpy neighbor who lived next door to Teddy. This neighbor had several apple trees in his backyard, and I would occasionally help myself to a few of his apples. He had one prize tree, right next to his back porch. One day he warned me to never remove an apple from that tree. He may have been planning to enter them in the County Fair. Anyway, I took his warning as a challenge. One late summer morning, I climbed into his prized tree, ate two of the best-looking apples I could find, then used some string to tie the apple cores back onto the tree, about where I had found them. I figured, if caught, I could argue that, technically, I didn't remove the apples from his tree.

Two school friends and I were once asked to do some yard work by a neighborhood oil executive. We worked for hours in the summer sun, mowing, raking, and pulling weeds in his backyard. When we finished, he paid us each a dime. A dime? Even in the mid-1950s, a dime didn't go that far. I would have been happy with fifty cents. But at least I learned to establish the expected pay before you do the work.

I did earn some good money with my paper routes. At age eleven, I got my first real job, delivering *Tulsa World* newspapers to about seventy customers in my neighborhood. The papers were delivered to our house on Jennings around 5 am. I would fold them, put a rubber band around them, and load them into the baskets on my bicycle. My bike had three wire baskets, one on the front handlebars, and two alongside the back wheel. On Sunday mornings, when the papers were too large to load onto my bike all at once, my dad would divide up the papers, put the stacks in his car, and spot them strategically along my route. Otherwise, I was on my own. I enjoyed the work during nice weather. But one cold winter morning my bike crashed after hitting an icy spot on the sidewalk, sending me into a pile of snow, and my newspapers scattered around me. I tried not to cry as I gathered up my papers to resume my deliveries.

One fall, Bartlesville, alone in the State, went on its own version of daylight savings time. The change was made because the top Phillips executives wanted their Bartlesville headquarters to be on the same time as their New York office. The local time change meant that my *Tulsa World* newspapers arrived an hour late, not leaving me enough time to deliver them before school started. (With this time change, you could drive to Tulsa in nothing flat, but it took you two hours to get back.) Apparently, other people had similar problems, and our local time warp did not last long.

The Dog That Didn't Bark

The low point of my paperboy career came early one crisp autumn morning as I was delivering to one customer's garage apartment, tossing the paper up to his second-story porch. Like Sherlock Holmes, I was warned by the dog that didn't bark. Normally, when my paper hit his porch, a big German Shepherd would start barking, and I would be glad he was kept upstairs. When I didn't hear him bark, I looked around and, sure enough, he was coming after me. I took off as fast as I could pedal my little bike. But my bike was so small and so loaded down with newspapers, he caught up with me easily. We raced down the street, eye to eye, until he bit my right ankle and called off the chase.

Later that morning, my mother dropped me off at Doctor Beachwood's so he could examine my dog bite. After he applied some ointment and bandages, I asked him if it would be okay for me to play in a grade school football game scheduled for that afternoon. He said no, I shouldn't play. When my mom picked me up, she asked what he said. I told her he said the bite wasn't bad, and it would be okay for me to play in the football game. I played. We won. I made a touchdown. (It's all about risk/reward.)

Dad played first clarinet in the Frank Phillips Men's Club Orchestra. I endured their occasional performances, but was proud that Dad was first clarinet, not second or third. He also played his clarinet in a little German band that performed many summer nights in the City Park. I would run around the park, eat popcorn and cotton candy, and ride the kiddy rides while he played. My favorite was a little boat ride in a small, above-ground pool.

Coming home from the park one night, I was sitting in the back seat of our car and watching a full moon in the western sky. As we drove down Jennings, I asked my dad why the moon was following us. He gave me a serious answer, explaining that the moon was so far away that, even though we had driven a mile down Jennings, we hadn't gone far enough to change our perspective. So, the moon seemed to be following us. I made a mental note that Dad must be a smart guy.

Dad earned his master's degree in chemistry from Oklahoma A&M (now Oklahoma State University) at the age of twenty. After working as a teacher and high school principal during the Depression, he moved his family to Bartlesville in 1941 to work for the Bureau of Mines. He later joined the research-and-development department of Phillips, where he received a critical occupation deferment from military service during World War II. Phillips was working on finding a petroleum-based substitute for natural rubber, since the Japanese had taken over most of the rubber plantations in Asia, and rubber was a critical material for the war effort.

On warm summer evenings, after playing outside with our friends, my brothers and I would sometimes take up a chant: "Let's go get a root . . . beer! Let's go get a root . . . beer!" Our folks would usually give in and take us to the A&W Root Beer stand on the south edge of town, on the road to the country club. Root beer, served very cold, in frosted mugs, was our favorite summer treat.

On trips to visit Dad's parents in Guthrie, we would take a series of narrow highways that wound in a southwesterly direction through small towns like Pawhuska, Cleveland, and Hominy. As we drove through Hominy, my mom would inevitably break into song: "Hominy hearts have you broken . . . with those great big, beautiful eyes?" On the nighttime drives home we would listen to the popular radio programs of that era, such as *Bob and Ray, Amos 'n Andy,* and *Fiber McGee and Molly.* And we would sing along with Rosemary Clooney, Snooky Lanson, and other pop stars as they sang the nation's most popular songs on *Your Hit Parade.* After a long car ride, I was always thrilled to see the city lights of Bartlesville as we emerged from the Osage Hills. Despite its small size, our town's tall office buildings gave it an impressive skyline, seemingly popping up in the middle of nowhere, only 330 miles southeast of the geographical center of the country.

My friends and I played a lot of baseball during recesses and after school at McKinley. We usually played "Work Up," a game in which a batter who strikes out, flies out, or is put out on base goes to right field, and the fielders all rotate up one position until they have worked their way up to becoming a batter. We managed to play this game, unsupervised, for several years. We played for fun and were usually able to resolve any disputes that came up. In one game, a close play at first base resulted in a shouting match, with some of the kids yelling "safe" and the others yelling "out." The shouting match may have been more fun than the actual game, because we kept it up until a ringing bell marked the end of the recess.

The baseball fun ended when the adults took over, drafting boys aged ten to twelve from all over town and assigning us to Little League teams. They bribed us with uniforms, lighted playing fields, score boards, umpires, and concession stands. I was insulted, feeling like we had been having a lot of fun on our own.

I reluctantly went along with the new regime, playing shortstop for the Frank Phillips Men's Club team. Unfortunately, I was afraid of bad hops while attempting to field grounders, so I would look away instead on watching the ball go into my glove. Too often, my blind stabs at the ball would miss, and it would go between my legs into the outfield.

I loved our Colorado vacations. We would usually stop in Denver to ride the roller coaster at Elitch Gardens amusement park. Then we would drive into the Rocky Mountains to a resort called Rabbit Ears, where we could ride horses and fish for rainbow trout in a deep, clear lake, using a shiny lure called a Christmas Tree. On one trip, while my dad and brothers were fishing, my mom and I decided to start a fire to warm up our cabin. Unfortunately, neither of us was aware that one should open the flue to the chimney before lighting a fire in the fireplace. I brought in a few logs from a stack by the cabin, crumbled up some newspapers, and lit the fire. To our surprise, the cabin immediately began to fill up with smoke. We bailed out, yelling, "Fire!" Luckily, someone from a neighboring cabin came over and put out the blaze before much damage was done.

My basketball career began heating up in the fourth grade. I was asked to play on the fifth-grade team, and I also played on teams at the YMCA and in a league for boys whose dads worked at Phillips. The Phillips 66ers belonged to the Amateur Athletic Union (AAU) and played in the highly competitive National Industrial Basketball League (NIBL). In those days, college All-American basketball players often chose to take a job with a big company and play for their NIBL teams, instead of joining one of the teams in the financially shaky National Basketball Association. When Phillips built the Adams building in 1950, it included a large gymnasium with seating for 2,600 basketball fans. The gym was sold out when the 66ers hosted their league rivals, including the Akron Goodyear Wingfoots, the Peoria Caterpillars, the Denver Truckers, and the Wichita Vickers.

In 1954, I saw a movie called *Go, Man, Go* about the early days of the Harlem Globetrotters. The scene I recall features Marques Haynes, who starred at Langston University, about a dozen miles northeast of Guthrie. He knocks on the door of the hotel room of team owner and coach Abe Saperstein, wakes him up, and asks for a tryout. Abe tells him to come back later, but Marques claims he can dribble past him in the hotel's narrow hallway, so Abe, still in his pajamas, steps out into the hallway and assumes a defensive stance. Marques, using an array of behind-the-back and between-the-legs dribbling moves, gets past him three times, convincing Abe to give him a spot on the team.

I got my first taste of playing basketball in front of large crowds when I played for the Phillips 33ers during halftimes of the Phillips 66ers games. In one of my earliest basketball memories, I was dribbling down the court on a fast break during a 33er game when an opponent suddenly blocked my path. I gave the ball a hard bounce, ran around him as the ball soared over his head, retrieved the ball, and continued dribbling down the court. This move drew my first reaction from a basketball crowd, probably a laugh.

Ninety-nine Bottles of Beer on the Wall

Buddy York, a Phillips 66er player, coached a team called the Phillips Peewee All Stars. We crammed into his car for a very long trip to the Texas Panhandle to play the Cactus Peewee Boys, another team of Phillips kids. According to a story in the Bartlesville newspaper, we staged a late-game rally, but lost in overtime, 24–23. Apparently, we were unfazed by the loss. On the ten-hour drive back home, we sang countless refrains of the same song:

"Ninety-nine bottles of beer on the wall . . . ninety-nine bottles of beer

If one of these bottles should happen to fall . . . there'd be ninety-eight bottles of beer on the wall

Ninety-eight bottles of beer on the wall . . ." Etc.

Down to: "No more bottles of beer on the wall."

Coach York somehow survived the Cactus trip and coached me in the local YMCA prep basketball league, playing in the Y's cracker box gym against local teams coached by volunteer 66ers. A story in the local newspaper reported: "Buddy York's quintet defeated Wayne Glasgow's forces 19–14 behind eight points of Bill Dutcher." At age ten, that may have been my first press clipping.

My heroes were the star basketball players on the Bartlesville Wildcats high school team. While I was in grade school, it seemed like the entire town would crowd into the College High field house for Wildcat basketball games. I would go to the games early, to get a seat on the front row. One Wildcat point guard, Dallas Dobbs, went on to star at the University of Kansas and later played for the Phillips 66ers. After him, my favorite Wildcat players were David Baker and Bobby Joe Green. They were known as the "20-point twins," as they each averaged more than 20 points per game, until late in their senior season, when they each scored over 30 points in one game and were promoted to the "30-point twins." Dobbs and Green each had smooth, long-range jump shots, while Baker would drive to the basket and spin underhand "scoop" shots off the backboard and into the basket.

Our dad took Del and me to Oklahoma City to watch the Wildcats play in the State Championship game in 1955. Baker and Green played great, but they couldn't stop the Norman Tigers' Denny Price, who poured in 43 points, hitting 15 of 18 field goals, most from near the basket, when the keyhole was shaped like one. I was heartbroken when Norman fought off the Wildcats' furious late-game rally and squeezed out a one-point win, 60 to 59. (Denny Price went on to star at OU and become an AAU All-American with the 66ers in Bartlesville, where his son, future four-time NBA All-Star Mark Price was born.)

My favorite cheer at Wildcat home games went:

"Clap your hands . . . stamp your feet
Bartlesville Wildcats can't be beat!"

One winter night, someone must have forgotten to sweep the floor before the game. As the fans dutifully stomped their feet at the cheer's command, dust began rising from the floor, like a fog, until the players were knee-deep in dust. The referees had to stop the game until the dust settled, literally.

Another popular cheer in those days, long before the introduction of bitcoins, went:

"Two bits . . . four bits . . . six bits . . . a dollar
All for Wildcats stand up and holler!"

During halftime of the Wildcat games, students would conduct fundraisers for local charities. Instead of passing the hat, the students would spread out white sheets and carry them along the sidelines, so the fans in the stands could toss coins into the sheets.

When the fans would miss their target, coins would start rolling all over the basketball court. Kids like me would scoop up the loose coins and throw most of them into the sheets.

A Caddy Debacle

My folks didn't belong to the Country Club when I was a kid, so I didn't know anything about golf. That didn't keep me from going along with some of my friends when they said they were going out to the Club to caddy. I sat with some black boys my age on a shaded hillside near the eighteenth hole, waiting to be selected to caddy by one of the ladies who would be playing in the tournament. I had rarely been around black kids before. Our schools were segregated until I started junior high in 1956. One black boy, about my age and size, asked me to bend my arm while he rubbed the top of my elbow with his hand. He rubbed in small circles for a few minutes, then stopped and told me I could straighten out my arm. I tried but couldn't. His rubbing had twisted the hairs on my arm into little knots. He and his friends had a good laugh as I tried to undo the knots. I had to admit he got me on that one.

Eventually, a nice lady selected me to be her caddy. I may have been the last one left. I couldn't give her any advice, since I did not know one club from another. But at least I could carry her golf bag, which wasn't too heavy, at first. After a few holes, the strap of her bag started rubbing my shoulder raw. I stuck some leaves under my shirt, hoping to provide a cushion for my shoulder. When this didn't work, I started dragging her bag behind me. I began to melt in the hot summer sun. By the time we reached the ninth hole, she was carrying her bag. If we hadn't made it back to the club house, she would have been carrying me. She was very nice about the whole ordeal. I hoped she found a new caddy for the back nine.

We moved from Jennings Street to a new home on Osage Street when I was eleven. Our new home was an old two-story brick house, built in 1912. It was a farmhouse until the city grew up around it. The houses of our next-door neighbors were not built until 1938. Our gravel driveway descended along the south side of the house and curved into our garage at the basement level. I had my own room, which looked out over the front porch to the street.

Soon after we moved in, Dad bought our first family television. It was a Huffman model. It came in a big cabinet with a large, green screen. (I would bet that a salesman had convinced Dad that a green screen was easier on the eyes of the viewers.) One of our neighbors was a shortwave radio operator, and our new television antenna picked up his transmissions. Our programs were often interrupted with his booming voice: "This is Baker, Baker, Able . . . calling . . . Roger that . . . Baker, Baker, Able." My Dad seldom got mad, but he clearly was not a fan of Baker, Baker, Able. And it took months to get rid of this interference.

Looking for Uncle Bob

The new television immediately brought some excitement into our lives. One of my mom's sisters, Margaret, was married to Bob Harris, who was a member of the Ray Charles Singers, a popular vocal group that appeared weekly on the nationally televised *Perry Como Show*. We would crowd around the new television in our small den hoping to catch a glimpse of Uncle Bob happily singing, "Doo waa . . . doo waa" in the background. Depending on the staging and camera angles, we would see him more often in some shows than in others.

"There's Uncle Bob!" we would shout, as his face would pop up briefly on the screen.

Uncle Bob and his family came to visit us one summer when I was around twelve. During their visit, I had a memorable conversation with Uncle Bob, possibly the first adult kind enough to take my views seriously. Our topic was: which is more important to a professional baseball hitter: confidence or ability? I don't recall which side of this chicken-and-egg argument I was on. The important thing was that we were discussing this issue, man to man.

During their visit, I ran some races in our front yard with my cousins Bob, Ed, and Paul. Cousin Ed, then about five years old, was a very fast runner for a little kid. His speed must have helped him as a football player in high school and college, and possibly later in his acting career. (Yes, the famous Ed Harris.)

My mom's father, William Sholl, was a Presbyterian minister who passed away too soon for me to remember him. Her mother, Lilly Sholl, would come to visit us in Bartlesville. She was a pleasant woman, but she was easily shocked. If someone said something of questionable taste, she would exclaim: "Ooo . . . I never heard of such a thing!" This expression became a family saying, often invoked when someone made a controversial remark.

Mom may have been a bit of a rebel herself. She was quick to tell people that her father had been too strict. As she often put it: "He called dancing 'hugging to music' and would not let me go to a dance, even when my friends, whose parents were deacons and elders in the church, could go."

Both of my parents had a good sense of humor. On a hot and muggy afternoon, Bartlesville was under a tornado warning. I had heard that Circle Mountain (some foothills southwest of town) would protect us from tornados, so I wasn't worried. I suggested we should have a tornado watch party.

"What fun'll that be?" Mom asked.

Dad and I liked to watch Westerns like *The Lone Ranger* and *Have Gun, Will Travel*. On one Saturday morning show, a cowboy told his friend: "Your problem is that you are planting tumbleweeds. There's no profit in it." Before the friend could respond, Dad beat him to the punchline: "Yes, but think of the turnover."

On Sunday afternoons, I loved to watch the Bud Wilkinson show, featuring the University of Oklahoma Sooner's charismatic football coach. With All-American players like Heisman Trophy winner Billy Vessels, Tommy McDonald, and Clendon Thomas running Bud's T-formation offense, the Sooners dominated college football in the mid-1950s, running off a forty-seven-game winning streak between 1953 and 1957, ended by a heartbreaking loss to Notre Dame.

As a fifth grader and avid fan, I entered an essay contest in which I had to write, in twenty-five words or less, why I watched his show. I wrote three different versions and sent them in. One of my entries won a prize. A man from Meadow Gold Milk came to an assembly at our school and gave me a basketball. Why he gave me a basketball instead of a football was a mystery to me.

When we had enough kids, we played touch football, three on three, in our front yard. I would make up plays in our huddle back. As we got older, our football games got rougher. We played tackle-the-man-with-the-ball, which is played just as its name implies, without pads. I developed my game as a grade school running back, dodging my friends as they tried to bring me down. We finally quit playing this game when one of the guys started running with his head down, charging the would-be tacklers like a battery ram, as if he were wearing a helmet. Even at that age, we could recognize a concussion waiting to happen.

No Way to Block a Punt

For our grade school games, we all had helmets and shoulder pads, but played in our jeans and tennis shoes. One fall afternoon, during football practice at McKinley School, we lined up in punt formation. I was a ninety-pound halfback, standing up behind our line to protect the punter. Bruce, a big-for-his age fifth grader, was on the defensive line. When the ball was hiked to the punter, big Bruce broke through our line easily, hit me at full speed, and sent me flying back into the punter, just as he was punting. The punter kicked me instead of the football, sending me rolling around on the ground in agony. It was the worst pain I had felt since I fell onto the hot water vaporizer. Mr. Snyder, our coach and school principal, stood over me and asked: "Did he kick you in the stomach?" My response, which remained an inside joke among my football teammates for years, was: "God damned no . . . it's my balls!"

As if football wasn't rough enough, we also had front yard piggyback fights. Some of the older kids in the neighborhood would serve as the horses, and the little kids like me would ride, piggyback style, on their backs. The objective of the game was to push, pull, or shove the other horse-and-rider pairs until one or both ended up on the ground. The game was like a medieval joust, without the lances. A couple of the older kids played on the high school football team, so they made steady mounts. I took a lot of spills as a rider in these piggyback fights, but if you are going to be an athlete, it is important to learn how to fall.

Old Man in the River

My twelfth birthday party was a classic. My dad drove a carload of my friends and me to Circle Mountain. After roasting hot dogs, we played a game of "King of the Mountain," in which the simple objective was to climb to the top of a big mound of dirt and stay there while everyone else tried to throw you off. This rough and tumble game resulted in all the boys getting dirty, but no one was hurt.

On the way back into town, we stopped along the steep banks of the Caney River, where some old oak trees were laced with heavy vines. My friends and I would pry a vine loose from the trees and hang on while we swung out over the river and back to its banks. My dad, who was not exactly an outdoorsman, decided that this looked like fun. He grabbed a vine and swung out toward the river. Unfortunately, with Dad being heavier than the average twelve year old, the vine snapped. He dropped to the ground, then began slowly sliding down the steep bank toward the river. I watched helplessly as he grabbed little plants to try to stop his slide, but only uprooted them as he continued his descent. Still holding a handful of tiny plants, he splashed into the river. The water was only about waist deep for him, but on a cold January afternoon the water was frigid. We were able to fish him out and, since he was the driver, his slow-motion, plant-grabbing slide into the Caney River brought a comical ending to my party.

My sixth-grade teacher was an uptight, unpleasant woman who had trouble maintaining discipline in her classes. Under her demerit system, if you did something wrong in class, she would give you a certain number of demerits. When you accumulated enough demerits, you would face some penalty, such as having to stay in class during recess. Steve Crutchfield and I soon got into an ornery contest, trying to see who could rack up the most demerits. My favorite ploy, a few minutes before recess, was to ask if I could go into the hallway to do some research in the encyclopedias kept in a nearby closet. I would take a brief look at one of the research books, then sneak down the hall to a wooden box that held the playground equipment. Taking my favorite basketball, I would sneak outside to the basketball court and warm up before the other boys could come out for recess. The dirt court was on a slope, with ridges caused by the rainfall runoff. (If you could dribble on that court, you could dribble anywhere.) The basket at the bottom of the slope was effectively lower than the one at the top, and I would stake my claim to the low basket.

Phillips Petroleum Company's international headquarters consisted of an office complex with three tall buildings in downtown Bartlesville. As a kid, I liked to explore their buildings, during working hours. It seemed that Phillips ran such a tight ship that the employees were chained to their desks, so I could walk through the halls and ride the elevators without ever encountering an adult. I once set a goal of seeing how far I could get across downtown without ever going outside. I entered a tunnel that began in an employee parking lot on the west side of the complex and extended under a building full of mechanical stuff like boilers and generators for the office complex. After sneaking through this building, I continued through a tunnel under Jennings Street to the basement of the Adams Building. The basement contained, among other things, the Frank Phillips Men's Club and the locker rooms for the swimming pool and gym. Then I found a tunnel under Keeler Street to the basement of the original Phillips Building, where I was able to take an elevator to the second floor. On that floor, there was a walkway, across an alley, to a bank building. Once in the bank, I walked down some stairs to the lobby and walked out the front door, on Johnstone Street. Mission accomplished.

Exploring downtown Bartlesville led to my discovery of an adult magazine shop, tucked away in a small space that could be entered from Johnstone Street through a pool hall, or from Third Street through a newsstand. I once wandered into this shop innocently enough, but departed a little less innocent, and possibly in shock, after sneaking a few peaks at the photographs in their racy magazines.

A Chip Hilton Fan

When I wasn't out exploring, or looking for fun in all the wrong places, I liked to lay down on the sofa in our living room, under the window air conditioner, and read. Other than the newspaper sports pages and funnies, my boyhood reading focused largely on several books from the Chip Hilton sports stories, a twenty-two-volume series written by Clair Bee. The author was a highly successful college basketball coach in the 1930s and 1940s. The series begins with "Touchdown Pass," published in 1948 and covering Chip's sophomore year in high school football. The series follows his exploits through his high school and college seasons in football, basketball, and baseball. Chip was a star quarterback, forward, and pitcher. His friends, Speed Morris and Biggie Cohen, are often his teammates, playing whatever sport is in season. Chip's teams often won whatever championship they were competing for, overcoming difficult challenges in each season. With Chip Hilton as my fictional hero, I developed not only a love of competition but also an expectation of winning.

During my sixth-grade year, my good friends Mike Hewitt, Bob Blaker, Paul Curd, Bill Turner, and I formed a secret group modestly called "The Five." We made ourselves some handprinted membership cards. Our activities included hanging out and playing games. In a poker session at Paul Curd's house, we played a version of seven-card stud we called "Dizzy Maurine Going Down the

River Drinking Dr. Pepper." The game had so many wild cards you needed at least four of a kind to win. I lost five dollars that night, but Paul's mother made my friends give me back my money. We valued our membership, as it allowed us to confer some status on ourselves, and as late as our high school graduation, we still considered ourselves active members of "The Five."

— • — • —

CHAPTER TWO

A REBEL
WITHOUT A CLUE

A*fter departing grade school*, I added a new group of friends. These guys had gone to Garfield grade school and had older brothers and sisters. Unlike my McKinley friends, they "knew what was going on." I knew something was going on, but I didn't know what. I suspected it had something to do with "sex," whatever that was. They would tell jokes based on an entirely new vocabulary. Not wanting to admit I didn't get the jokes, I would laugh without knowing why. I seemed to be missing a few key facts. Later that year, when I passed through puberty, I asked my dad what was wrong with me. After his explanation, I suddenly got the jokes. The facts I had been missing turned out to be the facts of life.

A Church Camp Caper
During the summer before the seventh grade, I attended a one-week Methodist church camp near Tahlequah, Oklahoma. Bored by the camp routine after a couple of days, I decided to hitchhike to Muskogee, a town that inspired the classic country and western song,

"Okie from Muskogee," and was also an archrival of Bartlesville's football and basketball teams. Not far from the camp entrance on Highway 62, I hitched a ride on an eighteen-wheeler and was dropped off in downtown Muskogee. I found the local YMCA and shot a few games of pool. Then I had lunch at a nearby drug store and went to a movie. After the movie, probably a Western, I walked to the bus station and took a bus going to Tahlequah. I asked the bus driver to drop me off shortly before the bus reached the church camp.

As I headed back to my cabin at the camp, I noticed an unusual amount of activity. I asked a kid what was going on and was surprised to learn that some boy named Bill Dutcher was missing and that they had been searching for him all afternoon. I found the camp director and told him that I had gone for a hike in the woods and had gotten lost.

Soon I was back home, attending Central Junior High for my seventh-grade year. Kids from their neighborhood grade schools all over town were funneled into Central for their early teen years. By the start of the school year, I was in full rebel mode. I bought a pack of Lucky Strike cigarettes, telling the clerk they were for my mother. I tried to smoke one, but the smoke burned my eyes and made me cough. I just rolled the pack into the sleeve of my white T-shirt and walked around town like the tough kid I aspired to be. I sometimes joke that I gave up smoking to go out for eighth grade football, but, in truth, one cigarette was enough for me.

At the time I had no idea of what I was rebelling against. While James Dean was starring in the movie *Rebel Without a Cause*, I was a teenage rebel without a clue, feeling some vague objection to the authority of the authorities.

My dad was easy going, believing in positive reinforcement and encouragement. But he had his limits. I tested them frequently during my seventh-grade juvenile delinquent period. Late on Saturday nights, the Osage theater featured what we called the Shock movies, which were horror shows like *The Thing*. I was not permitted to attend these movies. When I went anyway, I was shocked to see Dad coming down the aisle to pull me out of the audience, much to my embarrassment and to the delight of my friends.

This incident did not prevent me from taking my class clown routine to the movies on Saturday afternoons. Some friends and I were watching a movie about a very poor family, struggling to survive the Depression in a ramshackle cabin. There was a knock on their door, and the mother got up to see who it was as her family looked on expectantly. Just as the door opened, I popped off, with perfect comedic timing and just loud enough for the entire theater audience to hear, saying: "My name is Michael Anthony."

The entire audience cracked up at my comment. In those days, with only three national television networks, most people watched the more popular shows, so everyone got my joke. In a program called *The Millionaire*, a wealthy benefactor named John Beresford Tipton would write a cashier's check for one million dollars each week. He would give the check to his executive secretary for delivery to some needy family. When making the delivery, the secretary would knock on the recipient's door and introduce himself, saying: "My name is Michael Anthony."

One of my new friends, Jimmy Hess, and his dad took me to Tulsa to see a new rock star, Elvis Presley, at an outdoor concert. I was rocking out, excited to see Elvis singing, "You ain't nothing but a hound dog," and "Don't step on my blue suede shoes." *The Tulsa World* reported: "All it took was a little shake of his hips to ignite a wave of screams from the throngs of teenage girls crowded around the stage."

One evening I tagged along with two of my new friends as they stopped by to see a smart and pretty girl named Dona Beesley. She was a year older than us and lived in a large home that looked like a small castle. I was impressed that my new friends even knew someone that rich. Strangely, before our visit was over, Dona had persuaded us to sit still while she curled our eyelashes. (I never suspected that one day Dona would marry Del and become my sister-in-law.)

My rebel tendencies were eventually overcome by my competitive nature. I wanted to make good grades to show that I was smart, and I wanted to excel in sports because I liked to win and because I thought it would help me with the girls. I got that idea from a 1930s hit song that went: "You've got to be a football hero . . . to get along with the beautiful girls."

An Undefeated Season

I was the player/coach of our seventh-grade basketball team. My first draft pick was Paul Curd, who was then the best athlete in our class. We played thirty-minute games, with a running clock, during the noon hour. I figured that five players playing thirty minutes would total 150 player-minutes available, which had to be split up among our eight players. Since Paul and I would play the whole game, that left ninety minutes to be shared by our other six players, or fifteen minutes each. I set up a substitution system that let the other players come into the game at a set time so I didn't have to worry about making substitutions during the game. Our team went undefeated, winning one game by 50 to 0, thanks to a full-court press that made it difficult for our opponents to advance the ball past half court. We won another game 76 to 8. My coaching career peaked early, as I never had another undefeated season.

That spring, the Phillips 66ers won the US Olympic Tournament, so the team's starting five made the US basketball team for the 1956 Olympics. Two of my favorite players on that team were Chuck Darling and Burdette Halderson, both post players with beautiful, sweeping hook shots that seemed impossible to guard. The team picked up some serious help from a couple of University of San Francisco All-Americans, Bill Russell and K. C. Jones. By adopting a basketball play known as "going back door," I was able to sneak into the Adam's Building gym to watch them practice.

I also watched the Harlem Globetrotters, starring Goose Tatum and Meadowlark Lemon, when Dad took me to Tulsa to see them play a team of College All Stars. I loved watching the Globetrotters, not just for their comedy routines, but for their amazing dribbling, passing and shooting skills. I came home with a goal of becoming the first white Globetrotter, immediately working on ball handling tricks in my bedroom.

Del started at guard for the Bartlesville Wildcats basketball team during his senior year, playing alongside the team's star player and future Kansas University Jayhawk Dewayne Ketchum. As we walked into the College High field house before a game, Del said I must be feeling pretty good walking in with a starter on the Wildcats. I agreed it was an honor, indeed, while thinking, "I'm going to make them forget all about you."

Del, whose high school nickname was "Buckshot," didn't play football because it interfered with hunting season. But he was easily the best baseball player in the family, starting at third base for the Wildcats. My own baseball career was hampered by the fear of getting hit in the face with a baseball. That summer, in a Pony League game, I hit the only over-the-fence homerun of my baseball career. Normally, I would bail out on curve balls, but this one was so slow and hanging that I was able to knock it out of the park. In those days, an athlete played whatever sport was in season, even if he wasn't very good at it.

A Shocking Discovery

My first junior high girlfriend was Jeanne Martini, who lived down the block from us on Osage Street. (Dorothy Ann, my first friend who happened to be a girl, and I had drifted apart after I moved away from Jennings.) At Jeanne's house, there was a small outdoor lamp by the side of the stairs that went from the front driveway to a sidewalk up to her front door. In the summer, neighborhood kids would gather in her driveway. Someone, possibly me, discovered if you held onto the lamp post with one hand and put your other hand on the concrete nearby, you could feel a weak electric current passing through your body. We also discovered if several of us formed a human chain, with one kid holding the lamp post and another kid at the end of the chain touching the concrete, the electric current was even stronger as it passed through all of us. This proved to be such a shocking discovery that we only did it once.

Changing Teams?

Our eighth-grade social studies class was taught by a white-haired woman who would write things on the blackboard for us to copy into our notebooks. Unfortunately, this method required her to spend a lot of time with her back to the class, which led to near anarchy. Once, a rebellious Westside kid threw a marble-sized firecracker that exploded when it hit the blackboard, causing our poor teacher to jump and the kids to laugh hysterically. I felt sorry for her, so I didn't feel a need to contribute to the chaos. Sure, I was ornery, and occasionally felt obligated to provide my classmates with some comic relief. But I wasn't mean. Just mildly disruptive, in the nicest possible way.

A few weeks into the school year, my English teacher, Mrs. White, asked me to meet her after class. She told me the social studies teacher was having a hard time maintaining control of her classroom, and she asked me to see what I could do to help her. I was surprised by this request. This was the first time an adult had asked me to change sides in what I had always seen as a battle between oppressed school kids and controlling, boring adults. Mrs. White's request made an impact on me. She seemed to imply that I could be a leader, and it was up to me to decide if I would be a force for good. The idea of changing teams had never occurred to me. She may have started me on a new path.

Mrs. White also introduced me to "A Psalm of Life," a poem by Henry Wadsworth Longfellow. There are three verses of the poem I can still quote today. My favorite goes:

> "Lives of great men all remind us
> We can make our lives sublime
> And, departing, leave behind us
> Footprints in the sands of time."

To me, leaving "footprints in the sands of time" seems like an ambitious, but worthwhile goal for a person's life.

My ninth-grade football season was forgettable. Our Central Cubs played against teams from small towns around Northeast Oklahoma and Southeast Kansas. For some strange reason, known only to our coaches, I played fullback. It may have been because our offensive line could only open very small holes, and, at 130 pounds, I was our only running back small enough to fit through them.

My best football play that year came in practice. The coaches decided to try our biggest tackle, Bruce, at fullback. (This was the same kid who had knocked me into the punter in grade school.) As the starting fullback, I viewed the idea of Bruce taking my position as a serious threat. I lined up at linebacker. Bruce took a handoff and charged right at me. Feeling like David without a sling shot, I met Goliath at the line of scrimmage and launched myself at his ankles, knowing that hitting him low and hard was my only chance of bringing him down. He hit the ground hard.

Mom, Dad and their three sons

After the play, our coach asked who made the tackle. He had thought it was one of our more aggressive defensive backs and was surprised when he discovered it was me. He probably realized my game was more about avoiding collisions than causing them. But this shoestring tackle saved my job at fullback.

For a project in my ninth-grade English class, I made an Ivanhoe newspaper, hand printed on four large pages. The newspaper covered events from the novel *Ivanhoe*, by Sir Walter Scott, set in England during the reign of King Richard the Lion-Hearted. I don't recall the stories, but hand printing them had an unexpected result. (To this day, any handwriting I do is in print rather than cursive.)

A passage in the Bible says: "When I was a child, I spoke as a child, I understood as a child, I thought as a child; but when I became a man, I put away childish things." It seems that my passage through juvenile delinquency came to end by the time I completed junior high. Heading to high school, I was far from mature, but I tried to put away my childish things. My view of life as an adventure, requiring an element of risk, stayed with me.

— • — • —

CHAPTER THREE

GLORY DAYS

My *primary interests in high school* were focused on sports and girls, not necessarily in that order, with academics a distant third, and very little, if any, thought given to what life beyond graduation might hold.

College High, once a combination high school and junior college, offered a rigorous academic schedule, designed to prepare its graduates for college. Bartlesville claimed to have more PhDs per capita than any other town in the nation due to the academic achievements of the many chemists, geologists, engineers, and other scientists working in the international headquarters of Phillips Petroleum and Cities Service. With so many smart parents in town, I had a lot of smart classmates. I was able to make decent grades by paying attention in class and doing my homework, but academics, in general, were an afterthought.

My sophomore year at College High kicked off with the dreaded two-a-day football practices in the broiling heat of late August 1958. Our head coach, Burl Stidham, was short and stocky, with a steely glare that seemed to look right through you. If a player began to make an excuse with an "I thought . . ." Coach Stidham would cut him off, saying, "That's what the little boy thought." Rumor, or possibly locker room humor, had it that during one August practice session, a player, lying on the ground, told Coach Stidham, "I think I broke my leg." His reputed response: "Don't just lie there . . . do push-ups." During another grueling practice, an overweight lineman took off his helmet, turned to Coach Stidham, and complained: "I don't mind the heat . . . but the humility is killing me." Even our tough old coach had to laugh at that one.

As a scrawny sophomore running back and outside linebacker (in those days, we played on both offense and defense), I didn't get to play in the Varsity games that year. I did start on the B team. Our football season ended in late November. Bartlesville never competed in the statewide football playoffs, which ran well into December and would have conflicted with the start of basketball season. Many of the Wildcat athletes competed in both sports, so football players had only a week of practice before the basketball season began.

On the first day of basketball practice, I noticed that two black sophomores had come out for the team. One of these players, Eugene Edwards, looked like a great athlete who hadn't played much basketball before. The other, Calvin Washington, looked like a great basketball player with impressive range on his jump shot. Unfortunately for our team, Washington quickly dropped out of high school and joined the Navy. Eugene stayed and developed into a great player by his senior year.

All the sophomores played on the B team. A few sophomores, including me, practiced with the A team and suited up for the Varsity games, but didn't get much Varsity playing time. The Varsity coach was Bailey Ricketts, who was well into his many years of coaching the Wildcats. The players called him "Father," a tradition that must have started when his son Rodney played on the 1955 team that went to the State Finals. Father was calm, but firm. He could get his point across without yelling at the players. He ran our practices from a seat in the stands, often sipping coffee from a thermos, occasionally venturing onto the court to demonstrate plays.

At practice during my sophomore year, I somehow dislocated the little finger on my right hand. I walked over to Father and said, "I think I broke my little finger." I showed him the finger, which was bent up in the opposite direction from how it normally bends. Without saying a word, Father grabbed my finger and gave it a good yank, nearly straightening it out. The finger remains crooked to this day, but at least I didn't miss the rest of that day's practice.

One B game that season was played in a small, basement gym at Tulsa Central High School. Tulsa, Oklahoma's second largest city, was then known as the "Oil Capital of the World" and had four high schools in our conference. Our B team was coached by Sid Burton, a young, energetic, and enthusiastic coach not long out of college. Coach Burton started our sophomore group, and we built a lead in the first quarter. He substituted a group of juniors, most of whom were better at football than at basketball, and they lost our lead by halftime. The same substitution pattern continued in the second half, and we ended up losing the game. For Paul Curd and me, after being undefeated in school basketball games during the fifth, sixth, seventh, eighth, and ninth grades, this was our first loss. I didn't know how to act after the game. I was used to telling our defeated opponents "nice game" or "good game" in a way that implied "nice try." I didn't know what to say after a loss, so I didn't say anything.

The Exuberance of Youth

On my sixteenth birthday, I made a big mistake. After a long A team practice, Coach Burton was topping off another hour of B team practice by having us run full-court wind sprints. Feeling good, and possibly a little cocky, I told our young coach, "I can run these wind sprints as long as you can blow that whistle." That turned out to be wrong. After running countless sprints, I finally collapsed, exhausted. My teammates, realizing I was defenseless and it was my birthday, dragged my lifeless body into the locker room and gave me sixteen good-natured whacks with a gallon-sized can of Tough Skin (a lacquer used to prevent foot blisters).

As a sophomore, I saw limited playing time for the Wildcat's Varsity basketball team, which started four seniors and a junior. We made it to the State Tournament in Oklahoma City, but lost to El Reno in the semi-finals. Two of our seniors, Marvin Ogle and Grover Marshall, made All State. College High's first black basketball player, Larry Guerry, started at power forward.

That spring, the football coaches recommended I go out for track, since it would help me prepare for football season the following fall. I ran sprints, which in those days were measured in yards instead of meters. My times were not very good, so when guys would ask what I ran the sprints in, I answered "track shoes." I enjoyed running the 100-yard dash but struggled with the 220-yard dash. The 440-yard dash, or quarter miler, was a killer. At about the 330-yard mark I would run out of oxygen and feel as if I had hit an invisible wall of air resistance. I would push myself to the finish line gasping for air.

Making a Wave

One of my favorite high school sports stories, the ones I have replayed in my mind hundreds of times since, occurred in my junior year, early in the opening game of the Wildcats 1959 football season. We were facing Tulsa Central, and I was in the starting lineup, playing left outside linebacker. When the Central quarterback fired a deep pass to my side of the field, I raced back at full speed, but out of control. (Not unlike I had done in my first Varsity basketball appearance in the previous year.) The football bounced off the shoulder of the intended receiver, but I ran right past it in my over-hyped state-of-mind. "Damn," I said to myself after the play, "I could have had an interception if I had been under control."

Luckily, in the second half, a similar play unfolded. This time I was ready for the football when it ricocheted off the Central receiver, so I snatched it and, with a quick pivot, was racing down the sideline with the ball, right in front of the student-filled bleachers. What burned this play into my memory was the realization that I was touching off a wave among the students as they jumped to their feet as I ran by. The student wave followed me for about sixty yards, from our twenty-yard line to our opponent's twenty-yard line, infusing me with about eight seconds of ecstasy, until the opposition's pursuit finally ran me out of bounds about five yards short of the goal line.

Three months later, I was back on the basketball court as the starting point guard, running the same offense I had seen being run by my boyhood heroes, former Wildcats Dallas Dobbs, Bobby Joe Green, DeWayne Ketchum, and Bob Benz. In the seventh game of the season, at home against archrival Muskogee, we were facing a two-one-two zone defense that left me open at the top of the keyhole. My role as a junior was to be a pass-first point guard, moving the ball quickly around the perimeter and looking for entry passes to our star center, 6' 5" senior Eddie Clark. However, I found it difficult to turn down open shots, so I fired away, making four consecutive jumpers from long range during the first half. Our home crowd went wild. This hot streak marked my coming out party as a shooter and rivals my streak down the football sidelines with an intercepted pass just a few months earlier as my most euphoric sports moment. Those plays were my first taste of high school glory in each sport, and remain burned into my memory, long after those glory days have passed me by. Our team won the game, 38 to 37, and remained undefeated.

Overall, my junior basketball season was disappointing. We won 15 games and lost four during the regular season but failed to advance to the State Tournament. I scored in double figures in a few games, and ended the season averaging about seven points per game, fourth on the team. Surprisingly, I received Honorable Mention honors on the "All League Cage Roster" for our misnamed Oklahoma Six Conference, which had nine teams, including four Tulsa high schools.

That April, Dad drove Mom, Phil and me to St. Louis to see an NBA finals game between the Boston Celtics and the St. Louis Hawks. As an aspiring point guard, I kept my eyes glued on Celtics star Bob Cousy. What impressed me most was the precision of his passes, arriving to his teammates exactly where they needed to be.

Heading for home, Dad was having a hard time finding the highway back to Oklahoma. As we drove through an urban ghetto that looked like it had been hit by a bomb, I was shocked to discover that such abject poverty existed on such a large scale within the United States. While stopped at a traffic light, Dad asked Mom to roll down her window so he could ask the man driving a car in the next lane for directions to the highway. The man shouted out the requested directions. We had been sharing a box of banana cookies during the trip, and Mom reached out to the man who had given us the directions, saying "I'm going to give that man a banana cookie!" For many years, when someone did a favor for a member of our family, one of us would comment: "Give that man a banana cookie!"

A Case of Curve Ball Phobia

After an uneventful track season that spring, I played on an American Legion baseball team for a long summer season spent mostly riding the bench, watching my friends play ball. We played teams from Tulsa, and from a list of small towns around northeast Oklahoma, southeast Kansas, and southwest Missouri. When I did get to play, I found that I could hit fast balls, even from good pitchers. But curve balls were another story.

Perhaps my worst game of all time, in any sport, came against a team from Tulsa. Their pitcher, a lanky right hander named Richard Calmus, managed to strike me out three times on nine pitches. Each pitch was a hard-breaking curve ball, seemingly coming toward my head from third base. I either swung in self-defense or bailed out of the batter's box. Either way, the result was nothing but strikes. Calmus went on to become a major league baseball pitcher, as did his high school teammate Carl Morton. But Morton was a fast ball pitcher, and I did manage to hit a right field single against him. Ten years later, Morton was named the 1970 National League Rookie of the Year.

That summer, I worked in the mornings as a counselor for Coach Bill Holbrook's sports camp for boys aged eight through twelve. Coach Holbrook was the Wildcats track coach and football line coach. His camp offered play and instructions in a variety of games and sports, including track, ping pong, dodge ball, stick wrestling, archery, fishing, and others. At the end of the summer session, the campers voted for the Outstanding Camper in each age group.

That summer, my little brother Phil, at age eleven, won one of these awards. The prize for winning this award was a camping and fishing trip to the White River in Arkansas.

The coach drove me, Phil, and the other honor campers to the campsite, where we set up tents and a firepit for cooking. The younger boys didn't have much interest in fishing, but Phil headed straight for the riverbank and began to fish. He fished for several hours without catching any fish. But he didn't give up.

Coach Holbrook, an avid outdoors man, decided to give Phil a little help. He walked upstream, swam under the water with his spear gun until he found a large bass, and speared it. Then he swam under water to where Phil was fishing, found his hook, took off Phil's bait, hooked the speared bass onto Phil's hook, and gave Phil's line a yank. Excited, Phil reeled in his prize fish, a five-pound bass (with a small hole in its side). Phil put the fish on his stringer and lowered it into the river near the spot where he had been fishing, then resumed fishing. When Coach Holbrook returned to the campsite, Phil eagerly showed him his great catch, then asked him about the hole in its side.

"Turtles must have got it," the coach replied. (To this day, Phil still believes this speared bass is the biggest fish he ever caught.)

In early August, my friend Mike Hewitt and I began working out together, trying to get into good enough shape to survive the upcoming two-a-day football practices. Our workouts consisted mainly of running up and down the stairs of the Custer Field stadium, where our home football games would be played. Experience had taught us that it was better to show up for two-a-days in decent shape.

Mike and I, along with our center Scott Dalton, were voted tri-captains of the football team. The Wildcats had strong football teams during my sophomore and junior years but going into my senior year our coaches had very low expectations. Fortunately, they were wise enough not to share their preseason feelings of impending disaster with the players. After we had finished the season with a record of seven wins and three losses, Coach Stidham admitted that, before the season started, the coaches had feared we would win two and lose eight.

As a team captain, I got to kiss the Homecoming Queen, a beautiful girl named Tana Ware, during halftime of our Homecoming Game. The school tradition, which I readily approved of, was for the football captain to embrace the queen, give her a kiss, and bend her back, holding the kiss until her crown fell off. We were able to uphold the tradition flawlessly.

My performance as an outside linebacker was nothing to write home about, but a *Tulsa World* sports writer's coverage of a Wildcat victory over Tulsa Central noted: "Bartlesville halfback Bill Dutcher, who played a corking game as a corner backer, tackled Central's Jim Seabolt in the end zone for a safety with 1:40 left in the first period."

Tulsa Rogers's Revenge

For our last home game of the season, we faced Tulsa Rogers, a football powerhouse the Wildcats had upset in the previous three seasons. They were loaded with a least a dozen Division One recruits, generally bigger, faster, and tougher than our guys. Early in the game, I was playing left cornerback when a big tight end dove at my feet, trying to block me. I stepped back to avoid his block, but suddenly glimpsed a football shoe, cleats and all, coming right into my face. The single bar on my helmet, which in those days passed as a face mask, failed to stop the rising shoe, which smashed into my upper lip. I kept playing and kept a stiff upper lip about my swelling upper lip.

Late in the game, we were trailing 40 to 0, and we faced a fourth down, eight yards to go, near midfield. Our quarterback, Bob Blaker, called for a punt formation. For the first and only time of my football career, I objected to the call, maybe thinking that being a captain gave me the right to protest. (Or, maybe I had read too many Chip Hilton sports stories.)

"We shouldn't punt now," I argued. "That would be like giving up."

Our quarterback shot back: "You want to get beat 46 to 0?"

That shut me up. We punted, and the game ended with Tulsa Rogers on our three-yard line, about to score again. We had played on Custer Field, and our last stand ended badly.

After the game, Coach Stidham noticed my upper lip and took me to the hospital to have it sewn up. By this time, my lip had swollen enough that I could see it by just looking down. My dad met us there and took me home, more concerned about my lip than about our loss. At school on Monday, my lip was still badly swollen, and it wasn't exactly a "red badge of courage," given the way our team had been hammered by Tulsa Rogers.

Saving My Best Game for Last

My helmet was fitted with a plastic mask to protect my lip as we faced Sand Springs in what turned out to be my last, and best, high school football game. I was playing left halfback in the same T-formation used by Bud Wilkinson's Oklahoma Sooners to win three national championships. Running a play called "Twenty-five Stutter," our quarterback faked a handoff to our fullback diving over the middle. As their linebackers took the fake, I remained in my starting stance while our quarterback moved down the line. He gave me the ball as I hit a gaping hole in their line, allowing me to gain full speed as I charged toward their defensive back. I gave him an exaggerated fake right, then cut left, a move that in today's basketball terms would be called a Euro-Step. This move left him tackling air, and me with a clear path to the goal line, sixty-five yards away. I had never seen so much open field. I ran for the touchdown, surprised that no one caught me from behind.

Another memorable play in that game was a double reverse pass. Our right halfback, Randy Rudisell, took the initial handoff going left, then handed the ball back to me, going right. I was supposed to pass the ball downfield to a receiver, but all our guys were covered. Then I noticed Randy, ignored by the defense after handing me the ball, alone on the left flat, jumping up and down, waving his arms, doing his "I'm wide open!" dance. I threw him the ball, and he raced down the sideline, untouched for a sixty-yard touchdown.

We won the game, 48 to 14. Feeling euphoric as our team celebrated our win on the bus back to Bartlesville, I borrowed the driver's intercom and sang the Kingston Trio's hit song "The Tattooed Lady," much to the surprise of my raucous teammates.

A few days after the game, Coach Stidham called me into the football office and told me, "Bud Wilkinson knows who you are, but he does not have any openings at halfback for you at OU." However, he said that Kansas State was interested in me as a football player. At that time, Kansas State was the doormat of the Big Eight Conference in football. I thought, "If they are recruiting 150-pound halfbacks who run the hundred in eleven seconds, no wonder they can't win a game." I envisioned going to Norman as a Kansas State Wildcat and getting hammered by

OU, 55 to 0. I told Coach Stidham I wasn't interested. I felt like Groucho Marx, saying he wouldn't join any club that would have him as a member.

Meanwhile, back in the classroom, I enjoyed English classes, where we read novels like *Silas Mariner,* epic poems like *Beowulf,* and plays by Shakespeare. For a journalism class, I wrote a satirical piece for the school paper, *The Nautilus,* entitled, "If There Is Anything I Hate, It's a Sesquipedalian," which complained about people who use long words. I also wrote an editorial complaining about the school administration's cancelling of Sadie Hawkins Day, which, based on the cartoon strip *Little Abner,* was a day in the mythical Ozark town of Dog Patch when girls like Daisy May would chase the boys. I argued that the administration was trying to force an "unnatural adulthood" on us kids, who just wanted to have fun. Later, the school paper was printed, but not distributed, due to a cartoon showing an old lady, looking into the backseat of a convertible, and saying, "No wonder the Russians are ahead of us."

Starting Slow, Bouncing Back

My senior basketball season got off to an inauspicious start. With a mediocre record of four wins and four losses, the outlook for our season was not very promising. But the Wildcats went on a three-game winning streak in mid-January, averaging 79 points per game. A blowout victory over Sand Springs included my best performance as a high school hoopster. As reported in the *Bartlesville Examiner-Enterprise* sports page: "Growing hotter by the minute, the Bartlesville Wildcats unleashed a torrid scoring assault in the second half to batter Sand Springs 79–32, here Friday evening in an Oklahoma Six Conference game.

"Bill Dutcher, 5–11 sharpshooter, led the overwhelming victory with 28 points, his best effort of the season. The wiry Wildcat playmaker was virtually unstoppable in the final half, scoring 20 points. He turned in one burst of nine straight points at the third quarter's finish. Coming back stronger, he added 11 more points, including a seven-point span early in the period."

When Dutch had some hops

The *Tulsa World* sports page commented: "Lanky Bill Dutcher paced the Wildcat assault, pouring in 20 points in the last half and ending with 28 points. He canned 13 of 20 field goal attempts."

Don't tell me there is no such thing as getting hot. As our lead grew during our fifty-point second half, my confidence grew with it. I wanted the ball badly, as I felt every shot I put up would go in.

After the game, Coach Ricketts told me there was a man outside the locker room who wanted to see me. I immediately thought, "College scout! I'm being recruited for the first time!" I walked out to the hallway and was disappointed to discover the man was Bill Douce, then a high-ranking executive with Phillips Petroleum and once my dad's boss in the Patent Department. All he wanted was my autograph, on a popcorn box, for his son. Like me, his son was a big Wildcat fan growing up.

The Wildcats were riding high as we travelled to Sapulpa. The *Tulsa World* reported on the game this way:

"Bartlesville's amazing one-two punch, Bill Dutcher and Mike Hewitt, pumped in a combined 47 points here Tuesday night as the Wildcats clawed Sapulpa's Chieftains, 72–69. Bartlesville stunned the hometown gunners by connecting on 17 of 22 field goal efforts in the second half.

"Dutcher canned 11 of 15 and added three charities for 25 points. Hewitt hit 10 of 16 and two free throws for 22."

The *Bartlesville Examiner-Enterprise* added: "Big rally of the contest was the 'Cats 26-point spree in the third quarter, giving them a 56–50 margin. This was the quarter in which Dutcher hit five of five, plus two free tosses to throw Sapulpa into a panic. Driving downcourt, he let loose from 30 feet to rip the nets."

The Wildcat's regular season ended with a disappointing record of eleven wins and seven losses. As we headed into the regional playoffs, we were in no one's radar as a championship contender, or even as a dark horse.

A Second Season

Looking back over our senior season, it appears that while Mike and I showed some gradual improvement, our other three starters improved a lot. By the start of the playoffs, Stan Ogle, Eugene Edwards, and LeRoy McDonald were ready to step up.

Fortunately, Bartlesville was the host of the Class AA regional tournament that year. In our first tournament game against Tulsa Nathan Hale, Stan Ogle exploded for 19 points, including 17 in the second half. In our second tournament game, we beat Tulsa Central 43 to 36. Advancing to the regional finals, we faced Tulsa Edison, a team that had already beaten us twice that year. With a trip to the State Tournament at stake, the field house was packed, and the noise was at aircraft carrier levels. The student section chanted:

"Come along and bring your Wildcat cheer . . .
"Come along and bring your Wildcat cheer . . .
"Come along and bring your Wildcat cheer . . .
"We're going to go to State this year . . . we're going to go to State!"

Tulsa Edison fielded a tall lineup, so it was surprising that we won the game by dominating the boards. We also had the most balanced scoring attack of the season. I led the team in scoring with 16 points, followed by Hewitt with 15, Ogle with 13, Edwards with 9 and McDonald with 8. For the first time all season, all five starters played the entire game. The *Tulsa World* observed: "Once again, unheralded Stan Ogle came through with a stellar floor game and his fast breaks netted him 13 points."

When the buzzer sounded to end the game, the Wildcats were leading 61–54, and the student body spilled out of the stands and rushed onto the court, jumping and shouting in what seemed like a long and rowdy group hug. I was thrilled to be in the middle of this spontaneous celebration. We were all looking forward to a trip to Oklahoma City for the State Tournament.

A Classic Upset

The following Tuesday, I realized what we had gotten ourselves into. That evening's *Examiner-Enterprise* reported that in the first game of our "State trek" we would "Face State's Number One Prep Quint," Oklahoma City Douglass. (A quint is a set of five, in this case, basketball players.) "The classy Douglass quint sports a 22–3 record." Their lineup featured their All-State senior center, James Gatewood, a future teammate of mine on the University of Oklahoma freshman basketball team, and Ben Hart, a future OU and Canadian professional football star receiver.

For some strange reason, the "Forty-Fourth Annual Oklahoma High School Championships" were held on a makeshift basketball court, laid down over the orchestra pit and a few front rows of seats in Oklahoma City's municipal auditorium. The team benches and scorer's tables were nestled on the court, in front of the stage. The fans sat in comfortable chairs, normally used by the patrons of the city's ballet and orchestra companies. The hardwood court itself was okay, if you did not fall off, as I nearly did while chasing a loose ball. But the shooting background was terrible, especially from the corners. It seemed like the basket was just suspended in open space.

Watching the Douglass team warm-up, I noticed that most of their players were dunking the basketball. We had one player, Eugene, who I was pretty sure could dunk, but I had never seen him do it.

Our game against the heavily favored Douglass seemed like a track meet. Most Oklahoma high school teams in that era played at a slow, deliberate pace, in the style coached by the legendary Hank Iba at Oklahoma A&M. But Coach Ricketts favored a fast-breaking attack, so we may have been one of the few teams who dared to run against Douglass. It seemed like we were behind in the score for most of the game, but we kept running and gunning with them, and they refused to slow down the pace to protect their lead. Somehow, when the game ended, we had squeaked by for a 55–52 win, in what was surely one of the biggest upsets in the history of the Oklahoma state basketball tournament.

In one memorable play, I passed the ball to Hewitt just past mid-court. As he started to go up for a very long shot, Gatewood came flying at him, attempting to block it. Mike adjusted his shot in midair, slinging the ball at the basket like a quarterback throwing a long bomb. Swish. (Gatewood later told me when that shot went in, he knew they were in trouble.)

But the biggest factor in the Wildcats' win was Eugene's rebounding. In one play, I had fired off a long-range jumper that hit the back of the rim and bounced high above the top of the backboard. A crowd of defenders went up to get it, but Eugene out-jumped them all, grabbing the ball at its apex. My jaw dropped. I had never seen anyone snatch a rebound above the top of the backboard. In the locker room after the game, I told Eugene, "I have never seen you jump so high before!"

Eugene shrugged and replied: "I never had to."

Hoop Dreams Dashed

Saturday, March 11, 1961. A night that will live in infamy in my personal basketball history. We faced the Norman Tigers, a team with a 21 and 3 record, for the State Class AA Championship. Norman was led by their All State point guard, Butch Roberts, another teammate of mine on the OU freshman team the following season.

We were trailing 47–45 with four minutes and thirty-five seconds remaining in the game when Eugene, who had been busy controlling the boards, fouled out. The Tigers hit two free throws to build a four-point lead, then went into their delay game, which they ran with the military precision of the Texas A&M marching band. Of course, in those days, there was no shot clock.

What ensued was possibly the longest two minutes of my life. The Wildcats employed what we called a "three-two chaser" against their delay game. As the name suggests, we played a three-man zone around the basket, while the two guards chased the ball, hoping to double-team the man with the ball and force a turnover. Unable to figure out their passing scheme, I raced around the court, chasing the ball for nearly two minutes until I was exhausted and had to stop to rest. I was standing near the top of the keyhole, bent over with my hands on my knees, trying to catch my breath, when their center, John Fever, caught the ball, pivoted, and threw it directly to me. His eyes widened as he released the ball and realized his mistake. I caught his gift and took off, full speed, down the court. But as I approached our basket, I felt too winded to attempt a layup, so I brought the ball back out to the perimeter to set up our offense. We failed to score, and Norman went back to their delay game, scoring on back door layups, and finally winning by a score of 59–47.

Growing up reading Chip Hilton sports stories, I had developed an expectation of winning. I was devastated by the loss, even though I realized I had left it all on the court. It just wasn't the way my senior year was supposed to end. Knowing we were only two points down with 4:35 left on the clock made it feel even worse.

After the game that night, a bunch of the Bartlesville kids crammed into a downtown hotel room for a season-ending party. One of the cheerleaders attempted to cheer me up as we slipped quietly into a bedroom and made out on a pile of coats covering a bed. Riding home on the team bus, I thought I might have found a new girlfriend. But when I called her the next day, she said she had decided to go back to her longtime boyfriend.

Launching a long jumper in State Finals

Burdette Payne, sports editor for the *Examiner-Enterprise*, in a column wrapping up our season, wrote: ". . . few people ever expected them to get to State, let alone bring back a second-place trophy. In gaining it, the Wildcats knocked over the state's number-one ranked prep team, Oklahoma City Douglass. And like in the Regionals, they scrapped hard to do it.

"Unlike several 'Cat quints of the past, this year's aggregation was more balanced—both in scoring and talent. The scoring drop between leader Mike Hewitt and Bill Dutcher was not a yawning gap. Playing in all 23 games, Hewitt wound up with a 16.5 average, getting 380 points. Dutcher tacked up 337 points in a like number of contests for a 14.6 average, giving Bartlesville one of the best 'one-two' scoring punches in the state.

"Big difference in the Norman loss seemed to come when Eugene Edwards fouled out in the final period. Up until that time, the 'Cats were rallying back, depending on his control of the backboards. For his efforts, the lanky forward was awarded a spot on the State All-Star team. Edwards got 24 rebounds and 18 points in two games. The only other Wildcat chosen was Bill Dutcher. He earned a spot on the second team by scoring 24 points in two games."

Despite my disappointing point total, I was the second leading scorer in the tournament, following Norman's Butch Roberts, who put in 41 points, mostly from mid-range jumpers. Not that it matters, but most of my shots would count as three-pointers today.

Based on our overall performance, I was hoping Hewitt and I would make All State when the season's honors were announced. But we were named All State alternates, which meant that we might be invited to play in the annual All State game if one of the original All State players were unable to play. The *Tulsa World* broke the bad news this way: "Bartlesville's scoring twins, Bill Dutcher and Mike Hewitt, both drew top consideration. There was very little to choose between the two as they led Bartlesville to the state AA finals."

Our local sports editor Burdette Payne came to our defense with a column later that summer, writing that the North All State team "needed a nip of Wildcat brew, or something just as potent" as they were blown out by the South All Star cagers 77 to 47.

He continued: "Bartlesville was not represented in the hardwood duel, mainly because we had a 'one-two' punch instead of the usual 'hero and four' situation. Both Bill Dutcher and Mike Hewitt did roll up better scoring averages than the majority of the North team. Add to this fact Bartlesville won runner-up honors at State for a real mystery—how the 'Cats could go un-noticed for a playing berth on the unit. Two of Oklahoma City Douglass's lanky charges made the South team. Douglass was the crew Bartlesville upset to meet Norman in the finale."

In my not-too-humble opinion, this column was possibly one of the greatest sports commentaries ever written. However, he should have mentioned our 6' 2" jumping jack, Eugene Edwards, who was overlooked as well.

Glory Days Are Winding Down

During the spring of my senior year, I tried to play on the baseball team since the football coaches could no longer pressure me into running track. I spent most of the baseball season warming the bench. I guess I just wanted to be on a team.

My prom experience that year was a disappointment as well. I had a date with a future Miss Bartlesville, but she was planning to head to Norman the next day to attend a fraternity's Fiji island party. In an apparent effort to look like a Fiji Islander, she had applied a tanning ointment on the day of our prom. After a few dances at the prom, her skin started turning orange, and, no doubt embarrassed, she asked me to take her home.

A lot of my friends in high school were "going steady" with long-term girlfriends. I seemed to be the guy the good looking, popular girls would date while they were in between serious boyfriends. I dated a lot, but never the same girl long enough for our relationship to qualify as a serious. I could get to first base consistently, but I don't believe I ever made it to second base as a high school student, or even understood the whole baseball analogy.

On a warm afternoon near the end of the school year, I found myself with some friends at the high school tennis courts. One friend, Jon Harkavy, was one of the smartest guys in our class, but not especially athletic. On a lark, I played him a game of tennis with my shoelaces tied together. This handicap required me to do some serious hopping around the court, but I somehow managed to win. This game remains the most fun I have ever had playing tennis.

During an awards assembly marking the end of my senior year, the school principal began his announcement of the winner of the award for the best Student/Athlete by saying the winner had lettered in three sports. That meant either Mike Hewitt or I had won the award. Irrationally, I hoped it would be me, even though I knew Mike beat me as a student and as an athlete. Sure enough, Mike won.

Although I had largely abandoned my class clown routine during high school, I did get a good laugh from the student body when the next award was announced. When my name was called as the winner, I walked from my seat in the audience to a curtain at the edge of the stage, noticed an exit sign above the curtain, and, pausing for effect, asked the school principal if it was okay to walk in an exit. When the laughter died down, I received the Robert Miller Kane award, given by a prominent local family in his memory, apparently for being an all- around good kid. The award included a $500 scholarship. Later Mike told me this was the award he wanted to win, because of the money.

— • — • —

CHAPTER FOUR

A SOONER BORN

Leaving high school, I didn't realize I had won the lottery at birth. With wonderful parents, an ideal hometown, great friends, freedom to roam a safe, quiet neighborhood, schools with great coaches, and intelligent teachers with high standards, all I had to do was skate through life without blowing my lead.

My ideas about my future were vague. I wanted to be the next Bob Cousy, or, failing that, the next Will Rogers. I wanted to write novels like Ernest Hemingway or plays like Neil Simon. As the manager of the technical branch of the patent division of Phillips Petroleum, my dad served as a technical interpreter between the company's research scientists and its patent attorneys. He once tried to explain to me some of the basic chemistry involved in the conversion of oil and natural gas into plastics, but he never whispered "plastics" into this graduate's ear or tried to steer my career path away from journalism and into chemistry. (And if I ever met my Mrs. Robinson, she was too subtle for me to pick up on what she had in mind.)

My parents always supported my love of sports, in their own way. They went to nearly all my high school football and basketball games, home or away. When I would see them after a game, they would say, "Nice game." Win or lose, hero or goat, it was always "Nice game." They were very casual sports fans and applied absolutely zero pressure on my athletic endeavors. Same for academics: "Nice report card." Same for college: "Where would you like to go?" They wanted me to make my own decisions and were willing to let me live with the consequences.

What I really wanted was a basketball scholarship to a major university, where I could study whatever seemed like a good idea at the time. When that didn't happen, I thought about going to a small college to play basketball. In a rare moment of good judgment, I decided I could get a better education at the University of Oklahoma (OU). Del was a freshman there, after spending four years in the Marine Corps. And Mike Hewitt was going there on a track scholarship, after winning a State Championship in the high hurdles.

Sid Burton, Wildcat baseball coach and B team football and basketball coach, was a graduate of Phillips University in Enid, Oklahoma. He told me he could get me a basketball scholarship there. When I told him I wanted to attend OU, he arranged for me to become an "invited walk-on" there.

I had not given any thought to joining a fraternity. Del was a member of Sigma Chi, and that sounded good to me. I was invited to a Sigma Chi rush party in Norman, where I drank my first beer, a Coors Light. I didn't like the beer, but the Sigma Chi's seemed like good guys, dedicated to enjoying their college experience.

That summer, I worked as a proofreader at the *Bartlesville Examiner-Enterprise*. Other than letting one day's newspaper be published with the wrong date, my proofreading experience was good. I even got to write a feature for the sports page on a former

Wildcat lineman playing football at OU, Dennis Ward, the older brother of my teammate, All Conference tackle Karl Ward.

Later that summer, I was awarded a $350 McMahon scholarship by the OU School of Journalism. Between my two scholarships and the money I had saved from my boyhood paper routes and other summer jobs, I was able to pay for my first semester at OU.

My mom encouraged my majoring in journalism, as she wanted to be a writer herself. She once received a job offer to be the Bartlesville stringer for the *Tulsa World* newspaper. But she had to turn down the opportunity, after she was warned by the wife of a Phillips executive that Dad would be fired if she took the newspaper job. Ironically, as a happy homemaker and busy club woman, she was opposed to the Equal Rights Amendment, feeling women were better off with the status quo.

Rush Week Was Greek to Me

Fraternity "Rush Week," held just before the beginning of the fall semester, was an interesting experience. Being a jock with good grades, I seemed to be somewhat in demand by the various fraternities. My first fraternity visit was with the Delta Tau Deltas. After touring their fraternity house, I found myself in an upstairs bedroom, with a few of their members, in what I later learned was called a "hot box." It seemed their agenda was to pressure me, in the friendliest possible way, to pledge to their fraternity, before I would be allowed to leave the room. If I was undecided before, their "hot box" approach helped me reach a decision, and I told them I was going to pledge Sigma Chi, because my older brother was a Sigma Chi. This cooled off the hot box and concluded my visit.

Next on my rush schedule were the Beta Theta Pi's. After shooting some baskets on an outdoor court, between their house and the Chi Omega sorority house, I was shown into the Beta's house, where I was promptly asked to join a tour of their facilities. As we toured the boiler room in the basement of their massive establishment, I looked around at the other guys in our group and realized I was on "squirrel patrol," designed to keep the socially awkward or not particularly cool guys away from the studs or at least somewhat sharp guys they really wanted to recruit. Not seeing myself as squirrel material, I assumed the Delta's had told them I was planning to pledge Sigma Chi, and the Beta's did not want me rushing their desired candidates.

On my next rush stop, I pledged Sigma Chi, and was soon surprised to find I was one of seventy-two new pledges, a huge class by OU fraternity standards. The pledge class reflected the membership, which could be sorted into three overlapping groups: jocks, brains, and party animals. Most were from Oklahoma or Texas.

As I got to know my pledge brothers, I began to realize I had grown up in a Bartlesville bubble, totally naïve about the outside world. Before classes began, there was a friendly confrontation, also known as a grab ass, between some Sigma Chi members and the pledges, on the front lawn of the fraternity house. I watched with pride as my pledge brothers, one by one, charged at Del, only to end up on their backs. Using their momentum against them, Del was flipping them over his shoulder, like they were little kids. They hadn't gotten the word that Del had served for four years in the Marine Corps and learned an array of judo moves during his two years in Japan. I was rooting for my real brother as he manhandled my pledge brothers in this boys-will-be-boys skirmish.

Many of my pledge brothers were good athletes. But if any of them bragged about their high school athletic feats, the standard response was, "Hey, everyone was a star in high school."

On the first day of OU's 1961 fall semester, I had an impulsive thought that maybe I should try out for the football team. After all, football was the big sport at OU. Basketball was an afterthought. Besides, I still thought of sports as something you did for fun. Games were to be played, not worked on. I had rarely touched a basketball all summer.

Football practice had already begun, and as I walked toward the practice field, I heard a series of collisions that sounded like small cars colliding at an intersection. I had played football since grade school but had never heard collisions like this. As a quick little scat back, my game was based on avoiding collisions, not running over opponents. As I got closer, I peeked through some evergreen trees lining the practice field and was able to see that the collisions were coming from a drill called the "Bull Ring" in which a player stands in the middle of a circle of other players, who take turns charging into him. As soon as he bounces off, or is run over by, one charging player, another one comes at him, for what seemed like a merciless number of hits. I watched this drill for a few minutes, noticed the size, speed, and toughness of the players, then walked on over to the field house to walk on for basketball, as originally planned.

Walking on Is Hard to Do

Although I wasn't recruited by OU, I was expected by the OU coaches, and they had a locker, complete with basketball shoes, socks, jocks, and a practice uniform ready for me. Official practices had not started yet, but I quickly suited up and went out to take some practice shots on the Sooner's home court. I was excited to be there, firing up long-range jump shots, hitting most of them, and hoping the coaches were watching.

The Varsity coach, Doyle Parrack, was entering his seventh season as OU's head coach. He had played for the legendary Oklahoma A&M coach Hank Iba on his 1945 national championship team. John Floyd, formerly the head coach at Texas A&M for five years, coached the freshman team. Both coaches seemed very old school, dedicated to a conservative style of play.

At that time, freshmen were not eligible to play on the Varsity team. Warming up for one of our early practices, I noticed that some of my teammates, including a couple of guards, were dunking the basketball, so I decided to give dunking a try. I dribbled to the basket at full speed, gripped the ball with my right hand, jumped as high as I could, and slammed the ball hard against the rim. My momentum caused my feet to fly up until I was nearly horizontal to the floor, and I dropped like a mannequin tossed from a second-story window, landing on my back with a loud thud. That experience was my first and only dunk attempt.

The preseason OU basketball media guide includes a brief profile of each freshman player. Mine reads:

"Bill Dutcher . . . member of Bailey Rickett's Bartlesville basketball team . . . captained club senior year, notching 15 points per game . . . a guard with accompanying dimensions: 5–11 and 155 pounds . . . journalism major at OU . . . son of H. A. Dutchers . . . father is a petroleum company employee."

If I had known what a big part of my life basketball would eventually become, I might have taken my basketball time at OU more seriously. At the time, basketball was just a game I played for fun and competition. My goals were to skate through four years of college, playing ball, dating the best-looking girls, and pursuing a degree in a major that seemed to offer the path of least resistance and promised the least interference with the first two goals.

That fall, I focused on basketball during our afternoon practices, which consisted of two hours of fundamental drills and scrimmages. Being on the basketball team was getting me out of countless hours of Sigma Chi pledge duties, not to mention Air Force ROTC drills and finding a part-time job to help pay bills. In a way, I was hiding out at basketball practice.

At practice one afternoon, the coaches had us walk over to the nearby OU swimming pool, take off our shoes and socks, and jump into the shallow end of the pool to play some half-court basketball. I loved the way the water held me up on my jump shot, as it gave me an extra second to aim and release my shot. I made several long jumpers during the game. As we headed back to the gym, one coach told me, "Dutcher, if basketball was played in four feet of water, you would be pretty good."

My best day as an OU freshman basketball player came early in the second semester, when Coach Floyd called the team together after practice. By then, the team was down to twelve players, and the coach was holding a list of the players' first semester grade averages. In those days, which preceded today's grade inflation, academic standards for athletes were relatively low. But this was ridiculous. OU was on a 4.0 grade system. He called out each player's name, followed by their grade average. My teammates' grades averaged around 1.8. He called my name last. My 4.0 brought a stunned silence and looks of disbelief. A little shocked by my teammates' grade averages, I said to myself, "I need to stay out for basketball . . . I may be one of the few freshmen eligible to play."

Admittedly, my perfect first semester grade average resulted from a combination of last-minute studying and luck. In American History, I had made a "C" on the midterm exam and needed to do well on the final. I crammed all night for the final, ate some breakfast, and trudged through the snow to my classroom. The essay test covered the period between the American Revolution and the Civil War. To organize my thoughts, I began my essay with a chart showing the name, term, and political party of each president during that era. Using this chart as a reference, and with the material still fresh in my mind, I was able to fill two Blue Books with all I could remember about each presidency. When I received my grade in the mail, it was an "A - - -." Despite the three minuses, it still counted as an "A." The professor added a note on my grade card: "Your final pulled you up."

When the senior members of Sigma Chi who were active in campus organizations learned I had made a 4.0 grade average, they immediately recruited me for various resume-building campus activities, such as the Model United Nations, where I quietly observed as the other members of our delegation pretended to represent some long-forgotten African nation.

Meanwhile, OU's freshman basketball team, nicknamed the "Boomers," journeyed to Oklahoma City in early February for the first game of our season. (Big Eight Conference rules limited our season to four games. Our opponent, the Oklahoma City freshman team, known as the "Little Chiefs," was playing its eighteenth game of their season.)

They ran us off the court, winning 81–62. During a brief run in the second half, I hit a deep, right corner jump shot, which turned out to be the only "official" shot of my OU career. It seemed I spent most of my time in that game as the only man back on defense against their fast break. The Boomers hosted the Oklahoma City and Oklahoma State freshman teams later that month, but I did not see any action in those games. I ended my OU freshman season as the team's leading field goal percentage shooter, with a 100 percent average.

Along with my token participation in campus activities, I did make a 3.6 grade average as a freshman and lettered in freshman basketball. This record gave my Sigma Chi campus leaders enough ammunition to get me named as one of the University's Top Ten Freshmen. I also placed second for an award for the top freshman at OU. By comparison, my grade average at College High ranked nineteenth among the 356 members of my graduating class, indicating my high school was tougher academically than OU.

A Happy Camper

That summer, I worked as a counselor at the Ozark Boys Camp, near Mt. Ida, Arkansas. I ran a cabin of eight rambunctious boys, ages eight to ten, and coached them in baseball and basketball, not to mention supervising other activities, such as archery, swimming, golf, horseback riding, water skiing, and other fun activities.

One of my more adventurous campers managed to get himself into an awkward predicament while we were horseback riding on some hilly, wooded pathways near the camp. He somehow bounced over the saddle horn and continued riding with his legs wrapped around his horse's neck. I was riding alongside him, trying to get his horse to stop, when suddenly he spun around, so that his feet were on the horse's neck, and he was face to face with the horse, close enough for a slobbery kiss, as we continued down the trail. I was finally able to get him down from his perilous perch, and he wasn't hurt, just a little shook up.

When the Ozark Boys Camp ended, I returned to Bartlesville for the rest of summer. I was running around with a pretty and popular high school girl named Sue Tyler. We were parked in her driveway after a date one night when a man in a dark suit walked up to the car. Sue rolled down her window and said: "Hello, Henry."

I looked over and was shocked to realize that Sue was chatting with Henry Bellmon, Oklahoma's first Republican Governor, who was strongly supported by her dad.

Soon after returning to OU for the fall semester of my sophomore year, I rode to Dallas with some fraternity brothers for OU-Texas Weekend. That Friday night, we watched a classic college football game between Southern Methodist University and the US Naval Academy. Navy's quarterback, Roger Staubach, put on the best display of scrambling and passing I had ever seen. I wasn't surprised when he won the Heisman Trophy that year.

After the game, I learned that Del had been in a terrible wreck on the way to Dallas with another carload of Sigma Chi's. Del was thrown from the car and suffered a broken neck. Some of the other brothers were badly injured as well. Del was taken to a hospital in Gainesville, Texas. Dad arranged to have a Phillips jet pick Del up and fly him back to Bartlesville, where he had a long stay in our hometown hospital.

Picking Up the Pace

OU made a coaching change for the 1962–63 basketball season, bringing in Bob "Go-Go" Stephens from South Carolina University. Excited about the chance to play in a more up-tempo style, I walked on again, only to be "red-shirted" and assigned to work out with the new freshmen team, as was my summer camp friend and OCU transfer Bobby Gregory.

I learned more basketball under the new coaches than I had learned as a freshman. Our coaches were Jim Stoddard, assistant Varsity coach, and Bud Cronin, a recent player at South Carolina. They taught a fast-breaking style of team play. With four scholarship guards from my freshman team coming back, and with taller and faster recruits coming in, it looked like my future as an OU basketball player would involve a lot more practicing than playing in games. So, in early December, I walked off, not realizing I had a lifetime of playing basketball ahead of me. As Robert Redford says in the baseball movie *The Natural:* "There are some mistakes you never quit paying for." Walking off was one of mine. After walking off, I would still drift back to the field house to play in some pick-up games, with guys like my Sigma Chi fraternity brother, George Kernek, who had played Varsity basketball for OU before leaving to become a baseball player for the St. Louis Cardinals. In one of these pick-up games that winter, I got hot shooting the basketball from my favorite spot at the top of the free-throw circle. Bud Cronin, my coach as a redshirt sophomore, was playing in the game, and when it was over he asked me if I would like to come back out for the team, but I turned him down, unwilling to admit I had made a wrong turn.

The best basketball experience of my sophomore year began one evening after completing my shift at Ma Packard's boarding house, where I made "bread burgers" for Arab petroleum engineering students. (Bread burgers are made by kneading bread into hamburger meat, to make it go further.) I walked through the snow to the OU field house, where OU was scheduled to play Missouri later that evening. I was one of the first fans to arrive. Coach Stoddard saw me and told me he needed an additional player for a game to be played before the Varsity game, between the OU freshmen and a group of OU reserves and redshirts. I said "sure" and suited up to play for his team.

The OU fans gradually drifted into the field house as the preliminary game progressed. Both teams were playing a fast-paced game, with no need for a shot clock. Coach Stoddard drew up a clever play for me to run. Although I had never seen this play before, I was able to run it successfully during the game, scoring six points on three layups. The Sooner freshmen won the game, 95–93. I scored 12 points, hitting five of ten field goals and two free throws. This turned out to be the most competitive game I ever played in.

After the game, Coach Stoddard told me he was leaving OU after the season to become head coach at Washburn University in Topeka, Kansas, and asked if I would like to join him there as his point guard. I was surprised by the sudden offer, but turned him down, saying, lamely, "I have a journalism scholarship at OU."

That summer, my dad got me my first real job, working on a maintenance crew at Phillips Petroleum's private airport. I say "real job" because I had to get a Social Security card before I could start. Although it was not intended to be fun, I enjoyed climbing around on the company's fleet of private jets, cleaning them up for their next flight.

Don't Tug on Superman's Cape

During my junior year at OU, I was invited to join a local AAU basketball team, awkwardly named the Moore Burgers. Our first game, played in the South Base gym near the OU campus, was against the Marques Haynes Magicians, a team led by the legendary Marques Haynes, who was known as "The World's Greatest Dribbler" during his career with The Harlem Globetrotters. Now he was barnstorming around the country with his own team.

My new coaches and team sponsors were Clark Hetherington and Charles Scallan, a couple of Norman businessmen. They must have noticed me hitting nearly every shot in the pregame warm-ups, because they let me start the game at point guard. Early in the first quarter, Marques dribbled the ball casually up the court, looking unconcerned. When I challenged him as he crossed the half-court line, he tried to drive by me with a quick cross-dribble, but I was able to get a hand on the ball, knock it away, then dive for it and flip it to a teammate. Big mistake. As Jim Croce sings, "You don't tug on Superman's cape . . . you don't spit into the wind . . . you don't pull the mask off the old Lone Ranger . . ." and you don't steal the ball from Marques Haynes. He made me pay for that steal for the rest of the game.

In possibly my most embarrassing moment in basketball, I was guarding Marques on the wing when he whipped the ball past my right ear, in what I assumed was a pass into the post. I turned my head only to realize he still had the ball, holding it in his huge right hand like it was a softball. He then reached around my head to grab the ball with his left hand. There I was, trapped, with his long arms around my head and the ball behind me. I couldn't move without fouling him. I must have looked befuddled. The fans were laughing at my predicament. Having gained his revenge for my steal, Marcus whipped by me on his way to the basket. I struggled to keep up with him for the rest of the game.

The Moore Burgers played several games against amateur teams around Oklahoma that winter. I played guard, coming off the bench behind former OU stars Eddie Evans and Mike Rooney. In one game that season Evans and Rooney each scored over 30 points.

By winning the Oklahoma State AAU tournament in March, the Moore Burgers advanced to the National AAU Basketball Championship Tournament in Denver. In what might have been one of the biggest mismatches in the fifty-seven-year history of this prestigious amateur event, the Moore Burgers faced the United States Armed Forces team in the first round of the sixteen-team, single elimination tournament. On paper, we were badly outgunned. They had more than three million men to choose from. All we had were a dozen guys who played ball for free hamburgers from the Norman Moore Burger stand, strategically located across the street from the OU jock dorm. But our team gave the Armed Forces team a tough battle, losing by only three points.

I had hoped for a chance to play against the defending AAU champions, the Phillips 66ers. I imagined the headline in the *Examiner-Enterprise*: "Former 33er upsets 66ers." And I might even have gained a small measure of revenge against AAU All-American Denny Price, the 66er guard from Norman who had lit up my high school heroes in the 1956 Oklahoma State Tournament.

California Dreaming

That summer, I convinced my folks I needed to broaden my horizons by going to California for the summer and finding a job once I got there. My mom arranged for me to stay with her sister, my aunt Mary, in Riverside, until I could get settled. I hitched a ride with a fraternity brother Gary Ely for a long trip, with our stuff crammed into his Volkswagen bug. As the song says, I was "going to California with a banjo on my knee." Literally.

My stay with Aunt Mary did not go well. After her husband became enraged when I beat him in a game of ping pong, I quickly moved out and rented a small apartment in nearby San Bernardino. The air pollution was so bad my eyes stung just walking through downtown.

I found a job as a door-to-door representative for Collier's Encyclopedias, placing "free" encyclopedias in people's homes, purportedly for advance word-of-mouth advertising purposes, before an official sales campaign began in the fall. All the customer had to do was pay a small fee of a few hundred dollars to keep their set up to date with annual yearbooks. All I had to do was stick to the script. I sold one set using this approach, and received a $75 commission, before I realized the sales pitch was somewhat of a scam. There was no sales campaign coming in the fall. This was the sales campaign and had been for years.

I must have been lonely in California. I wrote a letter to a friend saying there were ants in my apartment, but I didn't kill them because I needed the company. By mid-July, I was ready to quit my summer job and go home. Carrying my suitcase in one hand and my portable typewriter in the other, I hitched a ride on a truck headed for Las Vegas. Arriving there nearly broke, I dug into my billfold and pulled out my "emergency dime." I dropped the dime into a pay phone, called my dad, and asked him to wire me $35, the price of a bus ticket home.

When I picked up the cash in the Western Union office, I felt suddenly rich. Instead of heading to the bus station, I paid about $15 to rent a car for twenty-four hours and explored the city. I soon found myself in a casino playing blackjack for $1 a hand. I quickly lost $13 in fifteen hands of blackjack and was nearly broke again. I drove to the edge of town and found a trailer park where I could stay in a small trailer for about $5 a night.

The next morning, not wanting to ask my dad for more cash, I returned the rental car and resumed hitchhiking home. I soon caught a ride with a young sailor who had been a trumpet player in a San Francisco jazz band before he got drafted. He was racing back to his Navy duty station in Memphis, Tennessee, as the time on his pass was expiring. He said he had driven to Los Angeles to see his girlfriend and looked like he had been awake the whole trip. Driving through the desert Southwest at road runner speed, he got me back to Norman in a flash.

Back home in Bartlesville at mid-summer, I found another job as a mover for Milstead Van Lines. Loading and unloading the moving vans with people's furniture wasn't too difficult, but I somehow managed to break three mirrors in one month, enough for twenty-one years of bad luck. I am sure I would have been fired if I hadn't quit to return to OU.

— • — • —

CHAPTER FIVE

COURTING TERRY

As *the fall semester of my senior year began*, I ambled into a criminology class I had signed up for in case I ever became a crime reporter. I noticed a pretty and perky blonde sitting in the front row and slid into the seat next to her, trying to be as casual as I could manage. Slouching in my seat, I gazed up in her direction and observed how intently she seemed to be focusing on the professor's lecture. I also noticed what looked like a fresh scar on her left knee. I may have grimaced in a way that she interpreted as "that's disgusting," but my actual thought was "that must have hurt."

Somehow, I learned that her name was Terry Ridley and that she was a Chi Omega from Wichita, Kansas. Her recent knee surgery had resulted from a car wreck in Wichita, while she was still in high school. She had been a front seat passenger when a car raced through an intersection and crashed into her boyfriend's car.

Terry looked somewhat familiar, and I thought I might have seen her at the Sigma Chi house on a date with another Sig. Terry asked some of her sorority sisters from Bartlesville about me, and they assured her I was not as bad as the first impression I had made in our class.

Still assuming negative attention was better than none, I employed a few ploys to get Terry to notice me. Fortunately, the professor seemed oblivious to anything I might be doing, even though I was sitting right in front of him. He didn't seem to notice when I began reading a book by the humorist James Thurber during his lecture, but Terry did. When a test was scheduled a few weeks later, I came into class eating an ice cream cone, trying to look cool while Terry was doing some last-minute cramming.

Eventually, I asked Terry for a Coke date at the student union after a class. After another class, I asked her to walk with me to the student union again, but as we were waiting in line, I told her it was her turn to buy the Cokes. This caught her by surprise, but she did come up with the cash.

On our first real date, I drove my 1952 Buick, affectionately known as "Big Red," to a club in Northwest Oklahoma City. We had a nice dinner, and I kissed her gently on her cheek as we danced. Luckily for me, she thought that was sweet.

Terry and I were among the few OU students who supported Barry Goldwater for president in the 1964 election. I had read his book, *The Conscience of a Conservative*, at home in Bartlesville that summer. I agreed with his conservative principles and expected the "silent majority" of conservative voters to flock to the polls in the election that fall, but they somehow failed to show up. Terry, meanwhile, was actively supporting the legendary former OU football coach Bud Wilkinson, who was running for the US Senate as a Republican. She was a friend of Bud's family in Norman. We were disappointed when both of our guys lost.

An unexpected boost in my stock with Terry may have popped up as we were arriving at the Sigma Chi house for a party. Bill Rigg, a pledge from Bartlesville, had a date with a cute sorority pledge, also from Bartlesville. When he introduced her to Terry and me, she gushed something like, "Bill Dutcher . . . You're famous!" She must have been a Wildcat fan, back in my high school glory days, just three years earlier.

Terry invited me to the Chi Omega's annual ski party in December. We were an inseparable couple, wearing a red and white "tweater," sharing an arm hole in the middle of an oversized ski sweater for two. If nothing else, wearing a "tweater" makes it easy to keep track of your date. Before heading home for Christmas, I gave Terry my Sigma Chi pin. As I understood the custom, getting "pinned" meant you were serious, something like "engaged to be engaged."

My senior year basketball season was spent playing for the Sigma Chi team in OU's fraternity intramurals. Our team consisted of six seniors and one sophomore, and we were like brothers. All of us had played basketball in high school, and our top player, Linus "Gam" Williams, had played in junior college before transferring to OU. Games were played in an old gym on the North Base, a former US Navy Base during World War II, later taken over by OU. At times, OU sororities would bring their entire pledge class to watch the fraternity boys play basketball. Their attendance made the fraternity fan base more attractive than the sparse crowds showing up to watch OU's Varsity. I would take Terry to my games, and we would stop at a local Dairy Queen on our way back to campus.

Fortunately, our Sigma Chi team won the fraternity championship, defeating the Delts 58–38. Our center, Dennis James, led our team in rebounding and Gam was our top scorer. We also got some unexpected scoring from one of our forwards, Mike Thomas. He was a fun-loving, beer-drinking senior, not in great shape, but able to lumber down the court and launch long, overhead set shots from

Terry and I share a "tweater"

the wings, swishing them consistently. Shortly after winning the fraternity championship, I received a note of congratulations from the OU freshman coach, Bud Cronin. "You must have played real well to win by such a large margin," he wrote. He also invited our team to play a scrimmage game against his OU freshmen.

Our team accepted his invitation, but before the game I recruited a couple of former OU players who were Sigma Chi's and still on campus finishing their degrees: George Kernek, a St. Louis Cardinal baseball player, and James Kaiser, a 6' 10" center. Adding these two players to our Sigma Chi roster made our team surprisingly competitive with the OU freshman team, even though we lost a close game.

With my OU basketball playing days behind me, I turned my attention to dating Terry and finishing up my academic pursuits. Unfortunately, Terry's parents did not approve of me as a serious boyfriend for their only daughter. I seem to have made a bad impression on my first visit to their home when I left without thanking her mother for a ham sandwich. Apparently, judging me by my casual dress, fun-loving personality, and my professional writing major at OU, they had concluded that I would "never amount to a hill of beans." I found their assessment uncharitable but not unreasonable. They forbid Terry to see me. Fortunately, Terry had other ideas, but we had to work around the "ban" that spring as she was still living at home.

The ban nearly caused us to break up. Terry and I were visiting with some of her friends in an off-campus apartment when Terry somehow became concerned that her father was out looking for her. She insisted that I hide in a coat closet in case he came to the apartment. Reluctantly, I hid in the closet awhile, feeling humiliated. When I came out of the closet, Terry and I got into an argument as I struggled to regain my manhood. She took off a necklace I had given her and dangled it in front of me, daring me to take it back. I had a brief urge to snatch it but decided to give in instead. We made up, and never really fought again until we got married.

Terry gave me a copy of the book *The Prophet*, by Kahlil Gibran. This classic, published in 1923, reveals the wisdom of a prophet who, preparing to leave a city where he has dwelled for twelve years, is asked to respond to a modest request: " . . . tell us all that has been shown you of that which is between birth and death."

Terry and I were moved by two passages from the Prophet's responses. The first, on marriage, advises: "Let there be spaces in your togetherness . . . stand together yet not too near together: For the pillars of the temple stand apart, and the oak tree and the cypress grow not in each other's shadow."

The second passage we both appreciated was on children. The Prophet says that your children ". . . come through you, but not from you, and though they are with you, they belong not to you." He explains: "You are the bows from which your children as living arrows are sent forth. For even as He loves the arrow that flies, so He loves the bow that is stable."

I had been raised with "benign neglect" and had a strong sense of independence and a love of adventure to show for it. By the time I graduated from college, I was ready to fly, and my parents were at least willing, possibly eager, to fire away.

Terry's parents had been very strict and controlling, but they had not been able to smother her fierce independence or her longing for freedom. She was ready to fly, but her parents wanted to keep her in their quiver.

Her father had served in the Philippines during World War II, then graduated with a degree in journalism from OU in 1948. He seemed to realize that a journalism degree does not put you on the fast track to success. My apparent lack of direction and purpose bothered Terry's parents a lot more than her.

An English class that spring semester was extremely time consuming but very enjoyable. The assignment was to read ten classic American novels. My favorites included *Look Homeward, Angel; The Great Gatsby; Grapes of Wrath; Red Badge of Courage; The Scarlet Letter; and The Sun Also Rises*. I may have spent more time reading for that class than I had spent reading for several other classes combined.

Taking advantage of a gorgeous day in early May, Terry and I drove down to Turner Falls, tucked away in the Arbuckle Mountains, about sixty miles south of Norman. As we walked up a wooded trail to the base of the waterfall, I realized how much I loved her. She was pretty, vivacious, adventurous, and laughed easily and often. Our trip to Turner Falls was the date that clinched the deal.

Near the end of my senior year, I was sitting in a journalism class on filmscript writing when a group of OU senior men, wearing Indian chief headdresses, filed into the classroom. Their leader announced that I had been selected as a member of Pe-et, an honor society for OU's top ten senior men. I had been interviewed for selection into their society, but I did not know if I had been selected. Later, one of my fraternity brothers who was a member of Pe-et told me that my interview had nearly prevented my selection. During my interview, one of the members of the selection committee had asked me what I thought of OU's student government. I told him that I thought the student government was a farce, since the student leaders did not really have any authority to do anything. What I did not know at the time was that the guy asking the questions was the president of the OU student government. Apparently, my dismissive reply was not the answer he was looking for, but the Sigma Chi's had enough intra-fraternity political stroke to get me in anyway. My longtime friend and fraternity brother Mike Hewitt was also selected, hopefully with less controversy, as he was a track star and earned a chemical engineering degree in just four years.

Mountain Climbing for Dummies

About that time, Mike and his College High and OU girlfriend, Patty Mac Sloan, invited me to their wedding in Banff, Canada. I had a final exam for a journalism course scheduled for that week, but I wasn't about to miss their wedding. I arranged to take the final when I got back, even though this meant my official graduation from OU would be postponed until August.

Mike's dad was a top executive at Phillips Petroleum, and he arranged to fly the wedding party from Bartlesville to Calgary, Canada, in a company DC-3. This was my first airplane flight, and we bounced around so much in the turbulent air I was afraid it might be my last. Mike had invited five of his high school and college friends to the wedding. During the rehearsal dinner, we exchanged memories of our high school football days as Bartlesville Wildcats, including Bob Blaker's pointed question: "Do you want to get beat 46 to nothing?"

The Hewitts had arranged for the guys to stay in cabins in Banff National Park. After the wedding, we had a few days to explore around in the Canadian Rockies before heading home. One day the guys piled into a rental car and we drove to the base of a very steep mountain. Wearing jeans, a sweatshirt, and my Chuck Taylor basketball shoes, I decided to try a little mountain climbing. I walked up to a jagged rock face that tilted just enough to invite me to climb. Slowly, I scaled my way up, finding plenty of foot holds and places to grip. As I got higher, I realized that finding footholds on the way up was relatively easy, but I didn't really know how to find them going down. By then, if the mountain had been a building, I would have been up to the fourth floor. I was concerned, but not stuck. With no way to go but up, I kept climbing.

Fortunately, there was a small water fall to my left, and I could see that higher up the water had carved out a level area where I could climb off of the rock face, cross over a small pool, and reach an area with pine trees and grass, where I could just slide down the mountain on my rear.

As I carefully worked my way down the mountain, I noticed that a couple of Royal Canadian Mounties had joined my friends at the base. As I approached the group, I was intercepted by one mad Mountie. He said, in no uncertain terms, that idiots like me caused the Mounties to risk their lives doing helicopter rescues of people stuck on a mountainside like the one I had just climbed. Moreover, he said the climb I had just made requires five years of mountain climbing experience and the proper mountain climbing gear. Who knew?

— • — • —

PART TWO

"If the sky that we look upon
Should crumble and fall
And the mountains should fall to the sea
No, I won't be afraid, no I won't shed a tear
Just as long, just as long as you stand by me."

— MICKEY GILLEY

Newlyweds in Bartlesville

CHAPTER SIX

WELCOME
TO REALITY

U*nfortunately, while I was in Canada* for the wedding, Terry had to endure two more knee surgeries in Oklahoma City. Surprisingly, she was soon able to drive, even though she still had casts on both knees.

Once back in Norman, I rented a one-room garage apartment on Iowa Street in an old neighborhood near the campus. I started hunting for a full-time job, but with the Vietnam war heating up and the draft hanging over my head, my job prospects were limited. I had a vague feeling that I wanted to be a writer, but I felt I did not know enough about life to make writing a career. I could have written my version of "Animal House," based on my experiences as a Sigma Chi, but that idea never occurred to me until I saw the movie.

Eventually, I received offers for reporting jobs from two small town newspapers, one in northeast Oklahoma and the other in southwest Missouri. Each job paid $400 per month. When the Oklahoma State Highway Department offered me $410 per month to be the editor of their employee magazine, I snapped it up.

Adjusting to my long commute and eight-to-five job in the State Highway Department was not easy. The realization that I was on my own, financially, shook my confidence. I enjoyed the work itself, but eight hours working in an office seemed like cruel and unusual punishment.

Still sneaking around Norman, Terry and I decided we should get married. I never really took a knee and proposed. We just seemed to arrive at the same conclusion, at the same time.

While Terry's parents were on a long driving vacation on the East Coast, Terry and I got the blood tests required for a marriage license and went shopping for wedding rings. At a Zale's jewelry store in Norman, we found a pair of gold wedding bands and opened a Zale's credit account. (They cost $40 each. Making small monthly payments, we were able to pay for them by our first anniversary.)

The next morning, we threw a few things into Big Red and headed north on Interstate 35 to Wichita, Kansas. Terry had made an appointment there with an attorney who was representing her in a lawsuit over her knee injuries from her car wreck. Our plan was to find a courthouse and get married on the way to Wichita.

Speeding up the Interstate, my heart was joyful, and I burst into a medley of poverty songs. Possibly trying to lower Terry's expectations, or to give her fair warning that I was not particularly materialistic, I sang:

"I've got plenty of nothing
And nothing is plenty for me
I got no car
Got no mule
Got no misery

Folks with plenty of plenty
They got a lock on the door
Afraid somebody's gonna rob them while
They're out for making more

What for?"

Encouraged by Terry, who said she likes to hear me sing, I kept to my theme:

"Oh! We ain't got a barrel of money
Maybe we're ragged and funny
But we'll travel along
Singing a song
Side by side

I don't know what's a-coming' tomorrow
Maybe it's trouble and sorrow
But we'll travel the road
Sharing our load
Side by side"

When we reached the Guthrie exit off I-35, we drove into town and found the courthouse, but it was not open. We continued heading north on I-35, then took the exit to Perry. Their courthouse wasn't open either. There seemed to be a flaw in our plan. In Oklahoma, county courthouses are not open on Saturdays. We continued our drive to Wichita, where Terry met with her attorney. He told her getting married would not affect her lawsuit.

Early that evening, we went to Terry's parent's home in Norman to tell them about our decision. The discussion did not go well. While her parents did not exactly tell me to go to hell, they left no measurable room for my continued stay on this earth. Their anger did not hurt my feelings as much as it made me realize how badly Terry needed to get away. Like a silent movie heroine, she was tied to the tracks and it was up to me to rescue her. With Terry in tears, we headed for Bartlesville, where we received a warm and sympathetic welcome from my parents. They had met Terry on a trip we had taken to Bartlesville earlier that summer and seemed to realize that in marrying her, I was overachieving.

Monday was a busy day for my mom and dad. While Mom arranged our wedding, Dad traded Big Red in for a newer white Ford Fairlane and gave it to us as a wedding present. A small chapel at the First Methodist Church was reserved for 11 am on Tuesday, August 25th, and the church's pastor, Reverend Featherstone, was recruited to perform the ceremony. Friends and family were invited by phone. Terry wore a sleeveless, light blue silk dress with a white bow in her hair and a borrowed white veil. She looked beautiful as she walked up the aisle. When the reverend declared us man and wife, we kissed and stepped onto the roller coaster that would become our life.

Following a small wedding reception at the Bartlesville Elks Club, Terry and I were showered with rice as we headed out the door. We jumped into our new used car and drove away, just a couple of newlyweds destined for a poor couple's honeymoon at the appropriately affordable Western Hills State Lodge, in Northeastern Oklahoma, near Fort Gibson.

As we arrived at our room in the lodge, I turned on a small, wall-mounted, black and white television set just in time to hear

President Lyndon Johnson announce that being married would no longer result in an exemption from the draft. I started to joke: "Gee, honey, I'm sorry our marriage didn't work out," but in a rare moment of self-editing, I managed to keep this comment to myself, even as I realized this change in the draft regulations meant that I would soon be going to Vietnam. The only questions were when and in which branch of the Armed Services.

A Period of Adjustment

As newlyweds, there was no pomp in our circumstances. We rented a small, old, wooden house on Eddington Street, near the OU campus and affordable at $75 per month rent. However, we soon discovered that the house was affordable for a reason. It was located so close to a railroad track that when a train roared by, its vibrations would shake the house and make our bed scoot across the bedroom floor. Terry took a job as the advertising manager of the *Del City News*. For some strange reason, their offices were in downtown Norman.

After a few weeks of living on Eddington, we decided to move to a nice apartment complex near the Oklahoma State Capitol and the Highway Department headquarters. The move was easy, as everything we owned fit into our Ford Fairlane in one trip.

The rent at our new apartment was much higher than we had been paying in Norman, and it really strained our limited budget. As I watched the gas gauge in our car gradually move toward "empty," it felt as if the gauge were measuring a decline in my blood supply.

Our marriage required a little period of adjustment to differences that had not emerged during our courtship. We seemed to have loaded each other down with expectations of what a wife and husband should be. Terry was not bashful about letting me know where I was falling short. I had grown up receiving plenty of encouragement but very little criticism. When Terry would jump on me for what seemed like trivial offenses, I didn't know how to handle her complaints. This situation led to an iconic event in our early marriage. We were eating dinner in a little hamburger joint called the "Beef & Bun," and Terry was criticizing me about little things I viewed as minor offenses. She felt they were worth not just mentioning but beating to death. Frustrated and not knowing how to respond, I suddenly burst into tears, shocking Terry and embarrassing me. (As time passed by, the "Beef & Bun" incident became an inside joke.)

Terry had grown up in a house full of concerns about what other people should do and what they would think. I would ask Terry: "Who are these 'other people' and why should we care what they do or think?" Over time, Terry gradually became more relaxed about appearances and thanked me for freeing her from unnecessary worries.

I once asked my two bosses at the Highway Department to join me for lunch at our new apartment. All I had to offer them was toasted cheese sandwiches and Campbell's tomato soup. My boss's boss offered to make the toasted cheese sandwiches, and I watched in horror as he cut huge slices of our Velveeta Cheese for each sandwich. That cheese had been expected to last us until the next payday. When I confessed to Terry what had happened, I felt like Jack telling his mother he had traded the family cow for a few beans.

During the holidays, Terry and I were playing *Monopoly* in our apartment living room, and I was winning big, adding hotels on the best properties, and raking in cash as she landed on my collection of railroads. Apparently, I was enjoying my dominance a little too much, showing what looked to her like an unpleasant combination of avarice and competitiveness. When she had seen enough, she suddenly flipped over the board, and my unreal real estate empire went flying all over the living room. She accused me of getting greedy. I responded, "Of course I was getting greedy. That's the whole point of *Monopoly*." (We haven't played a board game since.)

In January, Terry resumed her classes at OU for the second semester, so we moved to OU's married student apartments just south of the campus. This was our third move in five months. Moving is easy when you don't have much stuff. A frugal couple next door showed us how to make a living room carpet out of free carpet samples. When her spring semester was over, we bounced back to the Statesman Apartments in Oklahoma City for our second stay.

Knowing that I had to deal with my military service obligation, I decided to apply to the Navy's Officer Candidate School (OCS). Given the nature of the expanding war in Vietnam, it seemed that the Navy offered the best chance of surviving the war. Apparently, a lot of married male college graduates around the country had reached the same conclusion and were competing to be accepted into the Navy OCS program. I took a difficult entrance exam in the Oklahoma City recruiting office and scored high enough to be accepted. I soon received orders to report to the Navy OCS in Newport, Rhode Island, in August 1966.

That summer, still needing to earn some extra cash, I signed up to be an umpire for Little League baseball games around Oklahoma City. One Saturday morning, I was assigned to call a game in a predominately black neighborhood in northeast Oklahoma City. I had played football and basketball with black teammates in high school and college for many years, so I wasn't concerned about the fans being black. I was concerned about them being Little League parents, as one of the teams was going to lose. It didn't help matters when the other umpire scheduled to work this game failed to show up.

Each team had several good players, which led to a high-scoring game. I called the balls and strikes from behind home plate, then sprinted around the infield to get into good position to call close plays on the bases. Fortunately, I was a little faster than the kids, so I could beat the runners to the base they were headed to. By the time the game was over, I was exhausted. The parents from both teams, winners and losers, could not have been more gracious, asking me to come back and call more of their games. They seemed to recognize hustle and decent calls when they saw them. My pay for umpiring the game was $3, and I earned every penny of it.

— ◦ — • —

CHAPTER SEVEN

YOU'RE IN THE
NAVY NOW

In early August, it was time for me to report to the Navy's Officer Candidate School in Newport, RI. Terry moved to another apartment in Norman, where she would stay with friends and finish the course work for her OU degree in sociology while I was at OCS. I flew to New York City and, while waiting to board the short hop to Newport, Rhode Island, I ran into Gary Williamson, my Sigma Chi fraternity brother at OU, who was headed for the same destination. We sat together on the flight to Newport and on a Navy shuttle bus to the OCS Navy base, conveniently located on the shores of Narragansett Bay. On arrival, we stepped off the bus and into a processing line. We were marched to get haircuts, pick up uniforms and gear, and move into our barracks. Still together, Gary and I were deposited into the same room and realized we would be roommates for the four-month grind of becoming Navy officers.

At that point in my life, I could be described a lot of ways, but those ways would not have included disciplined, organized, or militaristic. My biggest weakness was simply all things mechanical.

Gary and I were both athletic and used to working on teams, so that would help. We did not expect the physical part of the training to be a problem. Our initial deal was that Gary would help me with the military part, like cleaning a rifle or shining shoes, while I would help him with the academic part. As it turned out, he ended up helping me with both.

A couple of weeks into the program, I found myself having a hard time keeping up in a class on Navy organization. Most of my fellow officer candidates were still tense and possibly a little intimidated by their new military status. The professor, a young Navy lieutenant, was laboring through an explanation of a complex organization chart, when I raised my hand. He seemed a little surprised by this interruption but recognized me.

"I would like to change the subject," I said.

"Okay," he said.

"But I can't figure out what it is."

The classroom erupted in a boom of laughter. I had broken the tension that had been building up in my classmates for two weeks.

I was surprised by their outburst. I didn't think what I said was that funny . . . just true.

To his credit, the lieutenant took my little pin prick of the classroom tension in stride, perhaps realizing how a Navy organization chart must look to a new arrival. My favorite example of Navy organization was a sign I later encountered in the Philippines that read: FIC PAC FAC FAPL, which, of course, stands for Fleet Intelligence Center, Pacific Facility, Fleet Air Photo Lab.

Gary and I found that most of the other young men in our squadron were at lot like us: married, college graduates, and able to do well enough on the OCS entrance exam to make the cut. The military training was comparable to that received by the midshipmen at the

Naval Academy, only crammed into four months instead of four years. Somehow, I got through the program, but it didn't really take.

On a weekend pass, I drove to Cambridge, Massachusetts, where my friend Mike Hewitt was working on an MBA at Harvard. When I reached their student apartment, Mike was cramming for a test, so his wife Patty Mac offered to take me on a tour of some of the famous historical sites in Boston, including the site of "The Shot Heard Around the World." Patty Mac was obviously pregnant with their first child, and I was wearing my Navy OCS uniform. We kept getting sympathetic smiles from the other tourists, who seemed to be assuming I would soon be going off to sea, leaving my pregnant wife behind.

Near the end of my OCS training, I met with an administrative officer about my future assignment. I confirmed that I was requesting shore duty and that I was subject to sea sickness. He said I should do something in my Navy career besides just playing basketball. I had not known that was an option. With my journalism degree, I was hoping to be designated as a public affairs officer. Being from land-locked Oklahoma, I did not care much for those big grey things that go out on the water. My fear of being tossed around on some ocean for months at a time was so great that I would have rather been assigned to a river boat in Vietnam, like my classmate John Kerry was, than to any Navy ship smaller than an aircraft carrier. Luckily, I was assigned to report to the Subic Bay Naval Base in the Philippines for duty as a public affairs officer. My journalism degree was paying off already.

Gary was assigned to the Naval Air Station in Pensacola, Florida. He played wide receiver on a base football team quarterbacked by Roger Staubach, who won the Heisman Trophy as quarterback for the Naval Academy and went on to star for the Dallas Cowboys.

Gary and I turned out to be the only two members of our squadron to get shore duty. All the others were going to Vietnam or out to sea. This led to speculation that somewhere in the Bureau of Navy Personnel, there was a Sigma Chi looking out for us.

Leaving OCS, I was relieved that I had made it through the training program but did not feel prepared for active duty. Ready or not, I was commissioned as an ensign, the lowest rank for a Navy officer.

After a two-week leave in Norman, I packed up the Ford Fairlane and headed west on Interstate 40 for a long drive to the Presidio Naval Base in San Francisco. Almost through New Mexico, I stopped for the night and found my car battery frozen in the morning. Fortunately, an enterprising young man was in the parking lot of the motel jump starting cars with the same problem for $5 per start. I reached the Presidio late that night. The next morning, I arranged for the Navy to ship my car to Subic Bay and caught my first flight across the International Dateline. One thing I did learn at OCS was that when it's Monday in Manila, it's Sunday in San Francisco.

Philippine Time

My plane landed at Clark Air Force Base, located in a mountainous area of Luzon, the largest of the Philippine Islands. There were a few other ensigns on the two-hour bus ride to Subic Bay Naval Base. They seemed confident, maybe even cocky. I assumed they were graduates of the Naval Academy, because I felt unprepared for whatever might come next.

As we drove past jungles, rice paddies, and small villages, I recalled that I had been warned that there were communist guerrillas called "Huks" operating in the area between the two US military bases. I saw an old Filipino man, sitting on the back of a carabao, lighting up a Lucky Strike with a cigarette lighter, but he looked more like a rice farmer than a Huk.

Subic Bay indents the western coast of Luzon, just across the historic Bataan Peninsula from Manila. Only two days by sea from Vietnam, the Subic Bay base was the Navy's primary staging point for the war effort. The base's workforce consisted of 6,600 US sailors, marines, and civilians, plus more than 16,000 Filipino nationals, working together to provide logistical and maintenance support for all Navy ships in the South China Sea. Surrounding Subic Bay on three sides, the massive base covered more than fifty-six square miles of land.

More nervous than excited, I checked in for duty at the Public Affairs Office and met my new boss, Lieutenant Commander Van Ferguson, who was the Base Public Affairs Officer. We were on the staff of the base commander, Rear Admiral Fillmore Gilkeson, and our office was right down the hall from his.

Luckily for me, Lieutenant Commander Ferguson, henceforth Van, was not your typical Navy officer. He was an easygoing, free-spirited bachelor who put me at ease right away. He showed me the Bachelor Officers Quarters, where I would be staying until Terry was able to join me in March. We went by his room, which was cluttered with sheet music and papers filled with mathematical calculations. During his off-duty hours, he was working on a mathematical theory for composing music. He also showed me a book of puzzling poetry he had written while he was a "Beatnik" in the 1950s. One random line jumped out at me: "What time does this train get to Philadelphia?"

That evening, my boss and a friend of his, a Navy officer who was staying at the BOQ while his ship was being repaired, took me on a tour of Olongapo. This raucous Filipino city, just a bridge over polluted waters from the base, was home to thousands of Filipinos who worked on the base. However, Olongapo was better known for its dedication to serving the recreational needs of thousands of sailors who, after months at sea, poured out of their ships and into the town each evening. The main drag was lined with scores of nightclubs and bars, each employing dozens of "hostesses" eager to drink with the sailors and eventually go upstairs to trim their horns.

Later that night, we dropped by to see another one of Van's friends who lived in Olongapo. We had all had a few San Miguel beers, and the evening included howling at the moon and either a pushup contest or me being ordered to do push-ups. For whatever reason, I did forty. Finally, as part of my initiation into the Philippines, I reluctantly forced down a balut, which is a fertilized duck egg, incubated for two or three weeks, then boiled and eaten out of the shell. Luckily, the one I ate did not have feathers.

For my primary duty, I was assigned to manage the base newspaper and radio station. But I also assisted Van in media relations and community relations. As a young and still idealistic ensign, I wanted to manage the newspaper and radio station like they were independent news media, not promotional arms of the Navy. The sailors and Filipino civilians who worked for me seemed to like that approach. We launched a short-lived radio newscast, but after we reported that a high-ranking Navy officer had crashed his pickup into the entrance of the Officer's Club after midnight, the base commander cancelled our news program.

One local story that captured the essence of the Subic Bay/ Olongapo tango covered a Navy medical program aimed at protecting the health of the sailors on leave in the city. Navy medical personnel were tasked with giving free VD shots to the hundreds of hostesses employed in Olongapo's night clubs and bars. The hostesses, in uniform with their stiletto heels, mini-skirts, halter-tops, and heavy make-up, cheerfully formed a long line to wait for their shots.

To keep them from having to stand in the tropical heat for too long, the Navy had arranged to give the shots from a small building next to an outdoor amphitheater, where the waiting hostesses, howling in delight, were being entertained with Bugs Bunny and Mickey Mouse cartoons. To me, the sight of hundreds of scantily clad hostesses laughing their asses off watching Walt Disney characters was a bizarre picture of your tax dollars at work.

Once every couple of weeks I was assigned to Armed Forces Police duty, supervising the Navy shore patrol from a small building on the edge of the base, near the bridge to Olongapo. The enlisted men in the shore patrol were tough and experienced sailors who knew their jobs well. Navy regulations required the presence of an officer in certain situations, but as near as I could figure, my job was to stay awake all night and take the blame if anything went wrong.

The building had four jail cells. The shore patrol men would bring in sailors who had been misbehaving in Olongapo, usually in a drunk and disorderly way, and lock them up in one of the cells until a detail of their shipmates would arrive to take them back to their ships. Most nights were relatively quiet. Problems ensued when there were two aircraft carriers in port, swelling the number of sailors in Olongapo. This created a supply and demand imbalance in the city, with too many sailors and not enough hostesses in the nightclubs and bars. The additional fights that resulted from this market failure created hectic nights at the shore patrol office.

The dating situation was a little different for sailors stationed at Subic Bay. If they were shacking up in Olongapo with a Filipina girlfriend, they could take out "going steady" papers, which made them financially responsible for her, but only for the duration of their duty assignment in the Philippines. This arrangement made breaking up not so hard to do.

One of my first media relations efforts ended in disaster. Van and I were entertaining a *Manila Times* reporter named Manny at the Officer's Club. After dinner, we stopped by the bar, where Van ordered a round of flaming brandies. The bartender ignited a small blue flame from the fumes arising from our drinks, and Van demonstrated how to toss them down quickly, allowing the flames to shoot out of his mouth, like a circus fire eater.

Since the flames did not seem to bother Van, I copied his quick toss maneuver, with the same result. There's nothing like a flaming drink of brandy on a warm, tropical night.

Then it was Manny's turn, but he seemed conflicted about trying this new drink. He started to toss it down but hesitated at the last second and spilled flaming brandy on his Barong Tagalog (an expensive, open-collar, Filipino silk dress shirt). My eyes widened in shock as I realized his chest hairs were on fire. The bartender tossed Van a towel and he quickly put out the fire on our guest's chest. The next time I saw Manny, his chest was still heavily bandaged, but at least he was friendly and still able to work.

In February 1967, James Gordon, the first elected mayor of Olongapo, was assassinated. He had been in the city post office, mailing a letter, when a lone gunman walked up behind him and shot him in the head. The popular mayor, the son of an American Marine and a Filipina mother, had been in office a little over three years. By chance, a Navy hospital ship that had been serving in

Vietnam was docked in the base, and there were brain surgeons on board with experience in operating on soldiers who had been shot in the head during combat. The mayor, still breathing, was rushed to the ship for emergency medical treatment.

Van and I went to the ship to help deal with the media covering the shooting. The mayor did not survive the Navy surgeons' attempt to save him. Van sent me to the mayor's home in Olongapo to convey the bad news, give our condolences to the family, and see what our public affairs office could do to help. There were several armed guards in front of their home when I arrived. As I walked into their living room, it was apparent that the bad news had beaten me there. I asked to see his widow, Amelia, and I was pointed to a room down a hallway. I slowly opened the door and peaked in. A Catholic priest was trying to comfort Amelia, her long black hair tumbling down her back, tears flowing, wailing in grief. It was the saddest scene I had ever witnessed.

Terry Catches Up with Me

Terry joined me in the Philippines in March, after completing the course work and final tests for her BA degree in sociology. We rented a small apartment above a Sari Sari store, on curiously named Texas Road, in Olongapo. The store was like a miniature Seven Eleven, selling soft drinks, beer, candy, snacks, and various sundries. While we were living there, a landslide just a few blocks away crushed a home and killed a Navy sailor. We moved to a two-story duplex in the officer's section of base housing as soon as it became available.

Terry and I moonlighted preparing monthly newsletters for the Subic Officer's Club and for the Chief's Club. We worked together in the evenings, preparing the copy and photos for the newsletters, in the offices of the base newspaper. Although we occasionally argued about how to crop the photos, it was fun working together and earning a little extra cash.

One night, Terry visited with jet-lagged Johnny Cash and June Carter before their performance at the Chief's Club. June was feeling sick, blaming it on all the shots she had to get before taking the long flight to Philippines, but the show went on, as it must.

We soon learned the concept of Philippine time. We were invited to a program in Olongapo that was scheduled to begin at 6 pm. We arrived on time and found ourselves the only ones there. After we waited awhile, a group of Filipino men walked in and began constructing a stage for the event, which started a couple of hours later.

At Filipino parties, Terry and I learned to do a rhythmic dance called the "Tinikling." Two people, one at each end of two bamboo poles, bang the poles on a low wooden block in front of them, starting with the poles together, then spreading them about a foot apart. The dancers step in between the poles when they are apart, then step outside of the poles when they are brought back together. This can be a lot of fun once you catch on to the rhythm of the moving bamboo poles. Otherwise, possible side effects include tripping, falling, and sore ankles.

When we met Filipinos during community relations events, we were often asked if we had any children. When we said no, the response was often: "Oh, you must be newlyweds." When we again said no, all we got were sympathetic looks. Except once. When we told a Filipino doctor that we did not have any children, but were not newlyweds, he paused for a moment of thought, then concluded: "You must be practicing birth control!"

With Terry working, we found ourselves with a lot of disposable income, an economic situation we had heard about but never experienced. Many things were unbelievably cheap, especially things that normally included a high tax component in their price. Gasoline was eight cents per gallon; beer was a nickel a can; a fifth of champagne was $1.50. The prevailing wage for a full-time maid was $20 per month. Our maid, Helen, was able to supplement her

Tough duty: swinging at Subic Bay

income by taking home things like coat hangers and used coffee cans to sell in her barrio. Most importantly, we were able to buy a whole houseful of rattan furniture for $500. Later, we were able to buy luxuries like cameras, slide projectors, stereos, and eight-track tapes.

Terry and I enjoyed having dinner at the Officer's Club, which featured Perry De Guzman and his orchestra. His lead singer, a Filipina named Consuelo, loved to belt out "Black is black . . . I want my baby back." Our favorite guest artist was Filipina television and recording star from Manila, Pilita Corrales. The club also presented guest appearances by entertainers from the States, like Della Reese, The Four Freshmen, and The Platters. Officers whose ships were visiting Subic Bay, after months at sea, would sometimes ask Terry to dance, which was usually no problem. The only one who got a little too frisky on the dance floor was a Navy chaplain, and she was able to fight him off. Without kids to go home to, we sometimes stayed late at the club until finally hearing an announcement that "the club is secure." (This call has remained an inside joke for when we are ready to call it a night.)

As part of my media relations job, we sometimes had foreign reporters visit our home. Terry was in the kitchen one evening when a Japanese reporter arrived early. He had just sat down on our living room sofa when Terry ran by, wearing an old Sigma Chi football jersey, and hurried upstairs to change. The reporter inquired: "Is Number 40 your wife?" I wanted to reply: "One of them." But I was afraid he might not get the joke, so I just said "yes."

On July 29, 1967, a horrific fire broke out on board the aircraft carrier *USS Forrestal* as it was engaging in combat operations in the Tonkin Gulf. A chain reaction of explosions killed 134 sailors and injured 161. On the night of July 31, the ship arrived at the Cubi

Point Naval Air Station to undertake repairs. I was sent to help deal with the major national news media that was covering its arrival.

When I arrived at the scene, deceased sailors in body bags were being carried off the ship and loaded onto awaiting trucks. I recognized CBS war correspondent Bernard Kalb as he was directing his camera crew to film this depressing scene.

Unsure of how to handle this situation, I told him to stop the filming until I could go on board and get official approval. The veteran reporter looked at me, noticed the single ensign's stripe on my shoulder, and told his camera crew to go ahead with the filming. I figured he must have a lot more experience than I did in this type of situation, so I went on board the ship to see what else I could help with.

My First Comeback

While my media relations efforts were not going well, I seemed to be doing better at tying in my community relations efforts with my basketball coaching job. The base had a nice full-court basketball arena next door to the newspaper and radio station offices. I volunteered to be the manager/player/coach of the base basketball team, a so-called "collateral duty" that included responsibility for all basketball activities, including scheduling our team's games.

Having played very little basketball since I got married, playing on the Subic Bay team marked my first comeback. (I define a basketball comeback as resuming playing after going a year or more with little or no hoops. I hate it when life interferes with basketball.)

It did not take me long to figure out that our Navy players were not very interested in practicing, but they were eager to play in games. So, I scheduled a lot of games. We played games at home and away against Filipino teams, teams from the ships in port at Subic Bay, and teams from nearby Air Force and Coast Guard bases.

Basketball was a highly popular sport in Asia, even in the mid-1960s. The *Manila Times* covered the performance of the Filipino national team in Southeast Asian basketball tournaments as front-page news stories. It seemed that every little barrio within fifty miles of Subic Bay had its own team. Typically, we would be invited to play as part of a barrio's celebration of one of their countless holidays. Each barrio, no matter how small, had an outdoor area with a concrete basketball court and a stage on one side. The stage was used to crown the queen of whatever festival they were observing, then a basketball game would be played on a court ringed with hundreds of fans.

As player-coach, I installed myself as point guard. Our shooting guard was a stocky, talented seaman named Tom Lewis, who had made Catholic School All State in Pennsylvania. We were both long-range bombers who would have benefited greatly if the three-point line had existed in those days.

Our best player was ensign Larry Miller, a 6' 4" forward who had recently played for Indiana State. We also had a 6' 5" center, a Marine corporal who was a terrific rebounder, but will remain nameless for reasons explained later. Those two, along with our power forward, Eugene Barney, gave us a strong front line.

Early in my Subic Bay coaching career, while I was still an ensign, we were playing a game against a team from one of the Navy ships in port. One of our players, a lieutenant, became upset about his lack of playing time. He seemed to believe he was a great player, even though he only had a few post moves, and at 6' 2" was too short to use them against good competition. Much to my surprise, he jumped up from his seat on our bench, walked to the

Tropical hoops: Filipino style

scorer's table, and tried to put himself into the game as a substitute for one of our forwards. I immediately called time-out, outraged by this breech of basketball protocol, and told him to sit back down. When he protested, I shouted into his face: "You get out of this game, and you get out of this gym!" Surprised, he turned away and stomped back to the locker room. Later, I wondered if I had exceeded my authority, since he was a lieutenant and I was just an ensign. But I never saw him again, so I quit worrying about it.

Things did get out of hand in one of our Subic Bay home games against another ship team. I don't know what started it, but I was shocked when a good old-fashioned brawl broke out in the middle of the game. Both benches emptied and the visitors' shipmates poured out of the stands to join the fight. Soon there was a massive pile of basketball players and sailors at center court. The pile looked like the celebration of a baseball team that had just won the World Series. I started trying to pull my players out of the fray, which seemed like a group wrestling match, with no one seriously trying to hurt anyone else. Luckily, the Navy shore patrol was nearby, and those guys really know how to break up a fight. Soon, order was restored, but the game was cancelled.

Playing against Filipino teams presented different challenges. What the Filipino teams lacked in size they made up for in speed, quickness, and some surprising hang time. Many of the Filipino players had a highly individualistic approach to the game and were extremely creative in their attempted drives to the basket, as if they believed more points were awarded for degree of difficulty. Our games against Filipino teams were played using international rules, which apparently did not recognize the concept of a charging foul. The agile Filipino players took advantage of this difference in the rules by often driving hard for the basket, full speed ahead. If you blocked their path, expecting a charging foul to be called against them, you were disappointed. All you would get was a knee pad on your shoulder or a basketball shoe in your stomach.

Our games against the Filipino teams were often fast-paced, high-scoring contests, played in the tropical sun, with both the scores and the temperatures above the century mark. One of the better Filipino teams we played was the Payumo Selections, in Dinalupihan, Bataan. We beat them, 110 to 89.

But we didn't always win. Once we played a Chinese team in a steamy little gym above a bowling alley in Manila. We had a big lead for most of the game, but our players were beginning to melt in the fourth quarter, and the lead began slipping away. I kept checking the "official" game clock, a small alarm clock set next to the scorekeeper. The clock did not seem to be making much progress. Finally, I realized we were just going to keep playing until they got ahead. Sure enough, they took a one-point lead and a game-ending buzzer sounded before we could pass the ball in bounds. Since this was supposed to be a "friendly" exhibition game, promoting good international relations, I didn't protest their home-cooked timing strategy. I was just glad to get out of the sauna before I lost any more weight.

I did protest a "loss" to an Air Force team at Clark Air Base. We had a safe, three-point lead and the ball out of bounds under our own basket, with just three seconds left of the clock. I wasn't too worried when one of their players stole my careless in-bounds pass and dribbled the length of the court for a layup. As our guy retrieved the ball, out of bounds and under their basket, the final buzzer sounded, but one of their guys refused to accept its finality. He stepped out of bounds, wrestled the ball away from our guy, and tossed it in bounds to a teammate, who scored again. Even though all this post-game activity took at least ten seconds, the Filipino refs and scorekeepers, literally on the Air Force payroll, counted this belated basket and gave them the win.

Back in my office the next morning, I was still upset about losing this game. Even though I realized we were in the middle of the Vietnam War, and I should have something better to do, I wrote a lengthy protest letter about this egregious assault on the integrity of inter-service sports. To my surprise, officials governing the Philippine Interservice Basketball League awarded us a 102–101 win. According to a report in the *Stars & Stripes* military newspaper, "After conferring with both coaches, the referees and other witnesses, league officials upheld the Subic protest." They even provided the game officials with a face-saving, if flimsy, excuse, finding that when the disputed basket was made, "the final buzzer had sounded, but was not heard by the game officials because of the roar of the crowd." The verdict meant that our heated Navy-versus-Air Force rivalry ended the season with Subic Bay winning twice, 100–97 and 102–101, and Clark also winning twice, 108–86 and 118–82. We ended up tied for first place in our league.

On another basketball day trip to Manila, I wanted to bring Terry with me, and I told the other players they could bring a date. Most of them had Filipina girlfriends, so we had a crowded bus. When our bus pulled up to an outdoor court in the middle of Manila, it was surrounded by Filipino fans. Somehow, a rumor got around that we had Marilyn Monroe on the bus with us. As we climbed off the bus, I heard the fans buzzing about Marilyn Monroe. It turned out to be an understandable case of mistaken identity. Instead of the movie star, the pretty, petite blond on our bus was Terry.

In February 1968, our team won the Philippine All-Navy Tournament in games played at the Cubi Point Naval Air Station, just across the bay. In the finals, we beat a team from San Miguel Naval Communications Station by a score of 85–81. Larry Miller averaged 36 points per game in the tournament and was named Most Valuable Player.

By winning this tournament, we advanced to the All Navy Tournament at Pearl Harbor, Hawaii. We were able to pick up four of the better players from the other teams in the tournament, including Howard Clay, a guard from the USS Ajax and Jack Hornbuckle, a forward from San Miguel.

Unfortunately, we lost our center, who was in the brig. A Marine corporal, he was charged with looking the other way while Filipino employees smuggled equipment off the base. In a moment of bad judgment, I decided to go over to the brig and request that they let him out long enough to go to the All Navy Tournament, as we really needed his rebounding. I walked into the brig commander's office, where the commander, a Marine captain, was sitting at his desk. The left side of his face had been badly burned, most likely during recent combat in Vietnam. He gave me a skeptical look as I began to explain my request, and before I could finish his look had hardened into a penetrating glare, as if to say: "What war are you fighting in?" He never said a word.

"Never mind," I said, then saluted and quickly backed out in a hasty retreat. However, I didn't let my failure to spring our center ruin my enthusiasm for a wartime basketball junket to Hawaii.

Our team, minus one center, flew to Hawaii and took a bus to the Pearl Harbor Naval Base. Terry and I checked into the Bachelor Officer Quarters while the rest of the team settled elsewhere on the base. The next day, we had a shoot-around at the court where the games would be played. All we heard about from the local sailors was the fearsome full-court press to be applied by the powerful and heavily favored team from the Pearl Harbor Submarine Base.

In the spirit of inter-service rivalry, best seen in the annual football clash between West Point and the Naval Academy, each service maintained a stacked basketball team. In the Navy, if you had been a star high school or college basketball player as a civilian, there was a good chance you would be assigned to the Pearl Harbor Submarine Base. This assignment may have been what the officer at OCS was referring to when he said I should do something more than just playing basketball.

We drew the highly favored crew of submariners in the first round. Sure enough, they slapped on their killer full-court press. But we had an answer. We had two skilled young guards: Tom Lewis, the long-range gunner from our Subic Bay team, and Howard Clay, a quick and smooth guard and our best ball handler. I posted Larry Miller near the mid-court circle to give my guards a tall, athletic target for outlet passes. They hit him with sharp passes, then sped to the other end of the court. We were not content to just break their press. We took the ball to the basket and scored. At halftime, we were leading by ten points. That was the last we saw of their famous press.

For the first time in my Navy basketball career, I found it difficult to play and coach in the same game. I didn't play myself until the second half, and the only play I remember was going up for a long-range jumper and getting my shot blocked, for the first time ever. After benching myself to get back to coaching, I watched as the submariners, obviously the more experienced team, gradually clawed their way back into the game and eventually eliminated our Philippine contingent from the All Navy Tournament.

Later that spring, Terry's grandfather, affectionately known as "Daddy Charles," passed away in Oklahoma. The Navy was kind enough to fly her back to the States so that she could attend his funeral. I drove her to Clark Air Base for her flight. On my drive through a mountainous area on my way back to Subic Bay, our Ford Fairlane began struggling, then overheating. I pulled off the highway and crept along on dirt roads to a small barrio, where I asked a young man if there was an automobile mechanic in their town. He directed me to a small building with a dirt floor and a thatched straw roof, where the local mechanic looked under the hood and said he could fix my car. By then, my arrival had drawn a crowd of onlookers, including several men who offered their opinions on how to fix my car.

Knowing next to nothing about how car engines work, I stood by patiently, waiting to see if my car could be fixed. I did know that engine problems are often caused by the carburetor or the alternator, but I could not have picked either one out of a lineup. After an hour or so had passed with no solution discovered, the mechanic said he could not find a problem with the engine, so it must be in the fuel line. This required some disassembling, and I began to get worried after a couple of hours had passed and more and more of my car's parts were strewn around on a tarp covering the garage's dirt floor. However, by late afternoon, the mechanic had not only reassembled my vehicle, but also had fixed the engine.

Greatly relieved, I asked him how much I owed him.

"It's up to you, Joe," he replied.

All I had in my wallet was a $20 bill. I gave him the twenty and showed him my empty wallet. He seemed happy with this payment, and I was happy to get out of town. Although my car did not seem to be running normally, it did run well enough to get me back to Subic Bay.

When I got back to the base, I drove straight to the Navy's garage to have my car's engine examined. When I picked it up later, the Navy mechanic told me this was the first time he had seen a Ford fixed with Chevy parts.

Although I served on Admiral Gilkeson's staff, I did not speak with him directly on many occasions during my time in the Philippines. Tall and thin, serious and direct, he looked and acted the part of an admiral.

There were several officers between the admiral and me on the staff. But I was in the weekly rotation for all-night duty in the base's command office. Normally, the biggest challenge on this duty was staying awake. But one night, around 2 am, I was on duty when an urgent message came in from the commander of the Navy's Pacific Fleet in Hawaii. The message said an Air Force search and rescue operation was in progress in an area of the South China Sea where the Navy was planning a large training exercise involving an aircraft carrier and many other ships later that morning. After a mild panic, I decided that to avoid potential collisions, I needed to send an urgent message telling the admiral commanding the Navy exercise to call it off. This was a tough decision. I must have been more afraid of waking up Admiral Gilkeson in the middle of the night than I was of cancelling the Navy exercise.

The next morning, I was called into the admiral's office. By then, he had heard from the admiral in charge of the exercise, who had asked something like, "Who is Ensign Dutcher, and why does he think he can cancel a major Navy training exercise?" Admiral Gilkeson told me I had done the right thing and had made a gutsy call, but next time I should wake him up.

In another meeting with the admiral, he complained about the number of Navy pilots being injured doing the "chair launch" at the Cubi Point Naval Air Station officer's club. There was a bar in the club where the pilots from visiting aircraft carriers could drink while they waited for a table in the club's crowded dining room, located just a few steps down a stairway from the bar. The pilots, blowing off a little steam after dodging enemy missiles in the Vietnam war zone, liked to make a grand entrance into the dining room. They would sit in a lounge chair with wheels, and their buddies would launch them from the bar, so that they could fly into the dining room. If their flying lounge chairs did not land properly, they would suffer the injuries that Admiral Gilkeson was complaining about.

The admiral took a few members of his staff, including me, on a public relations trip to a small island near the southern tip of the Philippines. We were invited to dinner at the home of the local mayor, and I was surprised to find that even the mayor lived in a traditional Nipa Hut, on stilts with a thatch roof. At dinner, I noticed there were several gnats in my soup. At first, I thought that maybe this was a local delicacy, but the gnat population in my soup kept growing, so I concluded that they were uninvited guests. Clearly, the admiral was not a fan of the gnat soup, and I was glad I was not the person who had arranged this trip.

My Sea Faring Daze

Although I spent nearly all my four-year Navy career onshore, I did experience eleven days of sea duty. Luckily, I was on large ships in calm waters, so I did not suffer from sea sickness during this time. My sea faring days began in July 1968, when I departed Subic Bay on board the aircraft carrier *USS Constellation*, armed only with a Canon sixteen-millimeter movie camera and a Minolta thirty-five-millimeter camera. On my first day out, I positioned myself in a nook alongside the carrier's launching point, where I filmed the pilots pulling up in their jets, saluting the sailor manning the launching controls, and being slung off the carrier by what seemed like a giant, cable sling shot.

After four days on the *Constellation*, I was flown by helicopter to the *USS George K. MacKenzie* (DD-836), a destroyer participating in an operation called Sea Dragon, a few miles off the coast of North Vietnam. The ship was not large enough for my helicopter to land on, so I was put into a harness and lowered by cable onto the stern of the ship. Dangling in midair during this process, I got the feeling I was a real soldier. In sports, coaches often tell their players to "lose yourself in the game." During that moment, I felt that if I were in actual combat, I would be able to "lose myself" and focus on what had to be done. My ability to do that under fire was never tested.

The ship's mission was to destroy WBLCs, the Navy's abbreviation for waterborne logistics craft, that were moving weapons, ammunition, and other war supplies along the coastline to Viet Cong troops in the combat zones in South Vietnam. I filmed the *MacKenzie's* long-range guns firing high-cost shells at low-cost sampans and wondered about the economics. Then I realized that cutting off supplies to the Viet Cong could save the lives of our combat troops, so the expense was worth it. A story I wrote about the hard-working, sleep-deprived sailors on the destroyer appeared in the *Stars & Stripes* military newspaper. After two days on the destroyer, a Navy helicopter came to reel me back in and take me to my next stop, which was the *USS Wainwright* (DLG-28).

As the helicopter approached the *Wainwright*, I was glad to see it was large enough to have a flight deck for us to land on. Designated as a PIRAZ ship, which stands for Positive Identification Radar Advisory Zone, the *Wainwright* served as "the FAA of the Tonkin Gulf." Stationed within twenty miles of Hanoi, the *Wainwright's* mission was to maintain constant radar and visual surveillance of the Tonkin Gulf and adjoining coastlines, to identify all aircraft in the zone, and to direct defensive forces to intercept any possible enemy intruders. (After I had returned to Subic Bay, Van Stewart, an OU fraternity brother and Navy pilot, brought me a recording of a sailor onboard the *Wainwright* giving directions to a carrier pilot who was chasing an enemy MiG. The pilot says, "foxes away," which means he has released his air-to-air missiles. Then, after a few seconds, he exclaims, "I got that son of a bitch.")

On my last day on the *Wainwright*, I took a picture of a small, unmanned helicopter and mailed that roll of film, which included other pictures from my brief tour of sea duty, into Kodak for developing. Later, I learned that the small, unmanned helicopter was a recent invention called a "drone" and was classified as Top Secret. I was relieved to get the developed film back from Kodak with no indication that anyone had noticed my breach of security.

Another helicopter ride took me to the last ship on my tour, the aircraft carrier *Bon Homme Richard*. The next morning, I climbed into a small passenger nook on board a Navy jet for a quick flight back to Cubi Point. As we were slung off the flight deck, I felt the "g's" flattening my face for a few seconds during take-off. Before long I was back on terra firma with a new respect for the sailors at sea and a deep sense of relief that I was not one of them.

Touring Southeast Asia

Terry and I took a weekend trip to Manila in a Navy car with a Filipino driver. The two-lane highway was so clogged with cars, trucks, buses, carabao, and carts that it seemed more like a parade than traffic. When a truck in front of us hit a bump, its cargo of bamboo shoots fell onto the roadway in front of us. Our driver tried to drive through the bamboo, but our wheels became jammed with the bamboo and we came to a halt. After our driver managed to pry the bamboo out from between the car's wheels and fenders, we were back on the road.

One bizarre scene on the way to Manila was a group of so-called "taxi dancers." These were young, enterprising Filipina bargirls who would take a taxi into the countryside, and, with rock music blaring from the taxi radio, dance with rural Filipino men for a few pesos per dance. (The Olongapo nightclub and bar scene could count on an influx of mobile Manila bargirls if there were an unusually large number of sailors visiting Subic Bay.)

While in Manila, Terry and I visited a massive Chinese cemetery on the edge of the city. Individual grave sites covered an area the size of a small home and featured concrete and granite tombstones, fountains, and beautifully maintained gardens. The final resting places were so elaborate it was no wonder people were dying to get in there. In sharp contrast, the cemetery was surrounded by a sprawl of shanties and ramshackle huts. It seemed as if the dead Chinese people were doing better than their neighboring Filipinos.

During this trip, we bought two oil paintings by a well-known Filipino artist, Cesar Buenaventura. One of them depicts three Filipinos harvesting rice by hand with sickles. The other features a street scene in Manila, including a calesa, which is an open, two-wheeled, horse-drawn carriage.

For our next trip, we flew to Hong Kong with another couple, a Marine lieutenant and his wife. When we got off the plane we were greeted by an enterprising pair of clothing salesmen, who offered us a ride to our hotel if we didn't mind stopping by their clothing store on the way. I ended up buying a black cashmere overcoat that has lasted more than half a century.

Hong Kong was still under British rule and seemed to be enjoying a building boom. I was amazed by the sight of the construction crews, hundreds of feet above us, climbing around on bamboo scaffolding as they built the new skyscrapers.

On limited budgets, we decided to stay in a small hotel conveniently located above a Chinese laundry in the Kowloon area. One day we decided to have lunch on the Tai Pak Floating Restaurant in Aberdeen Harbor. We were ferried to the restaurant in a rowboat, powered by an old Chinese woman with a weathered face and a strong back.

One evening, after I had taken several time-lapse photos of ships in the bay, we took a tram that slowly crept up the side of a very steep mountain. We were hoping to get a majestic view of Hong Kong at night. By the time we reached the viewing spot, a dense fog had set in and our view was limited to about five feet.

In December 1968, with our time in the Philippines running short, Terry and I took a trip to Taiwan. We visited a huge museum that housed thousands of ancient Chinese artifacts that Chinese nationalists managed to cart off as they departed the mainland. Apparently, you can accumulate a lot of stuff if your civilization goes back many millenniums.

A few weeks later, Admiral Gilkeson called me into his office to ask me about a letter he had received from the Olongapo City Council, requesting him to extend my tour of duty in the

Philippines. I was puzzled at first, but then the explanation dawned on me. I told the admiral that the City Council didn't care about me. Terry had become close friends with the mayor's family during our stay, and they didn't want Terry to leave with me. The admiral found this explanation very believable.

Seeing the World

My next assignment was to the Chief of Navy Information at the Pentagon, just across the Potomac River from Washington, DC. My love of the sea was so great that I had agreed to extend my Navy career for an additional year in exchange for another assignment on shore.

Preparing to depart Subic Bay, we sold our Ford Fairlane for around $1,000. There was a heavy tariff on selling imported cars, but a relatively small cost if you paid the taxman instead of the tax. A Filipino friend handled this transaction for us, and we came out with enough money to finance our trip home.

With two weeks for travel time and another two weeks of leave available, and with our next assignment about halfway around the world from the Philippines, we decided to head west instead of east for our trip back to the States. We arranged to fly, space available, on a series of flights that linked various US Embassies in cities around the world. In January, 1969, we checked in at Clark Air Base for the first leg of our trip, only to discover that a bureaucratic snafu had created a problem with our flight plans. We learned that a few of the countries we planned to stop in on our trip required visas. And, to make matters worse, we had to be out of the Philippines within twenty-four hours. We couldn't leave, but we couldn't stay. We were a couple without a country.

Fortunately, we were able to find a solution to this dilemma. We learned that Thailand did not require visas for US servicemen, as it was a popular destination for those on leave from their duties in Vietnam. This meant we could take our scheduled embassy flight to Saigon, and then go on to Bangkok, where I could visit the embassies of the various countries requiring the visas. The brief stop in Saigon meant my income for that month would be tax free.

Our plane's descent for landing at Saigon's Tan Son Nhat airport was surprisingly steep and quick. Concern about possible sniper fire discouraged low, leisurely descents. We got off the plane briefly but remained nearby. We reboarded, our plane took off, and we made a steep and rapid ascent. I received a Vietnam Service Medal for my brief tour of sea duty in the war zone, but I don't consider myself a Vietnam veteran. I just happened to be in the Navy during the war. If I am a Vietnam veteran, so is Terry.

Once in Bangkok, I had a week to round up the required visas for the rest of our trip home. I visited the embassies of India, Pakistan, and Saudi Arabia and requested the visas in time to catch the next embassy flight. Meanwhile, Terry and I took in the tourist sites in the self-proclaimed "Venice of the East." Bangkok did have a lot of canals, but the comparison to Venice was a stretch. We took turns feeding a bunch of bananas to an elephant, then watched some folk dancing and kick boxing. We also discovered a sport that seemed like a combination of basketball and soccer, as the players kicked a small ball into a very high goal.

Visas in hand, we caught an embassy flight to New Delhi, India. On the bus ride to the hotel, I was shocked by the abject poverty of the deplorables . . . I mean untouchables. For dinner that night, I ordered a chicken breast covered by a red curry that proved to be the hottest thing I had ever put into my mouth.

We continued our journey the next morning on a flight to Karachi, Pakistan. All we saw of Pakistan was an airport gift shop where we bought what I thought was an exotic vase but turned out to be drug paraphernalia.

Our next stop was in Saudi Arabia, where once again we never left the airport terminal. Terry, still dressed for the tropics, was wearing a light, short dress, or miniskirt. The vast airport terminal was nearly empty, but a few Saudi sheiks, clad in heavy robes and turbans, wondered by and gave her inscrutable looks, possibly ranging from disapproval to lust.

Soon we were back in the air, heading for the Torrejon Air Base in Spain. After spending the night on the base, we found ourselves with two weeks to wander around in Europe, but with no reservations for either transportation or lodging. I have always valued flexibility above planning, and Terry didn't seem too worried about our lack travel plans either. The next day, we took a train to Madrid.

My Spanish vocabulary was extremely limited. On our taxi to our hotel, I told Terry that I had taken some early morning Spanish lessons during the sixth grade, but all I could remember was "El gato bebe leche." The taxi driver must have been eavesdropping, because he cracked up at my random observation that "The cat drinks milk." I had also taken a semester of Spanish at OU, where I learned to say, "No tango mucho dinero," meaning "I don't have much money."

In Madrid, everything was quiet in the midafternoon. This led me to believe there must be something to the concept of a siesta. Conversely, the traffic was loud enough to wake us up at 3 am. I looked out our hotel window at the heavy traffic below and felt like we were missing a big party somewhere.

We left Madrid onboard a train for Lyon, France. At a stop in a small village just inside France, an officious conductor came by to check our tickets and said we were on the wrong train. He told us we needed to get off his train and buy tickets for another train at the local station. Not wanting to cause an international incident, we complied with his exit demand and bought new tickets to Lyon. While we were waiting for the next train, we noticed a small group of locals gathered to watch two train cars being coupled on another track. My comment to Terry was "not much to do here."

At that point, someone pointed out that our train to Lyon was about to depart. We grabbed our luggage and ran, barely catching it on time. Terry was about three months pregnant at the time, so I felt bad about her needing to carry some of our luggage while we ran for our train. Fortunately, we were travelling light. We found a small, pleasant hotel in Lyon that night and caught a train to Geneva, Switzerland, the next morning.

A pensive Terry on a train in the Swiss Alps

In Geneva, we asked an English-speaking desk clerk in our hotel for directions to a tourist site. She gave us the directions and added that our destination was within walking distance. After we had walked what seemed like halfway across the city, we decided the European concept of walking distance was a lot farther than the American version. We also experienced a few problems with language differences. Terry wanted to buy some hair spray, but the salesclerk could not understand what she wanted. Terry held a hand above her head, made a hissing sound, and pantomimed spraying her hair. The clerk immediately got the idea, and we had a good laugh.

With brother Phil in Weisbaden, Germany

The next leg of our journey was a breathtaking train ride through the snow-covered Swiss Alps. Sitting across from Terry on the train, I took one of my all-time favorite photos, showing her, and her mirror image in the window, seemingly lost in a pregnant pause, as if she were wondering what she had gotten herself into.

Our train arrived in Zurich, Switzerland, that evening, pulling into the largest train station I had ever seen. I joked that we should go looking for gnomes, but the banks were already closed. The next morning, we took yet another train to Wiesbaden, Germany, where my younger brother Phil was an airman serving in the Air Force. Phil took us to a local tavern for a few beers while we caught up on each other's lives. Like our brother Del, Phil did his military service before college, so he was only nineteen at the time.

Our original plan called for us to fly from Germany to London before returning to the USA. But we were running out of money, so we decided to skip the London visit and go back to Oklahoma for a while. We flew from Rhine-Main Air Base in Germany to an Air Force base in New Jersey, then hopped another military flight to Oklahoma City. With Terry being pregnant and safely back in the States, her parents decided they could speak to me, for the first time since our elopement.

Back in the USA

While spending a few days in Norman, we bought a new 1969 Oldsmobile Cutlass from Jackie Cooper's Olds for $3,000. Then we drove to Bartlesville to see my parents and pick up our poodle. Chauncey had been shipped, under considerable duress, from the Philippines to my folks' home in Bartlesville. A sedative we had given him to calm him down before his departure from the Philippines had had the opposite effect. He was one angry poodle when his journey began, and we were worried that he would not survive his trip from halfway around the world. He was a tough little guy, and, as several veterinarians discovered, his bite was worse than his bark. Chauncey would lure the vets into a false sense of security, then give them a little nip.

Driving from Bartlesville to Washington, DC, Terry and I noticed a lot of road signs on the highways through Pennsylvania.

We decided it would be fun to consolidate the warnings. We ended up with: Beware Trucks with Oversized Loads on Narrow Shoulders in Construction Zones Swerving to Avoid Deer Hit by Falling Rocks While Crossing Icy Bridges.

Having avoided the various road hazards, we arrived in Washington, DC, in early March. A Navy friend we had met in the Philippines helped us find an unfurnished two-bedroom apartment in Alexandria, Virginia.

Reporting for duty at the Navy Chief of Information's offices in the Pentagon, I was assigned to the News Desk. My job was to respond to queries from reporters covering the Navy's activities around the world. Most of their questions concerned the Navy's operations in Vietnam. I was, in effect, a reporter's reporter, as the members of the Pentagon's vast military and civilian bureaucracy who could answer a reporter's questions either couldn't be found or did not want to deal with reporters directly.

The most exciting call I took on the News Desk came from Terry that August, about a month after Neil Armstrong and Buzz Aldrin landed on the moon. She told me to come home quickly, as she needed a ride to the hospital to give birth to our first child. I sprinted to our car and sped through late morning traffic on Interstate 95, narrowly avoiding a wreck as I took the exit to Alexandria at an excessive speed. After that near disaster, I told myself to calm down, and we made it safely to Bethesda Naval Hospital.

Terry was swollen with toxemia and had a difficult time giving birth. I waited anxiously, alone in a small waiting room, for about six hours. Finally, I was told that Terry was okay, but our baby girl needed to go to an incubator immediately. I was shown into an empty room and Terry was wheeled in, lying flat on a hospital cart. She was as white as a ghost. Without saying a word, she turned her head to one side and threw up. I passed out, slowly sliding down a bare concrete wall, until my rear end hit the deck.

Three long days passed before I could see Terry and our beautiful baby girl, Anne Elizabeth. We took her home to our apartment, and it wasn't long before she was standing up in her crib, holding the rail, with her red hair already down to her shoulders. Anne and I liked to crawl around the apartment floor, playing peek-a-boo. Unfortunately, she had a rough infant year, being hospitalized with pneumonia and having eye surgery. About the time she turned one, we were in our kitchen together and she stood up in her highchair, lost her balance, and plunged toward the kitchen floor. I snatched her by the ankle before her head reached the linoleum. My quick hands saved the day, but I should not have let her stand up in her highchair before her first birthday.

Chauncey adapted to apartment living with ease. In nice weather, he liked to lie in wait at the edge of our second-floor balcony. When a neighbor or visitor would walk by, he would wait until they had just passed his perch and unleash a torrent of shrill barks, causing the walkers mild heart attacks or at least minor panic attacks.

That winter, a young ensign in our so-called "Chinfo" office put together a basketball team to play in a Pentagon intramural league. I signed up to play on his team, not realizing there was a serious dearth of basketball players in our office. By then, I had attained the rank of lieutenant and, at age twenty-six, was in my theoretical athletic prime. I turned out to be the highest ranked and most experienced basketball player on our small roster. My new teammates were not nearly as good as my Subic Bay teammates had been.

In a game at the nearby Andrews Air Force Base, we were playing a Marine Corps team that was very tough and athletic, just not in a basketball way. Matched up against a Marine who looked about six years younger and four inches shorter than me, I was confident he would not be blocking my shots. With my teammates unselfishly feeding me the ball, I went into full "feel leather and fire" mode and scored a career high 39 points as we won the game.

One of my funniest basketball experiences occurred one misty spring evening after work, while walking from a bus stop to our apartment. Some kids, probably in their early double digits, were shooting baskets on an asphalt court in our apartment complex. Since it had been a cool, rainy day, I was wearing a London Fog raincoat. After we shot around awhile, I took the ball in the low post area and did a trick I had seen Goose Tatum do while performing for the Harlem Globetrotters. I gave the ball a hard bounce, catching it between my calves, just below my knees, but faking a sweeping hook shot and looking up, as if I expected to see the ball. When Goose Tatum pulled this little bit of deception, it often took a few seconds for the opposing players to locate the ball. But, since I was wearing my raincoat, I made the ball disappear completely. Every kid took the fake, and none of them could figure out where the ball had gone. I kept looking up in the sky, as if I were waiting for it to come back down. The kids were totally mystified. I finally pulled the ball out from under my raincoat, gave it to one of the kids, and walked off, laughing to myself all the way home. (I still use that move when playing with kids, but it doesn't work as well without the raincoat.)

After about a year on the Navy News Desk, I was assigned to serve as editor of *Direction* magazine, a monthly publication for Navy public affairs officers and their staffs. In August 1970, as part of an overall Navy reduction of forces, I was given the opportunity to leave the Navy about six months before my service obligation had been set to end. I jumped at the chance to return to civilian life. I felt I had been lucky to get shore duty. I had been given some challenging responsibilities at a young age, and Terry and I had been able to see a lot of the world. Our Navy experience had broadened our horizons, but I knew I wasn't really the military type.

— • — • —

CHAPTER EIGHT

AN OKLAHOMA HOMECOMING

When I told my coworkers and friends we were leaving Washington, DC, and returning to Oklahoma, they often asked: "What do they have in Oklahoma?" I would answer: "It's not what we have, it's what we don't have so much of: traffic, pollution, crime, a high cost of living, and high taxes." I could have added that when you meet someone you do not know in Oklahoma, the default mode is friendly, not defensive.

A Cub Reporter

Terry, Chauncey, and I crammed into the Cutlass and drove back to Norman. (We didn't forget Anne. She flew to Norman with Terry's dad.) My strained relationship with Terry's parents gradually improved, apparently helped by the fact that I was the father of their granddaughter. We soon rented a small condo on Cherrystone Street, and I took a job in Oklahoma City as a reporter for *The Oklahoman*. At the time, I saw reporting as a noble profession albeit a low-paying one. I would be a watchdog for democracy for $620 per month. I saw my job as seeking and reporting the truth in a candid and unbiased way, letting the chips fall where they may.

As a general assignment reporter, I was on the low end of the paper's reporting hierarchy. One of my first assignments was to cover the Oklahoma State Fair, a week-long event at the State Fair Grounds in Oklahoma City. My first story was about a rodeo cowboy with a trained buffalo. I was unimpressed with the buffalo's performance until its last stunt. The cowboy climbed into his pickup and began driving out of the arena. He seemed to have forgotten his buffalo. But the buffalo chased after him and jumped into the back of the fast-moving pickup as it sped out of the arena, leaving me and the rest of the spectators amazed.

My biggest story from the State Fair that year was an expose of a pyramid scheme called "Dare to be Great." I sat in an audience of gullible fairgoers and listened to the promoter's spiel, which boiled down to: "You can become great by buying into our program to convince other people that they can become great." Of course, if this program really worked, eventually everyone would be great. Once the market for greatness was saturated, the promoters could always come out with a new program, something like "Dare to be Magnificent." Anyway, I did some research, discovered this pyramid scheme had already been outlawed in several states, and wrote an expose.

After a few weeks, I was assigned to the business news section. In a story about a new Oklahoma City bicycle shop whose business was going great, I wryly noted that more bicycles were being pedaled—and peddled—than ever before.

Working in *The Oklahoman's* downtown headquarters building, I found myself one morning riding in a tiny elevator with publishing magnate E. K. Gaylord, the paper's ninety-six-year-old founder, and his son, Edward Gaylord, who was fifty but looked a lot older. I had a strong urge to whisper: "Someday, son, this will all be yours." But I managed to stifle this comment.

By December, I found myself truly enjoying my work as a reporter, especially roaming around town looking for news. I concluded that my job was so much fun, it was no wonder that it didn't pay much. I was making about half the salary I had been making as a Navy lieutenant.

Eventually, with a wife and one-year-old baby at home, the financial pressure built up to a point where I decided I needed to make more money. I knew the public relations people bringing me news releases at the business desk were making a lot more than I was, even if most of their publicity pieces ended up in the trash. That didn't seem fair. But in a free market economy, the advocates are normally going to make more money than the reporters, just as the players are always going to make more than the referees.

On my last day as a reporter, marking the end of my meteoric four-month reporting career, one of the news editors wished me luck, but predicted I would find public relations work "sterile." He was right.

Serendipity at OU

Although it did feel like I was selling out, I took a new job in Norman at the University of Oklahoma's Public Affairs Department, as the director of print media relations. While working at OU, I was able to "moonlight" on the GI Bill by taking graduate courses, some at night and some during the day. My first GI Bill check, about $240 tax free, covered my tuition and books for nine credit hours in the fall semester. The same monthly check for October through January was pure profit. As a fringe benefit, OU allowed its bureaucrats to take courses during working hours. I was able to take journalism courses that required writing magazine articles that I could sell. Talk about serendipity: at times I was getting paid three times for the same work.

Waves of outside agitators washed up on the OU campus in 1971, as if the 1960s were arriving late to our remote university, ensconced near the center of fly-over country. But protesters like Abbie Hoffman failed to generate as much excitement as the football team did.

In an evening human relations class, I looked so out-of-place that my pot-smoking, hippie classmates must have thought I was an undercover narcotics agent who didn't bother with a disguise. The professor looked like comedian George Carlin, performing as the Hippie Dippy Weatherman, but was not as funny. Not wanting to seem oppressive to his students, he told us in the first class that we should set our own goals for the course, then grade ourselves at the end of the semester on how well we had achieved these goals. I immediately set a self-fulfilling goal to make an A in the course. Since he did not want to offend his students by taking roll, I seldom went back to this class.

A Veterans Administration loan made it possible for us to buy our first house with no money down. We bought a three-bedroom home on Cinderella Street, in a quiet neighborhood near the campus, for $30,000. Terry's dad and I built a wooden fence around the backyard, with him doing most of the work. At the time, Anne was two years old and Terry was pregnant with our second child, to be named later.

Terry shot a video of Anne and me lying on the carpeted floor of our den, playing with her alphabet blocks. We lined the blocks up in rows, but Anne would scoot over to my line and make corrections if she didn't like the way my letters were facing. (She's been editing my stuff ever since.)

The Governor's Limo

Each October, a spirited clash between two longtime rivals, the football teams from OU and the University of Texas, is held in the Cotton Bowl in Dallas, during the Texas State Fair. Mike Davis, an OU fraternity brother working for Oklahoma Governor David Hall, invited Terry and me to join him and his wife as they chaperoned the governor's two kids and two of their friends on a trip to the big game. They picked us up in the governor's long, black limousine and we had a pleasant ride, straight south on Interstate 35 to Dallas, until we got stuck in a massive traffic jam on the Stemmons Freeway. The traffic had come to a complete stop, and we were parked in 100-degree heat behind a large tour bus.

Suddenly, our limousine's engine caught fire and the limousine began to fill with smoke. We gathered up the governor's kids and their friends and got them safely to the side of the highway. The driver in the bus in front of us noticed the smoke, grabbed a fire extinguisher, and put out the limousine's engine fire. Gradually, the traffic began to crawl ahead, at a snail's pace. The wives and kids got back into the limousine, and Mike and I decided push it out of the freeway's middle lane and over to the shoulder.

As the driver steered, the traffic began clearing up, and as we pushed the limousine over the crest of a hill, it suddenly took off faster than we could run. This left us standing in the middle of Stemmons Freeway for no apparent reason. As our fellow Sooner fans whizzed by, they waved and yelled "Boomer Sooner!" They didn't seem surprised to see us there. Mike and I dodged our way to the freeway shoulder and walked to the bottom of the hill, where the limo had come to a stop. Two Texas Highway Patrol cars delivered the eight of us to the front gate of the Cotton Bowl. We received some curious looks from OU fans as we climbed out of the patrol cars.

Pulling into our driveway on Cinderella one evening, a thought crept into my mind: "My gosh, I'm twenty-eight and I've got it all. A family. An air-conditioned home. A car. A refrigerator. A stove. A washing machine. A clothes dryer. A color television. A stereo. What else is there?"

That moment of satisfaction didn't last long. I felt a need to stir the pot, advance the plot, make something happen.

On the Road Again

After nine months working at OU, I started looking for a new job with more upside and found one as a public relations executive with Ackerman Advertising, one of city's largest advertising and public relations firms. Ray Ackerman, the firm's founder and CEO, had been a Navy pilot and was a respected civic leader in Oklahoma City. I had sent him a resume while I was still in the Navy, and I guess that eventually led to the job offer.

Ackerman's firm had a subsidiary called Public Relations Southwest, where I became one of three public relations executives. My first major client was Midland Mortgage, a mortgage banking firm headed by George Records. I wrote a speech that he delivered to the American Bankers Association.

On the Thanksgiving Day following my job change, I joined nearly 62,000 football fans in Norman to watch number-one ranked Nebraska play number-two ranked OU in "The Game of the Century." Even before kickoff, the OU fans had worked themselves into a frenzy that bordered on mass hysteria. The game was a knock-down, drag-out brawl, putting the crazed fans on an emotional roller coaster as OU's quarterback Jack Mildren played a terrific game directing the Sooners' "Wishbone" offense. But the play of the game was a dazzling punt return for a touchdown by Nebraska's Johnny Rogers, and the Cornhuskers prevailed 35 to 31.

After working at PR Southwest for about a year, I received a life-changing request to meet with a possible new client, a management consulting firm called the Resources Analysis and Management (RAM) Group, in their downtown Oklahoma City headquarters. One of their principals was Breene Kerr, the son of former US Senator and founder of Kerr McGee Oil Company, Robert S. Kerr. The other was Alex Aven, an MIT graduate and oilman. After brief introductions, their client, a young, independent oil and natural gas producer named Robert A. Hefner III, came bounding into the room. The scion of a prominent Oklahoma City family, he seemed so excited, and radiated so much energy, I feared his head would hit the ceiling.

When they asked me to write a news release about something called a farm-out agreement between one of Hefner's companies, Gasanadarko, Ltd., and El Paso Exploration Company, I had no idea what they were talking about. Undaunted, I said something like: "Sure. You all go to lunch and I will have a draft news release for you when you get back." They left me a copy of the agreement and headed out the door. Fortunately, the agreement was self-explanatory. In summary, Gasanadarko had assembled a large block of oil-and-gas leases from mineral owners in Roger Mills County in Western Oklahoma. The leases covered an area near the western edge of the Anadarko Basin, a huge sedimentary basin containing vast quantities of natural gas. El Paso Exploration had been drilling successful natural gas wells in the Texas Panhandle and wanted to extend its drilling to the farms and ranches covered by the Gasanadarko leases. When El Paso drilled these wells, they would pay Gasanadarko overriding royalties, in addition to the normal royalties to be paid to the original mineral owners. After El Paso recouped their drilling and operating expenses, Gasanadarko's overriding royalty percentage would double.

When Hefner and the two RAM Group executives got back from lunch, they quickly approved my news release and seemed impressed I had written it so quickly. This led to my getting Hefner's main company, The GHK Company, as a public relations client.

Hefner had received a degree in geology from OU in 1956. He founded GHK in 1959. GHK stands for Glover, Hefner, and Kennedy. Hefner was the general partner. His limited partners were wealthy New York investors, David O'D. Kennedy and Laurence Glover.

GHK had established a large oil-and-gas lease position near Elk City, a small town on Interstate 40, in Beckham County. In 1967, Hefner had arranged for Northern Illinois Gas Company, a large natural gas distributor serving the Chicago area, to finance the drilling of a deep exploratory well called the No. 1 Green. The well was drilled to the Springer geologic formation, more than four miles deep, at a cost of $6.5 million. The Green was a huge natural gas discovery, producing more than nine billion cubic feet of natural gas in its first seven years, proving the natural gas producing capabilities of the Deep Anadarko Basin.

Hefner took me to the well site and asked the pumper to open the well's natural gas production to the atmosphere. Escaping from nearly four miles beneath the surface, the natural gas blew into the air, screeching like a dozen Concorde jets all taking off at once. The brief demonstration was both impressive and deafening.

Hefner's point was not just that deep natural gas was a tremendous resource, but that it could not be developed as long as natural gas remained under federal price controls. As a voice in the wilderness advocating the development of the Deep Anadarko Basin's vast resources of natural gas, Hefner was a prophet without a profit.

— . — . —

CHAPTER NINE

A BARTLESVILLE
HOMECOMING

That *August, my dad called* and told me there was an opening for a speechwriter in the public affairs department of Phillips Petroleum Company's headquarters in Bartlesville. In a meeting with Ray Ackerman, I said I really liked working at his firm, but the job at Phillips paid more. Then I added, naively, that I could work harder for him if he would agree to pay me more. "That usually works the other way around," he replied. Good point. I took the job at Phillips.

This was my fourth new job in the two years since I left the Navy. It didn't take much of a raise to convince me to move on to new opportunities.

Terry was about four months pregnant with our second daughter, so we decided not to move to Bartlesville until after the baby was born. I commuted between Norman and Bartlesville for about six months, staying in my old room at my parent's house during the week, and spending the weekends at home in Norman.

On my first day at Phillips, I was given a summary of my benefits to be received as a Phillips employee, including vacations, health insurance, and a retirement account. What jumped out at me was my retirement date in January 2008. I was twenty-nine, and they had my entire future worked out for me. All I had to do was work there for another thirty-six years and I could comfortably retire. The idea of working at the same place for thirty-six years seemed more like a sentence than an opportunity.

Our daughter Emily was born in Norman in January 1973, just three days before my thirtieth birthday. Her birth was less dramatic than Anne's. This time, Terry was fine, but Emily developed some jaundice and had to stay in the hospital a few days.

On a cold Sunday evening later that month, we decided that Anne should go with me as I drove back to Bartlesville so that she could spend some time with me and her other set of grandparents. Anne, then about three and half years old, was happily standing in the front seat of our Cutlass as we left home. A light mist was falling as we pulled onto Interstate 35 leaving Norman. As I started to gain a little speed on the Interstate our car spun out of control, did a full circle on the highway, and slid onto a wide space in the median. Luckily, there were no barriers between the northbound and southbound lanes at that time, so we came to a stop on the grass-covered median without colliding with anything or anyone. Anne had been able to keep her balance as the car spun around, so she wasn't hurt and didn't even cry. I told her the highway had iced over, so we would not be driving to Bartlesville. Cautiously, we crept back onto the highway and returned home safely.

After spending a few months in a two-bedroom apartment on the east side of Bartlesville, we bought a small house in the Kenilworth addition, an area near the Hillcrest Country Club generally populated by the families of oil company executives and other high-income professionals. We used a $3,000 gain from the sale of our house in Norman and a small loan from my dad to come up with the down payment. At the time, my job at Phillips paid $1,400 per month, more than twice what I had made as a newspaper reporter.

Shortly after moving in, I answered the doorbell and a nice lady asked me if my parents were home. I suspected we had broken some unwritten rule concerning the appropriate place in the company's management hierarchy required for home ownership in that neighborhood. Buying a small house in an exclusive neighborhood made sense to me as a real estate investment, and, feeling like Bartlesville was my home turf, I felt confident about my career prospects at Phillips.

The oil and gas industry had been in the doldrums for most of the 1960s and early 1970s, so Phillips had not done much hiring during those years. As I walked around the company headquarters in the early days of my employment, I got the feeling that one day I would come to work and find I was the only one there. Everyone one else would have died or retired. Two men about my dad's age headed up the editorial division of the public affairs department. They would give writing assignments for speeches, news releases, financial reports, and other promotional literature to me and two or three other staff writers.

Ghostwriter in the Sky

The speech assignments would come with ridiculously easy deadlines, so that I was given time to do extensive research on whatever topic the executive giving the speech would address. It was almost like I had been given an academic scholarship to study the oil and gas industry from a management perspective. The fun part was trying to make company policy in the speech. If I could get the executive to say something, it could become the official company position. The high point of my speechwriting career was reached with a speech I wrote for William Martin, the Phillips chairman of the board, to deliver at the annual meeting of the National Association of Regulatory Utility Commissioners in Seattle, Washington. In his speech, delivered in August 1974, Mr. Martin warned that the Arab members of OPEC could embargo crude oil shipments to the United States. When they did just that two months later, the oil price jumped from $3 per barrel to $12 per barrel.

Flying back to Bartlesville on a company jet with Chairman Martin, President Bill Douce, and two other senior executives, I was trying to project a professional image but was a little uncomfortable. They were the top bananas, and I was just a ghostwriter in the sky. Mr. Douce, who had once been my dad's boss, told a story that went something like this: "I remember young Bill here. My wife and I were at his parents' house playing bridge, and he came running out of his bedroom. He was about two feet high, and he didn't have a stitch of clothes on."

Another executive chimed in: "Didn't you used to be my paper boy?" A third executive added: "Didn't you used to date my daughter in high school?"

I didn't recall streaking by the bridge game, but I replied "yes" and "yes" to the two questions. None of these images from my boyhood were going to help my career.

Soon after the Arab oil embargo was launched, Oklahoma Governor David Hall requested a comprehensive study on energy in Oklahoma. My former clients at GHK and the RAM Group asked the Phillips Vice President of Public Affairs if he could make me available for a couple of weeks to edit this study. When he turned them down, they asked Governor Hall to call Phillips Chairman William Martin and repeat the request. This time, the request was granted, and I headed to Oklahoma City to work on the study. I holed up with my portable typewriter in a hotel on Lincoln Boulevard, near the Capitol Building, and began editing and re-writing reports from various Oklahoma energy companies and trade associations on their respective roles in the state's energy picture.

The coolest part of the study was a so-called spaghetti chart, put together by The RAM Group, that showed the various components of Oklahoma's energy sources, primarily oil, natural gas and coal, on the left side, and how these supplies flowed to consumers, such as residential, commercial, and industrial, on the right side. The width of the connecting lines indicated the amount of energy flowing from each source to its end users.

The report was submitted to the governor and the Oklahoma State Legislature by the Oklahoma Energy Advisory Council, with credits to Robert A. Hefner III as chairman and William W. Talley II, a new member of The RAM Group, as executive director. As a friendly ghostwriter, spirited into town from an oil company, my name was not mentioned. However, the governor was kind enough to send me a letter thanking me for my work on the report. His letter concluded: "In recognition of your contributions it is a real pleasure to commission you an Admiral in the Oklahoma Navy."

This was a nice gesture, but Oklahoma does not really have its own Navy.

In the mid-1970s, Phillips Petroleum was the subject of a report on CBS's *60 Minutes* program which painted Bartlesville as the ultimate "company town." Their story included some black-and-white footage, probably shot in the late 1940s, of a military style "pass in review" with Phillips employees, mostly men in coats and ties, marching past a group of company executives sitting on a stand in front of the company headquarters, as if they were generals reviewing the troops. The employees, many of whom were World War II veterans, were grouped by departments. They marched at least as well as an average high school band.

There was a women's exercise class held in the company gymnasium that was normally attended by a few wives of company employees. When the word got around Bartlesville that *60 Minutes* was going to be filming this class, women seizing the chance to appear on national television filled up the gym. The program implied that the exercise class was mandatory for the wives of company employees. (Actually, Terry had taken some fencing classes there, as she had at OU, and remains quite adept at verbal fencing.)

Bartlesville may have been the quintessential company town, but a lot of its citizens bailed out on Friday evenings. Terry and I called them "The Lake People." They spent their weekends with their cabins and boats at Grand Lake, a man-made reservoir about an hour's drive northeast of town. We ventured there once with some of our "lake friends." Terry went water skiing, zipping along behind a speeding boat, despite her bad knees. This was a sight I thought I would never see.

Not content with my public-relations job, I started taking some night classes at Tulsa University, with the goal of earning a master's degree in business administration. Once again moonlighting on the GI bill, I took several business classes that were required before I could get into their MBA program. I struggled with statistics and accounting, but really liked a finance course that proved to be very valuable as my career gradually shifted from public relations to business.

My Second Comeback

My eight-to-five working hours at Phillips also allowed me time to resume playing basketball. I launched my second comeback playing during the noon hour in very competitive pick-up games in the Adams Building gym, where I had played as a Phillips 33er. I often matched up against another point guard about my size and age, a computer programmer named Merle Atherton. He was quicker and a better ball handler than me, so I had a hard time keeping up with him. Merle had been selected as an Oklahoma All-State basketball alternate in 1961, the same year I was. He played at Phillips University in Enid, Oklahoma, along with some of my former high school teammates.

Merle and a Phillips lawyer named Mel Bloomfield formed an AAU team and asked me to play on it. The Phillips 66ers had been disbanded in 1968, as high-level amateur basketball could no longer compete with the professional leagues for top players. (Between 1948 and 1964, eleven 66er players and two 66er head coaches won Olympic gold medals.)

One of our first games was played in the high school gym in the nearby town of Dewey against the McAlester Prison All Stars. I drove to the game, after work, still wearing a coat and tie, not to mention some professorial looking eyeglasses, and arrived at the same time the prisoners were departing their bus. They looked athletic, but not particularly menacing. While we were suiting up, I joked to a teammate that one of the older-looking prisoners was a twenty-year letterman.

The game was a fast-paced, gun-and-run shoot-out. We escaped with a narrow win. As I was leaving the arena, one of the prisoners, a wiry young guard I had been dueling with for much of the game, told me, "Man, you look like an old man in your clothes, but you move like a cat on the court." I took that as a backhanded compliment. I may have looked old at thirty-one, but I didn't feel old.

Apparently, I was not above a little ageism myself. Prior to entering the 1975 Dewey Invitational Tournament, an annual clash for AAU teams from Oklahoma and Kansas, Merle told me he had been able to get Phil "Red" Murrell to play for our team. I knew that Red, a 6' 6" power forward, had been a college All-American at Drake and a 1960 AAU All-American for the 66ers. I even recalled him shooting his patented baseline jumper, fading away while extending his left leg to hold off defenders. But he was, gasp, forty! I told Merle, "That guy is forty! You can't play basketball when you're forty . . . he'll have a heart attack!" Fortunately, Merle ignored my advice, and Red helped us win the tournament. Despite my blatant ageism, he played great and did not have a heart attack.

A little basketball reality set in during an AAU tournament in Ponca City, Oklahoma, home of Conoco Oil Company. Our Phillips team was playing Athletes in Action, a team of college-aged players that often competed in exhibition games against college teams. I was back on defense against their three-on-me fast break. I set up in the paint and sized up the situation. There was a 6' 5" guard racing toward me with the ball. He had a 6' 8" forward on each wing, streaking toward the basket. In this situation, I usually watch the eyes of the ball handler. If he looks right, I go left, and vice versa. I am betting he is going to look one way, then pass the other. If I guess right, I get a steal. But this guy didn't do either. He just lobbed the ball high above the rim for a teammate to snatch and throw down an awesome slam dunk.

That's when it came to me. Parameters. We were playing the same game of basketball, but the younger players were playing with a new set of parameters: taking off from the free-throw line, soaring above the rim, slamming down rebounds as well as alley-oops. I felt my days as a basketball player were numbered, and they were. (It just turned out to be a much larger number than I expected at the time.)

Family life in Bartlesville was good. When Anne was five, she began taking ballet classes. Her teacher was a strict disciplinarian, and Anne's early ballet training led to many years of ballet performances. Emily was a low-maintenance baby and toddler. While Anne had liked to crawl around, exploring every nook and cranny of our Alexandria apartment, Emily seemed content to sit in front our fireplace, playing with her toys, smiling and observing whatever was going on.

Anne with baby Emily in Bartlesville

Terry and I were friends with several couples we could do things with, and Marie, a bright young neighborhood girl, was available to baby sit while we went out. One night we dusted off our swing dance moves and won a dance contest, which passed for excitement by Bartlesville standards. While my hometown was a place where a family could live happily ever after, not many of my high school friends came back to live there after college.

One summer we took a family outing to Eureka Springs, Arkansas, about a three-hour drive from Bartlesville. After touring some expansive caves, we stopped by a gift shop and bought Emily a T-shirt that read: "My Daddy is a Truck Driver." The gift shop featured a black myna bird fond of saying: "Hello . . . sucker" to the customers. The bird's greeting became an ongoing family joke, invoked when the conversation mentioned shady salesmen.

Del and his family lived down the street in our neighborhood, but they also spent a lot of time on their ranch a few miles east of Bartlesville. During a visit to their ranch one hot summer day, three-year-old Emily was walking through their horse barn and commented: "Your garage stinks!"

Del invited me to go dove hunting on his ranch that fall. Although I wasn't a hunter, I agreed to give it a try. Using a borrowed shotgun, I got off a few shots and accidentally killed one innocent dove. I felt terrible about it and haven't been hunting since.

Terry Runs The Gamut

In 1976, Terry and I took a vacation trip to Santa Fe, New Mexico. On a little shopping spree one afternoon, we came across a gift shop called The Gamut. The store featured gift items from around the world, mostly handcrafted pieces like woven baskets, jewelry, artwork, and blankets. Terry loved their stuff. She began talking with the owners about individual pieces, asking where and how they were made. The owners, a married couple in their mid-fifties, seemed a little surprised by Terry's enthusiasm. By that evening, we had made a deal with them for Terry to open a store like theirs in Bartlesville. Terry would buy her inventory from them at wholesale prices and sell the items in her store at retail prices. Before we left Santa Fe, Terry walked the aisles of their store and selected her initial inventory in what seemed like the ultimate shopping spree.

Terry found an affordable place for her store on the second floor of an old two-story home on Dewey Street, just a block south of the Price Tower, an historic nineteen-story office building designed by Frank Lloyd Wright. We drove to Tulsa and bought display cases and glass shelves for her merchandise. We set up shop and put an ad in the local newspaper, announcing that The Gamut was open for business.

Terry's store got off to a great start. She ran the store herself while Anne was in first grade and Emily was in preschool. She hired a few friends to keep the place open when she couldn't be there. After a few weeks, a pattern emerged. With her knowledge of and enthusiasm for her merchandise, Terry could sell the stuff easily. She thought it was all very fascinating and each item had its own story. But the customers only wanted to buy from her. Her employees couldn't sell enough to cover the modest cost of their salaries.

Terry would bring home the proceeds from each day's sales. Each evening before bedtime, she would dump the checks and cash on our bed and we would add up the loot. With Terry's degree in sociology and mine in journalism, we were not overburdened with business acumen. It seemed like we were making money, as we were selling each item for much more than we paid for it, and our operating expenses were minimal.

The flaw in our business plan was exposed when the original Gamut owners drove to Bartlesville from Santa Fe with a load of new inventory for us. I believe they felt they had made a mistake in letting Terry cherry pick their store for the most saleable items, so they brought a selection of stuff that looked like it would be harder to sell. Anyway, that's when I realized we had not budgeted for inventory replacement, so The Gamut was not doing as well as we thought.

Driving home with a hot pizza one evening, I was pulled over by a local policeman for speeding. I lowered my window and the officer peered into a scene of family chaos. When Terry finished scolding me, she told the officer, "I told him to slow down!" Both girls were in the back seat, crying about the prospect of going to jail. The officer, possibly a family man himself, must have felt sorry for me, as he let me off with a verbal warning and no ticket.

In 1976, my dad reached the company's retirement age of sixty-five and retired. He had been with the company for thirty-two years. During his last five years as manager of the technical branch of the patent department, Phillips led the entire oil and gas industry, including giants like Exxon and Texaco, in the number of patents received each year.

Near the end of my Phillips career, I was assigned to write position papers on various public policy issues, such as oil-and-gas price controls, facing the company. The Arab oil embargo and subsequent federal price controls had caused long lines and high prices at gasoline stations across the country. Some liberal politicians blamed the problems on "Big Oil," claiming the industry was not sufficiently competitive. Their solution was called "divestiture," a proposed law to break up the big, vertically integrated oil companies whose businesses covered all stages from oil-and-gas exploration and production, pipelines, refining, and marketing. Phillips covered all these bases but was only the eleventh largest oil company in the US at that time.

The Brookings Institute, a Washington, DC, think tank, held a conference on this issue and I was sent to represent Phillips there. I argued that Phillips was a relatively small company in Bartlesville, Oklahoma, and accounted for only two per cent of the nation's oil production. As such, we were "price takers," taking the best price we could get. If we had any market power to control oil prices, it was news to us.

Although I enjoyed the eight-to-five hours and noon basketball games at Phillips, I began getting restless about my career. In some ways, Phillips was more bureaucratic and possibly more militaristic than the Navy. At one point, I developed a severe case of writer's block, but I eventually got over it. During a performance review, my boss, a contemporary of my dad, told me that I was doing well. Leaning forward, he added in a cautious whisper, "You know, Bill, someday you could become the Vice President of Public Affairs for Phillips Petroleum Company."

My internal reaction was, "Oh my god . . . he's right." I decided I needed a change.

— o — o —

CHAPTER TEN

A ROOKIE
LOBBYIST

In early 1977, I was contacted by Robert A. Hefner III, my former PR client, who was looking for a public relations man. We discussed the job briefly, and he asked me to write him a handwritten letter about why I would be good for the job. Although my handwriting is terrible, I wrote the letter as requested, and before long I had a new job. The pace of my life quickened as I began dividing my time among Oklahoma City, Bartlesville, and Washington, DC.

Hefner wanted a public relations guy for two reasons: he was considering running for the United States Senate in 1978, and he was lobbying for the federal government to deregulate the price of natural gas sold in interstate commerce. There was some question in Oklahoma oil industry and political circles about which of these goals was being pursued in support of the other.

On my first day on the job at GHK, Hefner and his land manager were meeting with an oilman named Raymond Plank, the chairman of Apache Corporation, an independent exploration and production company headquartered in Minneapolis. Apache raised drilling funds from small investors, typically doctors and dentists seeking tax-sheltered investments.

GHK had assembled a large oil-and-gas lease block near Elk City, Oklahoma. GHK's leases covered farms and ranches overlying some of the deepest potential natural gas resources in the Anadarko Basin. During their meeting, GHK agreed to assign part of their drilling rights on this lease block to Apache, who would then drill seven exploratory wells on these leases. However, Apache was only interested in drilling to about 17,000 feet, to test the Morrow formation. Apache offered several million dollars for the deeper rights, but Hefner made a fateful decision to keep them.

Shortly after making his deal with Apache, Hefner arranged a meeting with the heads of several Oklahoma oil and gas exploration and production companies to discuss forming a new group to lobby for natural gas deregulation. The companies invited were those whose primary focus was exploring for natural gas. Hefner believed the other state and national oil and gas trade groups were dominated by companies whose primary interests were in oil production and old natural gas fields they had found as a byproduct of looking for oil.

Looking around the meeting room, it seemed like I was the youngest man there, except for another youngster, Larry Nichols, who had recently joined his father's company, Devon. As a result of the meeting, an industry splinter trade group called the Independent Gas Producers Committee was created. Selected as its executive director, I registered as a lobbyist and headed to the nation's capital. Going in, I knew the natural gas issue well from my time at Phillips, and I knew how Washington worked in theory, just not in practice.

Hefner and I took the company jet to Washington, DC. Our first stop was the K-Street offices of Casey, Lane, & Mittendorf, a

New York City law firm whose DC branch was headed by Hefner's Oklahoma friend, Henry "Boots" Taliaferro. A true Washington insider, Boots had served in the Johnson Administration before opening this office. I was surprised to find my friend and former Bartlesville Wildcat three-sport teammate, Bob Woody, working there. Bob, like many Bartlesville kids, had attended the University of Kansas. He had recently left the staff of Kansas Republican Senator James B. Pearson, where he had been immersed in the still-unresolved natural gas legislative battles during the past several years. Boots provided a spare office I could work from to launch our guerilla campaign within the escalating natural gas war.

Early in the game, Hefner and I flew to New York City to have lunch with Robert Bartley, the editor of *The Wall Street Journal*, in the Windows of the World restaurant on the top floor of one of the ill-fated World Trade Center towers. Their editorial position favored total deregulation of natural gas prices. As journalists, they were free to advocate their free market ideals rather than having to deal with what was possible politically. But at least their editorial position helped frame the debate.

During his run for president in the 1976 campaign, Jimmy Carter promised to deregulate the price of interstate natural gas as part of his National Energy Plan. Hefner had been one of the few oil-and-gas executives in the nation to support Carter for president, which apparently gave him some access to the Carter administration as they drew up their plans for natural gas.

Soon I found myself in a meeting with Hefner and James Schlesinger, Carter's secretary of energy, in a cramped office in the Old Executive Office Building next door to the White House. Schlesinger had been secretary of defense under Presidents Nixon and Ford, so I was surprised to find him in such a small office.

With his white hair, square jaw, and serious demeanor, he looked like an old executive, so I guess he was in the right building.

President Carter's National Energy Plan was still being drafted, but Hefner was concerned that it would not deregulate the price of deep natural gas. Schlesinger said something like: "The problem with you producers is that you will not take 'yes' for an answer. I am telling you that we will deregulate deep gas administratively."

Hefner responded: "The fact that you will not put that in the bill makes me question your intent." At that point, I expected Schlesinger to kick us out of his office, but he did not seem upset by Hefner's candid observation. Instead, as an economist, he explained professorially, "If we deregulate a narrow part of the natural gas market, it will cause a hyper-inflation in a micro-economy." That sounded serious, so I made a mental note of his warning.

The natural gas market was a tangled mess at that time, due primarily to federal price controls. Natural gas production and reserves had been falling since the mid-1960s, and by the mid-1970s, many schools and factories in the Midwest and Southeast were forced to close, due to a natural gas shortage. Natural gas produced and sold within the same state was not subject to the federal price controls, but the limited size of intrastate markets kept the gas prices too low to encourage exploration.

At a convention of the Texas Independent Producers and Royalty Owners (TIPARO), I met an old wildcatter and asked him how his finding costs were.

"My finding costs are fine," he said. "It's the looking costs that are killing me."

At that time, the nature of the oil and gas exploration and production business was more about the high-risk "looking" part. The price needed to be high enough to justify the exploration risks, since a high percentage of so-called "wildcat" wells ended up as dry holes. Opponents of natural gas price deregulation argued that the nation was running out of natural gas resources, so higher prices would hurt consumers but would not result in increased supplies.

While the natural gas market was stifled, the politics of natural gas were convoluted. In those quaint times, there were conservative Democrats representing producing states like Texas and Louisiana, and liberal Republicans representing consuming states like Indiana and Ohio. Regardless of political party, most of the senators and representatives seemed more interested in representing the business and consumer interests of their home states than in advancing any political ideology.

President Carter's proposed Natural Gas Policy Act (NGPA) was included as part of his National Energy Act. On April 18, 1977, the president donned a sweater and appeared on national television to warn the nation that it would take "the moral equivalent of war" to combat the energy crisis.

"The oil and natural gas we rely on for 75 percent of our energy are running out," the president opined.

While consumer versus producer interests were at stake in his energy policy proposals, the politics seemed more driven by energy industry intramurals, such as coal versus natural gas, and petroleum industry intramurals, such as major oil companies versus independent producers. Within the independent sector, the positions of established oil and gas producers were challenged by deep natural gas explorers (that would be us).

As a newly minted lobbyist, I naturally had to spend most of my time in DC. I told Terry the lobbying effort would only take a few more weeks. Once the energy bill passed, I would be back home in Norman and commuting to Oklahoma City. Unfortunately, with so much at stake, the political battle over natural gas price deregulation dragged on for nearly two years. If Terry and I had known how long this legislative marathon would go on, we might have moved back to Washington, DC. But the bill would live, die, and come back to life in an altered state. After a few months, my persistent claims that my lobbying days were nearly over had lost all credibility at home.

President Carter's bill extended wellhead price controls to the previously unregulated intrastate market, kept low price caps on previously discovered "old" natural gas, and established a complicated set of price ceilings on various types of newly discovered natural gas. The so-called Maximum Lawful Price for new natural gas would be gradually increased until 1985, when the price controls on new natural gas would be lifted.

Hefner testifies for natural gas deregulation

Boots was able to arrange for Hefner to testify before various House and Senate committees about the natural gas issue. I worked with them to prepare his remarks.

Returning to Norman

While Anne was completing her second-grade year in Bartlesville, Terry and I were hunting for a new home. The Oklahoma City public-school system was less than ideal, and its private schools charged tuition as high as OU's, so we focused our house hunting in Edmond and Norman. Thanks to the inflation of the mid-1970s, we were able to sell our house in Bartlesville for about twice what we had paid for it just four years earlier. This windfall affected my views on real estate values and inflation, making me want to buy the most expensive house we could barely afford. I found one in Edmond, a two-story home with a tree growing in an interior courtyard. Terry found one in a new housing development called Brookhaven, in northwest Norman. This one featured a swimming pool instead of an indoor tree, so it was the one we bought.

I broke away from the political scene long enough for Terry and me to pack up our stuff and move from Bartlesville to Norman.

Terry and the girls quickly adjusted to life in our new neighborhood. Anne began taking French lessons from a French woman, Monique Johnson, who lived across the street. And she found a new ballet instructor, Marjorie Kovich. A girl Emily's age, Amy Kane, moved in next door. Amy liked to join us for dinner when she didn't like what her mother was cooking.

Returning home from another lobbying stint in DC, I took a Braniff Airlines flight back to Oklahoma City's Will Rogers airport, where Terry and the girls were waiting in our station wagon to pick me up. They seemed a little excited, as if something was up. As I slid into the driver's seat, I heard a scratching sound and a little "arf" coming from the floor of the back seat. My little family of co-conspirators tried to keep straight faces as I got out of the wagon, opened the backseat door, and discovered the newest member of our family, a puppy named Sugar. Terry said Sugar's mother was a registered schnauzer and her father was the notorious lease-law-violator, Stretch, a birddog and basset hound mix who roamed the neighborhood looking for love.

As a puppy, Sugar enjoyed chewing up the green Astroturf around our swimming pool. She also like to stand on the top step of the pool, half submerged, like a Filipino caribou. We had to keep an eye on her when she was out by the pool, because if she accidentally fell in, she would panic, swim to the side, and dog paddle furiously. I tried many times to teach her to swim to the stairs, but she just didn't get it.

Anne and Emily took swimming lessons from a neighbor and were soon enjoying the pool. Emily, at four, would make running jumps from the diving board and splash into the pool with reckless abandon. Anne, at eight, was a beautiful swimmer, but took a more cautious approach to diving. She would stand on the edge of the pool, staring into the water, as if she were contemplating the age-old question: to dive or not to dive. Eventually, she would take the plunge. Growing up, our girls were close as sisters. Their differences in personalities and activities allowed them to support each other instead of competing.

That fall, Emily started kindergarten and Anne started the third grade at Cleveland Elementary School. Terry and I were glad that Norman, a university town, had a good public-school system.

Unfortunately, I had to resume my shuttling to and from the nation's capital as the natural gas issue heated up again. With

Representative John Dingell, a Democrat from Michigan, chairing the House Energy Committee, the NGPA, largely as proposed by President Carter, was approved by the House on July 18, 1977. The House bill was strongly opposed by the Independent Producers Association of America (IPAA) and the American Petroleum Institute (API). The industry's two major trade groups backed a bill sponsored by Senator Pearson and Senator Lloyd Bentsen, a Democrat from Texas. Each senator represented a major oil and natural gas producing state. Their bill called for ending federal price ceilings on new natural gas onshore immediately, and on offshore gas after five years. It passed the senate on October 4, 1977. Philosophically, I favored the Senate bill. But politics is "the art of the possible," and I didn't believe the Senate bill would ever get past the House or be signed by President Carter.

Although a natural gas bill had passed both the House and Senate, their approaches to the natural gas shortage were extreme opposites. President Carter believed we were running out of natural gas, and his plan called for managing inevitable shortages. In a misguided attempt to protect consumers, price controls on old gas were to remain in place, while controls on newly discovered gas were to be phased out grudgingly, over a seven-year period. A few narrow categories of so-called "high cost" gas were given higher price ceilings, since these sources were not expected to have much impact on supplies. The high-cost menu included natural gas produced from new wells drilled in Devonian shale, coal beds, and deeper than 15,000 feet.

As the House and Senate conferees searched for a compromise, I found myself walking the halls of Congress, representing the Independent Gas Producers Committee, a group of fifty-five member companies who were spending a billion dollars a year in US onshore natural gas exploration. Concerned that deep gas deregulation had come to be viewed as his own pet project, Hefner decided to stay away from Washington for a while, leaving me there to advance our position and keep up with what was going on.

It did not take me long to discover that the senators and congressmen were busy people who lacked the time or interest to get involved with the details of legislation. However, they all seemed to have a staff member whose portfolio included energy, since this was one of the president's main concerns. Most energy staffers would give me a few minutes of their time if I stopped by to lobby them on the natural gas issue. Gradually, I developed what I called my H&R Block method of lobbying. This concept was inspired by a series of television commercials in which Henry Block, the head of the well-known tax preparation service, would give one of the "seventeen reasons" to use H&R Block. Realizing the busy staffers had short attention spans, I would drop by to give them brief position papers on the virtues of deep natural gas and to discuss the latest developments in the ongoing natural gas debate, which seemed to be inching through the legislative process at glacial speed. I often invoked the story of GHK's No. 1 Green well, which I had visited with Hefner some six years earlier. This well, drilled more than four miles deep, had turned out to be a terrific natural gas discovery, but an economic failure due to interstate price controls. When some opponents argued that deep gas didn't exist in significant quantities, I would reply that if deep gas drillers didn't find anything, it wouldn't cost consumers anything. I often pointed out to the liberals that deep wells only accounted for one percent of the drilling, while emphasizing to the conservatives that, according to the Potential Gas Committee of the Colorado School of Mines, more than half of the natural gas remaining to be discovered in the lower forty-eight states would be found deeper than 15,000 feet. In effect, deregulating deep gas would win half the battle.

Hefner had arranged for a meeting with the powerful Senator Russell Long, a Democrat from Louisiana and Chairman of the Senate Finance Committee. At the last minute, Hefner decided to send me instead. My only meeting with an actual senator was enjoyable, but probably unproductive. The senator and one of his senior staff members, apparently mistaking me for a college kid, launched into a filibuster about their raucous fraternity days at LSU. They obviously enjoyed their college shenanigans. I hated to interrupt their trip down memory lane, but I sensed that my meeting time was about to expire. Finally, I managed to get a word in about the fabulous potential for drilling deep gas wells onshore in Louisiana, not to mention Texas and Oklahoma.

One appointment with a key senator that Hefner did keep was a scheduled walk with Senator Ted Kennedy. Like a Hollywood extra in the role of a briefcase-toting staffer, I tagged along from a respectful distance behind as the patrician pair walked from the Hyatt Regency Hotel across the capitol grounds to the Senate office building. Surprisingly, the senator was without staff. Hefner, of course, was doing most of the talking. I could not hear what he was saying, but his monologue surely involved the virtues of deep natural gas.

And That's the Way It Is

As if lobbying everyone in Washington, DC, was not enough, Hefner sent Terry and me to New York City to attend an Upper Manhattan cocktail party being hosted by the Scientists' Institute for Public Information. As we mingled with scientists, journalists, and literati in someone's crowded apartment, I was surprised to see the author Norman Mailer escorting a tall redheaded woman whose fame, if any, had not yet reached Oklahoma. But I was even more surprised when I looked across the crowded room and saw Terry chatting amicably with the anchor of CBS television's national evening news, the iconic Walter Cronkite. (He had introduced himself to her, as if she wouldn't have known who he was.) I hated to interrupt their conversation. People have a way of speaking openly with Terry as she genuinely listens to whatever they want to tell her, even if it is sometimes more than she wants to know. As I edged closer, he was telling her about his broadcasting a University of Oklahoma football game in Norman very early in his career. Eventually, Terry introduced me to Mr. Cronkite. Needing something to report back to Hefner, I immediately launched into my pitch for deep natural gas. Sensing he was being lobbied, the avuncular broadcaster quickly excused himself and disappeared into the crowd. I apologized to Terry for scaring him off. (Only later did I learn she had already tossed him a deep gas pitch.)

Terry joined me for another lobbying opportunity when Hefner sent us on the company Lear Jet to accompany Senate Minority Leader Howard Baker and author Kitty Kelley on a quick trip from Oklahoma City to Washington, DC. Ms. Kelly, the author of *Jackie Oh!* and several other celebrity biographies, interviewed Senator Baker for most of the trip, so I didn't get in much lobbying.

By December of 1977, no workable compromise on the natural gas issue had been found. The House had voted for continued price controls, while the Senate bill called for deregulation. It was beginning to look a lot like Christmas would pass with no legislation in sight. Back in Oklahoma City for the holidays, I drafted a letter to Senator Henry "Scoop" Jackson, a Washington state Democrat and chairman of the Senate Committee on Energy and Natural Resources, suggesting ways a compromise might be reached.

On the first anniversary of President Carter's announcement of his National Energy Plan, the House and Senate conferees worked late into the night to finally reach a compromise energy bill. The competing natural gas bills were so far apart, and there were so many economic interests affected by the legislation, it took a bitter fight to finally reach a deal. The final bill was a complicated concoction of split differences, with each compromise introducing new complexities. It took the energy staffers nearly four months to convert these agreements in principle to actual legislative language.

Strangely, I cannot say how it happened, but somehow the deregulation of deep gas survived the meat-grinder and emerged as part of the proposed Natural Gas Policy Act. Apparently, the Carter Administration supported including deregulation of deep and other sources of high-cost gas as part of a coalition-building strategy. Without a single senator or congressman openly sponsoring our goal, it seemed like we had been given some type of Participation Award, as if to say: "Thanks for playing."

Unfortunately, my lobbying career was not over yet. We had to help make the President's National Energy Plan become the law of the land. With most of the oil and gas industry's considerable Washington forces aligned against the bill, our small band of natural gas explorers was the only producer group actively supporting the final passage of the NGPA. The IPAA challenged the deregulation of deep gas by saying it made no sense to go after the more expensive deep gas first, while holding back shallow gas exploration with continued interstate price controls, and, even worse, extending these price controls to the intrastate markets. They claimed the proposed new law was like telling producers to use helicopters to pick apples, when a small ladder would suffice.

While Hefner's political activities made GHK unpopular among most producers, the oil and gas service companies seemed to love us. They must have noticed all the business GHK was generating for them by promoting deep drilling in the Anadarko Basin. Hefner asked me to raise funds from service companies like Parker Drilling and Halliburton to finance a runway extension at the Elk City airport. Elk City was rapidly becoming the hub of deep gas drilling operations, so its airport needed longer runways to handle a sudden influx of private jet traffic. I wrote fundraising letters to a few dozen companies, and their donations came flooding in. Within a few weeks, we had raised over $100,000 for the runway extensions. To mark the project's completion, the Elk City airport was renamed for Robert A. Hefner III.

Meanwhile, the Administration stuck with the President's diagnosis that the nation was running out of natural gas. One newspaper headline quoted President Carter as saying, "Gas has had it." This view was supported by congressional testimony from a bureaucrat in the Federal Power Commission that "regardless of what happens to gas prices, production will not substantially increase nor will it remain at present levels for a sustained period." Based on this view, another new law, the Powerplant and Industrial Fuel Use Act, required new electric power plants to burn coal instead of natural gas. Agricultural interests also bought into the Administration's view that we were running out of natural gas. The farmers supported the NGPA because it protected their high priority status when natural gas shortages required the limited supplies to be allocated among end-users.

Hefner, on the other hand, told the House Energy Committee that vast quantities of natural gas remained to be discovered. The nation was not running out of natural gas. We were simply running out of natural gas that could be economically found and produced under the prevailing federal price controls. He explained, "Unlike oil, which is usually accumulated in geological structures, natural gas is pervasive in sediments. Throughout the United States, many known and potential natural gas reservoirs have been intentionally bypassed and ignored because federal price controls made virtually all natural gas not associated with oil production unprofitable to find and produce."

Working with the Administration to get the NGPA passed, Hefner and I had another meeting with Secretary of Energy Schlesinger, who by then had moved into a much bigger office. Hefner was pointing out that deep gas wells will require a huge amount of steel drill pipe. He called his friend Robin Fulton, an executive at Dresser Industries, a large manufacturer of drill pipe, and the conversation got off to an awkward start.

Hefner: "Robbie, I'm calling from Energy Secretary Schlesinger's office."

Robbie: "That's too bad."

Hefner: "And the secretary is on the speaker phone and would like to ask you a few questions."

Continuing to support the passage of the NGPA, I occasionally became involved in some oil and gas industry intramurals, since the major oil companies and most independent producers opposed the bill. Back in Oklahoma City, I debated a representative of the Oklahoma Independent Producers Association on a local Sunday morning television news program. This was my first time on television, and I thought I won the debate, or at least held my own.

But if I won the debate, Hefner won the lottery. The Senate approved the NGPA conference bill on September 27, 1978, and the House did the same seventeen days later. President Carter signed the NGPA on November 9, 1978. He was kind enough to send me a framed photograph of his signing ceremony, including one of his signing pens. Ironically, one reason the Carter Administration allowed deep gas deregulation to remain in the final bill was that they did not believe we would find any.

— ᴼ — ᴼ —

CHAPTER ELEVEN

THE DEEP
GAS BOOM

$\mathbf{B}$*ack home in Norman*, I encountered a reluctant angel. Four-year-old Emily was sitting on the sofa with her arms crossed, a frown on her face, balking at performing in a Christmas pageant. Eventually, Terry and I persuaded her to put on her angel costume and sing at the pageant. The next morning, we were surprised to find a big picture of her happily singing away, on the front page of *The Norman Transcript* newspaper.

When I returned to work at GHK's Oklahoma City office, Hefner gave me a significant bonus for my lobbying efforts. He also informed me that, since I knew more about the NGPA than most people, my new assignment at GHK would be Vice President, Natural Gas Marketing.

Hefner had recently purchased a World War II vintage DC3 passenger aircraft from the Wrigley family in Chicago. The plane still had its original interior décor, featuring numerous Wrigley logos. He invited my family and me to join him on a quick flight to Santa Fe, New Mexico, on this latest addition to his private air fleet. Hefner was a big supporter of the Oklahoma City ballet, and Anne, our nine-year-old aspiring ballerina, demonstrated some of her ballet moves for him on this trip.

Back in Oklahoma, with my lobbying days behind me, I decided to quit feeling guilty about my career change. I had felt I had sold out for money by changing from being an honest journalist and aspiring writer to becoming a lobbyist and public relations hack. I began to view myself as an oil and gas producer who wanted to make money by providing the energy people need to drive to work and heat their homes in the winter. I came to realize that there is nothing wrong with capitalistic acts between consenting adults, provided they are free to choose how to spend their time, efforts, and resources.

While the deep gas political battles had been dragging on in DC, Apache Corporation had been busy drilling deep gas wells under the farmout agreement covering GHK's Elk City Project Area. Apache drilled two prolific natural gas wells in the Carpenter Field, just north of Elk City. The wells, the Watkins 1–21 and the Gregory 1–29, were each completed in the Morrow formation at depths below 17,000 feet, so they qualified for deregulated deep gas prices.

My first task as GHK's natural gas marketer was to arrange for a long-term sales contract for wells in the Carpenter Field. Panhandle Eastern Pipeline Company had a major line in the area of the field, so I met with their gas buyer to negotiate a deal. The most important items to be determined were the price of the gas and the volumes to be sold. Since the pipeline companies needed natural gas to keep their lines full, they were willing to commit to taking 80 percent of the wells' annual production capacity or paying for that volume even if they did not take that much gas. These so-called "take or pay" contracts were designed to ensure that the producers could count on a certain level of revenues and to allow the pipelines to make up pre-paid volumes later.

While the take-or-pay requirements in these long-term contracts were common, the Panhandle gas buyer and I were in a new ball game on the price terms. We were both negotiating our first natural gas contract under the NGPA. For shallow gas, I asked for the maximum lawful price under the new price controls. For deep gas, produced from new wells below 15,000 feet, I asked for the price to be determined under a formula to equal 130 percent of the energy equivalent of No. 2 fuel oil, or the average of the three highest prices Panhandle paid to other producers in Oklahoma (a so-called "favored nations" clause). The gas buyer, who had an annoying habit on injecting the term "to be honest with you" in about every other sentence, asked how I came up with the No. 2 fuel oil concept. I explained that under the NGPA, the interstate pipelines are allowed to pay a price for deep gas of up to 130 percent of the energy equivalent, measured in btu's, of No. 2 fuel oil and roll the cost of this gas into their average cost of gas, which is used by the pipelines to set their prices to their customers. Given the huge volumes of low-priced, regulated gas they sell, including a relatively small amount of more costly deep gas would barely move their average price.

The Panhandle buyer replied, "To be honest with you, I've never heard of this idea. I'll have to check on this with our attorneys." He was, and he did. When GHK signed the contract in December 1978, the No. 2 fuel oil was selling for around 40 cents per gallon, so the deep gas price would have been about $2.90 per mmbtu (million British thermal units, a measure of the gas's energy content).

Fortunately for GHK, when the Shah of Iran was overthrown by the Iranian Revolution in February 1979, the oil price jumped up to $25 per barrel. This price spike brought the price of No. 2 fuel oil to 60 cents per gallon and the price of GHK's deep gas to $5.65 per mmbtu. Deep natural gas was the only domestic hydrocarbon that was not subject to price controls or President Carter's so-called "windfall profits" tax. And the deep gas drilling boom was born.

After enjoying a couple of gas marketing boondoggles sponsored by the gas-hungry pipeline companies, I negotiated a big gas contract for GHK with Southern Natural. Importantly, this contract did not include a "market out" provision, which would have allowed the buyer to back out of the contract due to adverse market conditions on the consuming end of the pipeline.

Get Money . . . Sell Gas

In the spring of 1979, GHK's vice president of finance left the company to work for another Oklahoma City independent producer. I was a little shocked when Hefner named me his new vice president of finance. However, as Hefner described the job, my main function was to raise funds for the company's voracious appetite for drilling dollars. My only relationship with the accounting department occurred monthly, when they issued my paycheck.

Hefner had a way of managing his complex personal and business finances that ensured he was the only person on earth who knew what was really going on. When he wasn't jetting around the planet, he would ramble through the company offices, giving executives and managers specific tasks, but there were never any management meetings to coordinate strategies or plans. Given my independent nature, I enjoyed the freedom his management style allowed. Reporting directly to Hefner, I seemed to have a four-word job description: "Get money . . . sell gas."

The combination of Apache's drilling success in the Carpenter Field and the soaring prices for deep natural gas allowed GHK to obtain a large production loan from the First National Bank of Dallas. Before the ink was dry on that deal, I flew to Chicago to arrange another multi-million- dollar loan agreement with energy lenders at Continental Illinois Bank.

In my fundraising role, I met a young, energetic banker named Bill Patterson. He was the vice president of energy lending for a nearby shopping center bank called Penn Square. Although I was about six years older than him, we had a lot in common. He was from Bartlesville, a Sigma Chi at OU, and Hefner treated us both like employees, tasked with raising millions of drilling dollars.

Running for the Prize

In July of 1980, the deep gas drilling boom was gathering momentum and the future was looking bright. Hefner, at age forty-three, liked to go on runs on the golf course of the Oklahoma City Golf and Country Club near his home. He had recently taken a physical at the Cooper Clinic in Dallas and seemed particularly proud of his time on a treadmill during a stress test at the clinic. In a challenge to certain GHK executives, he offered a $1,000 prize to any of us who could beat his time on the treadmill, and another $1,000 prize for achieving an excellent rating for our age category. In my case, it would take forty-four minutes to beat his time, which would also get me an excellent rating for my age. I was scheduled for an appointment in mid-August, but I knew there was no way for me to get into shape by then. Pleading too much work on my plate, I managed to get my appointment moved back until early October.

The next morning, I got up at 6:00, put on my jogging outfit and New Balance running shoes, drank some orange juice, and began jogging up a slight incline on Hidden Hill Road. I had intended to run around our block for a few times, but I couldn't even make it to the end of our block before I found myself walking. I knew I was out of shape, but this was pathetic.

Motivated by my own competitive nature, not to mention a possible $2,000 in prize money, I stuck to my early morning routine. Within a week, I was able to jog around our block without stopping. As the summer went on, I gradually expanded the circumference of my jogging circle, making slow, but steady progress.

In early October my appointment at the Cooper Clinic was drawing near, and I picked up the pace on my morning jogs. By the time the big day arrived, I was able to jog twelve miles without stopping.

My stress test on the treadmill at the Cooper Clinic began at an easy stroll and gradually speeded up to a brisk walk. When I passed the forty-four-minute mark, I knew I had won both prizes, and thought I would really blow Hefner's time out of the water. But just as I was enjoying that thought, the treadmill speeded up. Running faster to keep up, I noticed the track I was treading on was beginning to incline. Soon I was sprinting up hill. My sprint did not last long, and I stopped with a time of forty-four minutes and forty-five seconds, enough for a moral as well as financial victory. With my $2,000 prize, I bought a ring for Terry, bicycles for the girls and a watch for me. But perhaps the biggest benefit was that all the running had gotten me back into good enough shape to resume my basketball career.

My Third Comeback

In 1980, I embarked on my third basketball comeback, this one involving as much coaching as playing. I joined a team sponsored by Penn Square Bank, competing in an Oklahoma City business league. Its games were played in the Northside YMCA gym. In an early season game, I had only been playing for a few minutes when I became totally winded. Unable to catch my breath, I had to call time-out to take myself out of the game. A visit to a heart doctor revealed that I had developed an irregular heartbeat. When it would kick in, usually while exercising, I would have trouble breathing. The better my conditioning, the longer I could play without becoming short of breath. My game came back gradually, and I managed to score 33 points for Penn Square as we defeated a team from IBM.

Although I was thirty-seven, my hoop dreams had not died. I began dreaming of becoming the NBA's first player-owner. With financial backing from Penn Square, I could buy an NBA team and install myself at point guard. The Dallas Mavericks, then a struggling expansion team, looked like a possible acquisition target. (Today, there is an NBA rule against owners playing for their own teams, which explains why Mark Cuban is not the starting point guard for the Dallas Mavericks.)

The Billion-Year Gap

Trying to maintain a work/life balance was more difficult at GHK than it had been at Phillips. With deep gas prices rising toward $10 per mmbtu and with more deep gas wells being completed on GHK's Anadarko Basin leases, the company's revenues were shooting up fast. Many of the company's executives and employees were working long hours, and someone complained to Hefner about my leaving work "early" at 6 pm. In defense of my schedule, I told Hefner that if someone cannot get their work done between 8 am and 6 pm, they must not be very efficient.

Not that GHK was all work and no play. Hefner organized a five-day float trip on the Colorado River, running from Page, Colorado, through the Grand Canyon, toward Lake Meade, Nevada, for a group of a dozen friends, family, and GHK executives. We piled onto a huge raft built on rubber pontoons and floated down river. The geologists on the trip could point out rock formations on the canyon walls that were the same formations we were searching for in the Anadarko Basin, where they were buried more than three miles beneath the surface. At one stop, a geologist pointed out a "billion-year gap." He could cover with one hand a gap between one rock formation that was a billion years older than one lying directly on top of it.

We bounced around a little on the rapids as we floated down the river. At times, the rapids sent us heading straight into the canyon walls, but the pontoons smashed into the walls, then snapped back, thus absorbing what I had feared were impending collisions. At times, we would climb off our raft and explore canyons and caves along the river.

More terrifying than the rapids was our helicopter ride out of the canyon. For aeronautical reasons, having to do with the summer heat, the helicopter, when loaded with passengers, could not fly straight up and out of the canyon. Instead, it had to work its way up, first flying directly toward a canyon wall, then reversing course and flying toward the wall on the opposite side on the canyon. Based on my time at Subic Bay, when I often had to write news releases about Navy helicopter crashes, I had a healthy respect for the dangers involved in flying on helicopters. I was greatly relieved when our helicopter landed safely and dropped us off at the top of the canyon.

When I got home from this excursion late one afternoon, I was wearing an old fishing hat, and my face was sunburned, swollen from bug bites, and covered with a five-day beard. I walked around to the back of our house and opened the gate to our pool area. Anne and Emily saw me and ran inside, yelling, "Mom, there's a man in our backyard!" It's bad when your own kids don't recognize you.

On another GHK excursion, Hefner and a few GHK executives hopped in the company Lear Jet and flew to Aspen, Colorado, for a little skiing. I had never skied before but figured I could teach myself. How hard could it be? It's all downhill. I rented some ski boots and skies, took the lift to the top of the mountain, and managed to stay vertical as I hopped off the lift.

I skied over to the top of a beginners' slope and headed downhill. Noticing that I was gaining a little speed, I thought back to my high school football days, where I was taught that to maintain your balance, you should bend your knees and widen your stance. This maneuver helped my balance, but it also greatly increased my speed. Soon I was racing down the mountain, struggling to maintain my cannonball position as my knees began to ache. Looking to my right, I noticed a large crowd of people strung out along a wooden fence. Glancing beyond the fence, I realized the people were ski fans, watching professional skiers race down the mountain.

Looking ahead, I saw that I was running out of snow, but couldn't see beyond the point where the snow ended. I aborted my first ski run by diving forward, sliding down the mountain on my stomach for about fifty yards. Shaken but unhurt, I climbed back up the mountain to retrieve my skies, then walked down to peer over the embankment where the snow ended. It appeared that if I had skied over that point, I would have been airborne awhile, then crashed into the ski resort's parking lot, probably setting off a few car alarms.

Always thinking big, Hefner sent me to a world energy conference in Montreux, Switzerland, where world oil executives were meeting in conjunction with an OPEC meeting nearby. Not wanting to waste my trip, I hoped to get in a plug for deep gas. During a Q & A session, in what was more of a comment than a question, I asked the panel if they were aware that deep gas in the Anadarko Basin was being sold for 130 percent of the energy equivalent of No. 2 fuel oil. Judging from their reaction, this was news to them.

That evening, I tagged along with a group of conference goers who were taking a boat across Lake Geneva, to have dinner at a fancy restaurant in France. When we were exiting our boat, I realized that I had forgotten my passport. When I explained my problem to the French border guards, they let me in on the strength of my Oklahoma driver's license.

At a Houston conference attended by several hundred oil and gas industry people, I was on a panel discussing recent events in the natural gas market. A long-winded gentleman rose to ask me a question that he apparently felt required an extensive amount of background information. I waited patiently as he rambled on for several minutes, totally unaware that the large audience was growing restive. When he finally quit talking, I asked, matter-of-factly, "Can you repeat the question?" The audience erupted in laughter. As the poor guy sat down, justifiably embarrassed, I feared my asking him to repeat his question may have been the cruelest thing I had ever done. On the other hand, it seemed like the whole audience felt he deserved it.

Later that year, I was attending a reception in Oklahoma City's Skirvin Hotel for the famous economist Milton Friedman, who had recently published a book on free market principles called *Free to Choose.* I had a chance to visit with him briefly, so I told him I had really enjoyed reading his book. I added, however, that our dog Sugar had apparently misread the title as *Free to Chew* and had chewed up his book. Without pause, the diminutive economist replied: "Your dog has excellent taste."

Both of our daughters were born with eye muscle problems, so Terry and I often drove them to Dallas to see Dr. David Stager, a pediatric ophthalmologist. Dr. Stager had studied under Dr. Marshall Parks, who had done Anne's infant eye surgery when we were living in the Washington, DC, area.

On one trip to Dr. Stager's, each of the girls had undergone eye surgery, and we were staying in a motel near the hospital while they recovered. It was early on a Saturday morning. Both girls were nauseated from the surgery, so I rushed back to the hospital pharmacy to get them some additional medicine. I parked in a nearly empty pay lot, ran inside, and picked up their medicine. As I started to drive out of the parking lot, I noticed there was no one in the toll booth, but there was a coin-operated device that required fifty cents to lift a cross bar at the exit. Still hurrying, I dropped two quarters into the parking machine, but nothing happened. I put in two more quarters. Still no result. Out of quarters, I got out of my car, sized up the cross bar, looked around, and, seeing no witnesses, gave the cross bar the hardest karate kick I could muster. To my surprise, my kick had snapped the bar into two pieces, leaving me room to speed out of the exit, hoping there were no security cameras recording my escape. Besides, given the circumstances, I felt that no jury would convict me.

Being Rich Is More Expensive

With the deep gas drilling boom gathering steam, and with our recent experience with real estate inflation in Bartlesville, Terry and I decided to look for a bigger and better home in Norman. In August 1980, we found one only a few blocks away, on the aptly named Grandview Avenue, on the northwest edge of Norman. The terrain in most of Oklahoma is so flat that finding any home with a great view is difficult. But this home, designed by a locally famous architect, was more than 5,000 square feet, and rested on a bluff with a magnificent western view of a low-lying area called Ten Mile Flats.

By chance, the home was owned by Clark Heatherington, a local businessman who had cosponsored the Norman Mooreburger basketball team I had played on in college. As we were touring the house, we found a large closet full of wheelchairs, crutches, braces, and other injury-related devices. We asked the realtor what sport the owner plays. She answered: "Polo." He must have been a serious polo player, not just horsing around.

By then, I knew Penn Square Bank's aggressive energy lender, Bill Patterson, was eager to make loans. I wasn't surprised when he agreed to make us a home loan of over $400,000, which was the asking price plus an allowance for remodeling. Terry launched an extensive remodeling project for our new home. When we moved in a few months later, we realized we truly had one foot in town and the other in the country. The massive oak tree in our front yard was the home of an owl, while contingents of squirrels, ground hogs, and armadillos roamed our 4.25 acres, and made home gardening impossible.

Shortly after we moved in, we began adjusting to our new financial situation by buying a Bösendorfer piano for Anne. At that point, I was happy with our existing household stuff, best described as an eclectic mix of early marriage and early Philippine furniture, accented by Terry's unsold Gamut inventory of knickknacks from around the world.

Soon a large delivery truck from Cunningham Interiors arrived full of fine furniture and artful decorating pieces I didn't know we needed. Lyle and A. J. Cunningham and their staff went to work dispersing their high-class items around our interior. We were soon the proud new owners of a zebra rug, a porcelain watch dog named Butch, a new living room divan and easy chairs, not to mention scores of decorating items. When they finally finished unloading their truck and placing their inventory, I had to admit that our new home looked like a million bucks. Their bill, which required several pages, added up to only a quarter of that. But Terry and I really liked Lyle and A. J., and they assured us if we decided we did not want to keep any of their stuff, they would take it back. Anyway, since we were paying with Penn Square dollars, we bought the whole truckload. It was then that I first realized that, compared to my experience with being poor, being rich was going to be a lot more expensive.

One night during a frightening thunderstorm, Anne, Emily, and I sat out on a wooden swing on our covered back patio to watch an awesome display by Mother Nature. Accompanied by lightning bolts dancing across the horizon and thunder that sounded like the Gods were bowling, we sang our state song, "Oklahoma!" as loudly as we could. When we could get the timing right, a lighting flash or thunderclap would punctuate each line of the song. Our performance went something like this: "Oklahoma! . . . flash . . . Where the wind comes sweeping down the plains . . . rumble . . . And the waving wheat . . . flash . . . does sure smell sweet . . . distant explosion . . . when the wind comes right behind the rain!" (Whenever the conversation turns to our first boom house, that night's experience still comes up.)

Banking on Good Times

While the Anadarko Basin's deep gas drilling boom was heating up, much of the rest of the country was in a recession. Bankers looking for new loan business heard about the billions of dollars being spent on deep gas drilling in Western Oklahoma and converged on Oklahoma City looking for new loan business. My energetic and fun-loving friend Bill Patterson greeted these loan hungry big city bankers and helped them throw money at Penn Square's many cash hungry independent oil and gas producer clients.

The process went something like this. A young banker from Chicago would arrive in Oklahoma City looking for energy loans. If this was his first trip, he was encouraged to adapt to the local culture by buying cowboy boots and a cowboy hat, so that he would feel at home when invited to meet some oilmen for dinner and drinks at a local cowboy nightclub. Before the evening was over, the big city banker, in full "nouveau macho" mode, would be two-stepping around the dance floor, or riding a mechanical bull, feeling like John Travolta, starring in a real-life version of the movie *Urban Cowboy*. By the time the dealing was done, Penn Square would have made a $50 million loan to Billy Bob Jumpback, independent oil and gas producer, kept $2 million of the loan on its books, and sold the balance of the loan to his new and eager big city banker friend.

Patterson took it upon himself to always be the life of the party. One of his well-known hijinks was drinking beer from a cowboy boot. At times I wondered if he had escaped from the cast of *Saturday Night Live*. My favorite memory of his class-clown act occurred during a dinner meeting with the top management of Northern Trust Bank at their headquarters in downtown Chicago. GHK was discussing a multimillion-dollar loan from their bank, and Hefner, Patterson, and I were there to meet their executives. I happened to be seated across from Patterson at their long, formal dinner table. A procession of formally attired waiters marched stiffly into the dining room, with each waiter carrying a large dinner plate covered by a chrome dome. There was an individual waiter for each guest. Each waiter placed a plate in front of his guest and waited for a signal to dramatically lift the dome. Unfortunately for his waiter, Patterson jumped the gun and placed the dome on his head, where it looked a lot like a German helmet, and Patterson looked a lot like the guy on *Laugh-In* who would pop up unexpectedly and say: "Very interesting." Patterson's poor waiter had a truly panic-stricken expression on his face when the eleven other waiters pretentiously lifted their guest's plate covers at the proper signal.

Hefner had supported President Carter in 1976 because he thought the Georgia peanut farmer would win. For the 1980 presidential election, he put his money on Ronald Reagan, and suggested I do the same by becoming a Republican Eagle. As a disappointed Goldwater supporter and Watergate denier, I was fine with the Republican part of his suggestion, but the Eagle part was going to require me to make a $10,000 donation. I could remember being shocked when I learned that my parents had paid $50 per plate to attend a Republican political dinner in Tulsa during the 1950s. How could one dinner plate cost $50? However, in the spirit of pay to play, I came up with our $10,000 donation, which led to an invitation to a Republican Eagle election night watch party in a Washington, DC, downtown hotel.

Once again on the company jet, Terry and I flew to DC and landed at Washington National around 6 pm. Listening to the radio as our cab crawled along in heavy traffic, we learned that President Carter had conceded defeat surprisingly early. We checked into our hotel and immediately caught a cab to the hotel hosting the watch party. When we arrived, we discovered the hotel had become overcrowded with celebrating Republicans. Invited or not, we couldn't get past the fire marshals at the hotel entrance. Fortunately, I knew an Italian pizza place from my recent lobbying days, so we went there for dinner. The next morning, we headed home, joking that that was a long way to go for a pizza.

In December 1980, Hefner negotiated a deal with Mobil Oil Company that validated his long-held belief in the Deep Anadarko Basin. Under the deal, Mobil agreed to earn a half interest in GHK's acreage in its Elk City Project Area by making a large cash payment up front and agreeing to spend more than $200 million on a combination of high-risk exploratory and lower-risk development drilling. Hefner told me that Mobil was willing to pay millions more for the entire lease block, but he did not want to sell more than half. He could have just sold Mobil the whole package, declared victory, and moved on. But he had invested his whole career as a geologist in proving the deep gas concept and seemed to be as interested in this project's science as he was in its economics.

A few days before President Reagan's Inauguration, Terry and I joined a large flock of Texas and Oklahoma Republican Eagles, flying to DC on Dresser Industries' corporate 727 jet. President Reagan's Inaugural celebration included three days of formal dinners and events, leading up to the Inaugural Ball on January 20, 1981. As we arrived at Washington National Airport, a long line of black limousines awaited us on the runway. With each of the ladies in our party requiring three or more formal gowns for the festivities, unloading their luggage from our plane was a major task, resulting in an assembly of trunks and other luggage surely rivaling the arrival of a travelling opera company.

We made the rounds of several parties, performances and balls being hosted by various States around the city. My favorite event was easily a ball hosted by Texas. Terry and I were included in a group led by Hefner's friend and Dresser Industry executive Robin Fulton. When we arrived at the Texas ball, Robin informed a doorman that he was the governor of Texas, which was entirely believable, since he projected a sense of authority and looked like a man Central Casting would select for the part. The doorman dutifully ushered our party to the governor's reserved seats, a private viewing box just to the left of the orchestra. We ordered champagne and watched the Texans dancing to music not composed with a two-step in mind. Occasionally, a dancer would shoot us a glance, as if asking, "Who in the hell are you people?" But we stayed awhile without incident, finally moving on to the next event. (I never learned if the real Texas governor ever showed up, or how he was greeted if he did.)

My basketball season that winter was limited to a few games playing with a team called the Norman Mormons in the Norman Open League. After one of our games, a teammate who was still in high school asked me how old I was. I told him I was thirty-eight. He responded, "I hope I can still play basketball when I am thirty-eight."

After a family skiing vacation in Aspen, we were in downtown Denver one evening doing some window shopping. Eight-year-old Emily noticed a policeman who seemed to be watching us. She walked up to him and explained, "It's ok, I'm just a streetwalker."

The Boom Heats Up

Shortly after President Reagan took office, a deep gas well being drilled by a small Oklahoma City producer called Ports of Call grabbed the nation's attention by erupting like a small volcano. The well, the No. 1 Tomcat, blew out natural gas at a rate of more than 100 million cubic feet per day from just below the magic 15,000 feet depth needed to qualify for deregulated prices. Located near the eastern edge of the Deep Anadarko Basin, about fifty miles west of Oklahoma City, the well supported Hefner's geologic thesis that "anyplace else in the world, the entire Anadarko Basin would be considered one giant gas field."

In April 1981, GHK's fortunes took another leap up when Apache completed the K. C. Cattle Company 1–34, an important deep gas discovery in the Atoka formation, near the southwest edge of Elk City. To celebrate, GHK threw a party at the wellsite for employees, royalty owners, contractors, bankers, and others involved in the well. Some of Hefner's friends from France had invested in the well and brought a giant bottle of Champagne to toast the occasion. As a country and western band played, a huge flare of burning natural gas shot up from the well into the night sky, dramatically demonstrating the well's prodigious productivity. While our party flare was nothing compared to the torch from the Tomcat blowout, it was still impressive.

While the Tomcat had put on a spectacular show that stirred the industry's new-found lust for deep gas, another deep gas play in the Fletcher Field emerged to fulfill Secretary of Energy James Schlesinger's prediction that deep gas deregulation would "create a hyper-inflation in a micro-economy." Located in Comanche County about fifty-three miles Southwest of the Tomcat, the Fletcher play was focused on the Springer formation, at depths below 20,000 feet. Wells penetrating this formation unleashed natural gas molecules that had been trapped there for millions of years, under tremendous pressure, and eager to escape to the surface. The high initial production rates from the early wells in the play set off a bidding war for leases in the area, and GHK and other independent producers like Saxon Oil of Dallas bid up lease prices as high as $10,000 per acre.

The Fletcher deep gas play soon attracted Oklahoma City's largest oil company, Kerr McGee. The company launched a $150-million-dollar drilling program, described as "an invasion force of rigs, men, and equipment probably unmatched in the history of oil and gas exploration in the United States."

By August 1981, GHK needed additional financing for its lease buying and drilling programs. Terry and I flew to New York City to see some investment bankers who had been raising funds in London to invest with independent producers in the United States. The bankers and I worked out the basic terms of a deal for their investors to loan $35 million to GHK in the form of debentures subordinated to its bank debt. After our meeting, the investment bankers took Terry and me to Le Cirque restaurant for dinner. Our hosts casually ordered a bottle of Chateau Suduiraut 1969, a dessert wine from Sauternes, France. One glass of this bold and sweet wine was enough to make me feel a little buzz. I knew I couldn't finish my second glass and still walk out of there upright. I felt bad about leaving what I feared was a small fortune's worth of wine in my glass as I staggered outside. Fortunately, Terry was unfazed by the wine or the deal, and we made it home okay.

A few weeks later, Terry and I were in New York City's JFK Airport, hopping on a Concord jet for a quick flight to Paris. I took a small English-to-French language handbook on the flight and tried to learn a few key phrases. All I remembered from my high school French class was "La plume es sur la table," which means, "The pen is on the table." Unfortunately, the flight was unbelievably quick. Traveling at twice the speed of sound, we arrived in Paris in less than four hours, so I did not have time to learn much French. We were joined on this trip by a contingent of Penn Square bankers, consisting of Bill Patterson, his wife Eve, two young executives who worked for Bill, and their wives.

Our destination was the eighteenth-century Chateau du Fresne in the Loire Valley of France. Hefner had given me a reserve report showing the current value of a group of GHK wells his French friends had invested in, and he had asked me to go over it with them. Judging by our travel companions, I assumed Penn Square had financed their investment. Our hostess was an American, the Marquise Suzanne de Brantes, whose French husband, Paul, was somehow related to the former French president Valery Giscard d'Estaing. At dinner one evening, the wine and champagne were flowing freely, and Patterson came up with a more sophisticated version of one of the stunts he employed when entertaining visiting bankers back home. Instead of drinking beer out of a cowboy boot, he drank champagne out of a Gucci loafer. Apparently, his reputation preceded him, because no one seemed surprised by his antics.

One night after dinner, our group of eight, led by the de Brantes's attorney, ventured out to a rural nightclub in what must have been a converted wine cave. As we walked in, the local patrons, possibly zoned out on their drug of choice, appeared indifferent to our arrival. Terry and I were shocked and amused by the local band, featuring a young man with a heavy French accent, singing the decades-old country and western ballad, "Red River Valley." Finding a French band playing country and western music in a cave in wine country seemed beyond bizarre.

As I said before, there is something about Terry that makes people want to confide in her. Total strangers would tell her their life story while waiting in a grocery line. I wasn't surprised when I saw the Marquise and Terry, sitting on the front stairs of the chateau, engaged in serious conversation. Terry later told me that the Marquise had remarked that she was "deeper than I expected."

Hefner and I flew to London a few months later to meet with the investors represented by the high-rolling New York investment bankers. I was surprised to learn that one of these investors was called something like the Scottish Widows and Orphans Fund. (I had always thought that taking money from widows and orphans was just a figure of speech.) The deal also required a trip to Florida for another meeting among GHK executives and attorneys and the investment bankers, before finally closing in February 1982. (In retrospect, I wondered if any other investment bankers had ever negotiated so long and hard to make such a bad deal.)

Seeking additional drilling dollars, I flew to Chicago on a cold February day to meet with John Lytle, the vice president for energy lending at Continental Illinois Bank. My mission was to convince him to loan GHK an additional $40 million, to be secured by GHK's retained interests in the development drilling program being conducted in the Elk City area by Mobil. After our meeting, we went out to dinner, where I continued to advance my case for the loan.

The next morning, he told me I could tell Hefner that I had gotten him the $40 million. Heading back home that afternoon, I was in an O'Hare airport terminal waiting for my flight, which had been delayed by a snowstorm. Still stuck at the airport that evening, I wandered into a bar to kill some time. After ordering a drink, I looked down the bar and was surprised to see Julius Erving seated at the bar, with just one empty seat between us. He was apparently alone, killing time like me. Seeing him as a stranded fellow traveler, I took the liberty of introducing myself. Dr. J seemed happy to have someone to talk to. He explained that he was traveling by himself, instead of with his Philadelphia 76ers team, due to his scheduled appearance in the NBA All Star game.

Trying to establish some hoops credibility, I mentioned that I had once stolen the ball from Marques Haynes. Dr. J, by then in his twelfth season of professional basketball, admitted that his knees were giving him some trouble. "It's not the dunking that causes knee problems," he explained. "It's the landing."

Oklahoma's oil and gas drilling boom continued to gain momentum. By December 1981, there were 871 rigs drilling in the Sooner State. (By comparison, in December 2020 there were fourteen rigs drilling in Oklahoma and only 346 drilling in the entire United States.) Good news is easy to absorb, and I quickly adjusted to my rapidly improving financial outlook. With Penn Square Bank backing my every move, I had acquired an interest in a GHK-related limited partnership called North Block Gas. I was also investing in a GHK drilling program and receiving a small interest in GHK wells through a company net profits program. At age thirty-eight, I thought I had made my first million.

Camelot Is Over

Feeling flush, Terry and I hired a local architect to design a 6,000-square-foot addition to our home, including an indoor/outdoor pool with a retractable roof, a home office, and an art gallery. After a few months of architectural digesting, we settled on a plan to more than double the size of our home.

On a pleasant afternoon in April 1982, I was sitting at my desk at GHK's Oklahoma City office, working on a natural gas marketing contract between GHK and El Paso Natural Gas Company. Hefner told me that his executive assistant, Tom Heritage, was going to escort a potential investor on a helicopter tour of GHK's drilling operations in the Anadarko Basin. He asked if I would like to go with them. I declined the invitation, saying I was too busy working on a gas marketing deal with El Paso. The next day, I learned that the helicopter had crashed early that morning, on its way to Elk City. According to press reports, the helicopter "exploded in the air and plummeted to the ground." Tom, the investor, and the pilot were killed. The crash was a tragic loss for their families and a near miss for me.

Terry said at the time that the helicopter crash marked the end of the boom. As she put it, "Camelot is over." Terry has a talent for making bold statements, apparently based on very little evidence, that somehow turn out to be true.

Dismissing Terry's warning, I remained in empire-building mode. The house next door to ours came on the market, and I considered buying it, since their lot included a wonderful tennis court that backed on to our backyard. My plan was to buy my neighbor's property, annex their tennis court, and re-sell the house and remaining lot. I told my plan to Bill Patterson and he said Penn Square would loan me the $2 million needed to do the deal. Fortunately, something caused me to change my mind before I pulled the trigger on my tennis court caper.

There were warning signs I should have picked up on if I had been more sensitive to the fact that markets can move down as well as up. One day I told Hefner that the head of our investor group had called and asked me to tell him that "our investors are getting nervous." Striding away down an office hallway, he called back over his shoulder, "How nervous does he want them to be?" The pipeline gas buyers were beginning to scale back the prices they were willing to pay for deep gas. This led to a disagreement between Hefner and me about a pending natural gas contract. I told him if he only wanted people who will always agree with him, he could hire them for a lot less than he was paying me.

To me, the end of the boom was marked by a telephone call I received in mid-June from a natural gas buyer with El Paso. He said his company, one of the major pipeline companies buying and transporting natural gas from the Anadarko Basin, was no longer interested in buying deep gas. Soon, El Paso and the other major interstate pipelines were renouncing their long-term deep gas purchase contracts. While natural gas was in short supply, the pipeline companies had been paying between $8 to $10 per mmbtu. The surge in deep gas drilling resulted in the pipelines being obligated to buy more deep gas than they could afford. As their average cost of natural gas increased, they began losing market share to competing fuels. In response, they ceased honoring their deep gas contracts and began offering around $1.50 per mmbtu, take it or leave it. The hundreds of millions of dollars that producers were spending on deep gas drilling were immediately rendered unprofitable, and the dominoes started to fall.

— • — • —

CHAPTER TWELVE

STOP THE
BULLDOZERS

O*n Monday, July 5, 1982, federal regulators* closed Penn Square
Bank. The popular conception in Oklahoma at the time was that
the failure of Penn Square caused the deep gas drilling boom to
go bust. I believe it was a confluence of difficult economic times
and convoluted federal regulations on the natural gas market that
allowed Penn Square to bloom. Under more normal circumstances,
there was no way Bill Patterson or anyone else could have flown
around the country and rounded up a quick $2 billion in energy
loans to a bunch of unknown Texas and Oklahoma oil and gas
producers. The national economy was in a recession, and interest
rates had spiked to 18 percent as the Federal Reserve battled inflation. Where would the national banks find borrowers willing and
able to pay such high interest rates? Only in the micro-economy
of Western Oklahoma, where no one blinked at 18 percent interest rates when loans were needed to drill deep gas wells. One
good Anadarko Basin well, like GHK's K. C. Cattle 1–34, could
flow 10 million cubic feet (mmcf) of natural gas per day, at $10

per mmbtu, thus generating $3 million of sales in a month. This would pay out a $6 million drilling cost in two months. (Forty years later, the well has produced more than thirty-seven billion cubic feet of natural gas and is still going strong.) With the lure of instant wealth generators like this, it was no wonder that eager bankers from all over the country flocked to Oklahoma City to throw money at Penn Square's customers.

Fortune magazine ran a long article in their August 23, 1982, issue, featuring Bill Patterson as "The Swinger Who Broke Penn Square." Patterson was a convenient scapegoat, and his work-hard, play-hard approach to boom-time banking may have fanned the flames of avarice, but his starring role in the Penn Square saga was created by powerful economic forces that sucked in thousands of profit-seeking, risk-taking players. Blinded by the prospect of quick fortunes, many of these players, including me, seemed to have been suffering from episodic megalomania, a mental state which commonly occurs when the participants in a boom mistakenly attribute their success to their own acumen, rather than to the strong winds at their back.

When I learned that Penn Square had been shut down, my immediate reaction was to call the builder who had just broken ground on the addition to our home. Almost shouting into the phone, I told him: "Stop the bulldozers!"

Our plan, to be financed, of course, by Penn Square, called for the second floor of the addition to be level with our existing one-story home. This plan required the builder to bring in bulldozers to carve out a good chunk of the hillside our home was perched on. If Penn Square had been closed a day later, instead of living on a hillside, we would have been living on the edge of a cliff. Taking one step out of our back door could have sent you into a twenty-foot plunge.

Shortly after Penn Square was shut down, an energy banker from Utica Bank in Tulsa came by my office at GHK and said he was looking to snap up some of Penn Square's best customers. His bank was too small for GHK's financial needs, but I told him I had some personal loans at Penn Square that I would like to refinance, since I didn't want to have to deal with their successor, the Federal Deposit Insurance Corporation (FDIC). Apparently, he subscribed to the common wisdom that the collapse of Penn Square was a banking problem, not an oil and gas industry problem. I let him snap up my personal business with an $800,000 loan, secured by my portfolio of GHK-related deep gas assets. I also borrowed $400,000 from a small Oklahoma City bank to pay off my Penn Square home loan.

When I walked into the FDIC's makeshift offices in what had been the Penn Square Bank building, a bureaucratic banker seemed shocked, and possibly a little suspicious, when I said I wanted to pay off my Penn Square loans. Apparently, they were not set up to handle loan payoffs in full.

In the wake of Penn Square's closing, the FBI was investigating possible fraud on the part of the bank's energy lenders. The investigators interviewed the petroleum engineers in the bank's energy lending department, since these engineers were responsible for evaluating the oil and gas reserves being pledged by producers as collateral for Penn Square loans. The higher the engineers' evaluations, the more money the bank could shovel out the door. An investigator was interviewing a strong-willed and free-spirited bank engineer, and the conversation went something like this:

Investigator: "Were you under pressure to inflate the value of the reserves so that the bank could lend more money?"

Engineer: "No."

Investigator: "How can you say that? The other engineers have testified that they were under tremendous pressure to inflate the value of the reserves!"

Engineer: "Some people handle pressure better than others."

As I began to adjust to the post-Penn Square era, it became clear that the "sell gas" part of my job description had suddenly become much more difficult. While most of GHK's natural gas reserves were under long-term contracts, the pipeline companies were not honoring them. To ensure producers a minimum amount of cash flow, these gas contracts included the "take or pay" provisions I mentioned earlier, which obligated the pipeline company to either take a minimum amount of gas annually or pay for these volumes, with a chance to make them up later. Instead of honoring these take-or-pay obligations, the pipeline companies were devising specious legal arguments for why they were not obligated to do either.

Meanwhile, the "get money" part of my job changed from finding new sources of drilling dollars to negotiating with banks and investors to buy time to work out new payment arrangements in exchange for Hefner and GHK tossing in additional collateral for these new loans. For a meeting with GHK's trade creditors, mostly drilling contractors and other service companies, we had worked up a forecast showing that the future value of GHK's deep gas reserves would be enough to solve the sudden cash crunch caused by the closing of Penn Square. All we needed was some time and enough financing to allow us to continue our current drilling program. During the discussions, someone mentioned that Hefner and Parker Drilling Company's CEO, Bob Parker, had been longtime friends. In response, a representative of the drilling company uttered what to me was a classic quote for the bust: "Friends are friends . . . and business is business." It was immediately clear that drilling our way out of financial difficulties was not going to be an option. With hundreds of millions of dollars at stake and a long list of creditors, a GHK workout was going to be a long and difficult undertaking.

Meanwhile, Terry had booked an August trip to Monte Carlo for her, Anne, and Emily, along with a close friend and her daughter. Since they had already paid for the airline tickets, they went ahead with the trip, Penn Square closing notwithstanding. By then, Anne was turning thirteen and Emily was nine. My favorite picture from their trip shows Emily in their luxury hotel suite, impersonating a monkey, bouncing high off her bed, her head nearly touching a chandelier.

Terry and I took a long weekend jaunt to Wyoming that fall. A new executive at GHK invited us to visit his family's vacation ranch near Jackson Hole in the Grand Teton mountains. It was a memorable trip for Terry, as she braved three activities she had said she would never do. First, we went horseback riding. Second, we took a ski lift to a mountain top, with no snow to cover the rocks below. These activities went smoothly, and Terry's fears were overcome.

But a raft trip down the Snake River was another story. I reminded Terry that I had been river rafting in the Grand Canyon, so floating down the Snake River should be no big deal. I was wrong. Our party of five climbed into a small rubber raft about a quarter of the size of the raft our GHK group had manned on our Grand Canyon expedition. Soon we were being bounced around on the Snake River rapids, hanging on for dear life. While these rapids were not as fierce as those I had encountered in the Colorado River, I learned that in river rafting, the key factor is the ratio between the size and speed of the rapids you are shooting and the size and structure of the raft you are riding. As we shot the Snake River rapids, I felt like I was riding a souped-up mechanical bull that was going to buck me off any minute. Terry and I each exhaled a huge sigh of relief when we were able to climb out of our dinky little raft and back onto terra firma.

Back to reality in Oklahoma, I found my personal financial situation mirrored GHK's, just on a much smaller scale. Dealing with my own financial problems needed to be done during the normal working hours, while I was being paid to work for Hefner. Even though Hefner had once told me that "people who don't have conflicts of interests don't have any interests," I decided to avoid this conflict by resigning from my position at GHK, to concentrate on my own problems.

Self-Unemployed

While the music from the John Travolta movie *Urban Cowboy* could have provided the soundtrack for the boom, another of his movies could have done the same for the bust. That movie was called *Staying Alive* and that was what a lot of natural gas producers were trying to do at that time.

My salary at GHK, relative to the depth of the financial hole I had dug myself into, was not enough to make much difference. While going broke at age thirty-nine was not any fun, it did teach me that an upside-down balance sheet is not the end of the world. As we say in Oklahoma, "There never was a horse that couldn't be rode, and there never was a cowboy who couldn't be thrown." I just had to dust myself off and climb back in the saddle.

One debt settlement we reached was both quick and painful, like ripping off a Band-Aid. Our friends from Cunningham's Interiors allowed us to return just enough of the furniture and décor they had delivered to us during the boom to cover the balance of what we owed them. They let us pick which items to return. The one item I hated to send back was a bronze statue of Jerry West dribbling a basketball, as depicted on the NBA logo. It was awkward trying to explain to Anne and Emily why the men from Cunningham's were carrying off about a third of our household stuff. I wanted to tell them that it was due to failure of the interstate pipeline companies to honor their take-or-pay contracts, but I feared that would sound too complicated. So, like everyone else, I blamed our troubles on the failure of Penn Square Bank.

Thinking about my debt situation gave me a feeling of déjà vu, bringing me back to my high school football game when my team trailed Tulsa Rogers 0 to 40, with time running out. This time, rather than punt, I decided to throw a "Hail Mary" desperation pass, by writing a novel based on the Penn Square debacle. I called my novel *The Best Little Bank in Oklahoma*, a vague reference to the 1982 Burt Reynolds and Dolly Parton movie *The Best Little Whorehouse in Texas*. Realizing that many of the participants in the Penn Square saga were bogged down in various bankruptcy, workout, and other legal proceedings, I decided a novel about the little shopping center bank could be done quickly, without naming names, while Penn Square's aftermath was still in the news. After completing the novel in mid-January, and feeling that time was of the essence, I took my 237-page manuscript to New York City, had several copies made, and began calling on publishing houses. My reception was underwhelming. The best response came from an editor who wrote: "I enjoyed reading your novel and found it very amusing and informative. However, we are presently review-ing a nonfiction book on the same subject, and we feel that the situation lends itself more to this sort of treatment than it does to the novelized form."

Terry's friend from her Monte Carlo trip invited us to join her for a skiing vacation in December. Her friend had access to a two-story home, owned by one of her relatives, near Lake Tahoe, Nevada. A few weeks before this trip, Emily had injured her left shoulder playing soccer. Since her injury would prevent her from skiing, I decided to take her to Hawaii to watch OU play in a basketball tournament. We left Terry and Anne at the ski resort and headed west. In Hawaii, as we checked in at a Hilton Hotel on Waikiki Beach, we heard a rumor that Eric Estrada, one of the stars of the hit television series *CHiPs*, was staying there as well. Since *CHiPs* was one of Emily's favorite TV shows, she wrote a note to Mr. Estrada saying she would like to meet him and get his autograph. As we left the note with a hotel clerk at the registration desk, I had very low expectations for Emily's getting a response. I rented a little yellow Toyota station wagon and we toured the main island. We found a remote rocky beach where we were able to go snorkeling, checking out the tropical fish in shallow waters.

That evening we joined a small crowd of OU fans who had made the trip to watch OU play college basketball powerhouse North Carolina. The heavily favored Tar Heels brought two All-American players, Sam Perkins and Brad Dougherty. At the time, OU's fantastic freshman Wayman Tisdale was not well known, but he surprised the North Carolina team by scoring 26 points to keep OU in the game. North Carolina had so much talent we didn't even notice their freshman, a kid called Michael Jordan. OU eventually lost the hard-fought game.

The next morning, I left Emily in our hotel room and went for a jog. When I returned, Emily said, matter-of-factly, "Eric Estrada called." At first, I thought she was kidding, but she explained he had received her note and had invited her to meet him on the hotel's beachfront area that afternoon. We tracked him down, and I was able to get a great picture of the handsome TV motorcycle cop with my beaming daughter. That night, we watched Wayman Tisdale score 44 points in an OU win over the University of Hawaii.

One advantage of being self-unemployed was that I had time to coach Emily's fourth grade basketball team. We played in the Norman Optimist League in a gym originally built as an aircraft hangar during World War II. In one of my favorite memories from this coaching era, Emily was dribbling the ball at full speed down the middle of the court. On her left, Shelley Cossart, one of our fastest players, was sprinting down the court. On her right, Lilly Peacock, a little girl from England, was skipping down the court, with a wide smile on her face, keeping up with our break, probably confident that Emily would dish the ball to Shelley. I was surprised that Lilly could skip as fast as Shelley could run, and happy that she was enjoying herself so much, so I did not tell her that there is no skipping in basketball.

Anne was still emerging as a graceful ballet dancer, which Terry and I encouraged, but did not try to coach. She was also a fluid runner and swimmer. She just didn't take to any sports that involved a ball. As she focused on ballet, Anne escaped the benefit of my coaching. Emily, on the other hand, got the full "Little League dad" experience. She played softball, basketball, and soccer, and I lived and died with each at-bat, shot, or kick. I wanted her to enjoy her own "moments" in sports, and to develop the close friendships often formed among teammates. I was probably sending her mixed messages, telling her to relax and have fun, while I went to her games and tensed up enough for both of us.

While coaching Emily's teams, I also tried to play some hoops myself. Playing in the Norman 30 & Over League, our group of not-so-recent college players won the championships in 1983 and 1984.

In early October 1983, I was shopping at our local Safeway grocery store and happened to glance at a magazine rack while pushing my cart down an aisle. Suddenly, I found myself face to face with my cousin, the actor Ed Harris, staring at me from the cover of *Newsweek* magazine. The cover headline read: "The Right Stuff . . . Can a Movie Help Make a President?" And a line in the lower right corner added: "Ed Harris As Astronaut John Glenn." My family had been following Ed's early acting career since the late 1970s, when he began appearing on television shows like *Hart to Hart*, *The Rockford Files*, and *CHiPs*, usually cast as the villain. But this role was Ed's big break. At the time, Ohio Senator John Glenn and former vice president Fritz Mondale were considered the front runners for the Democratic Party's nomination for President in the 1984 election. The *Newsweek* article asked: "Can an actor named Ed Harris playing a Marine pilot named Glenn help win for the real John Glenn his party's nomination in 1984?" As it turned out, the movie did more for Cousin Ed's career than it did for Senator Glenn's.

By the summer of 1984, I had given up on getting my Penn Square novel published. Perhaps inspired by the way my cousin Ed's acting career had taken off, I decided to convert my novel into a film script. The novel was a nom de clef, with thinly disguised characters recognizable to friends and family, but probably no one else. The film script was more of a romantic comedy, revolving around three young friends in Oklahoma City: Rusty, a struggling writer of country and western protest songs; his girlfriend Dolly, a television news reporter; and Billy Joe, an ambitious and free-spirited banker.

As soon as the ink was dry on my film script, I packed a bag, hopped into my copper colored, two-plus-two 280Z, and drove to Hollywood. Wanting to make a good impression on whoever I might meet there, I decided to check into the famous Beverly Hills Hotel on Sunset Boulevard. During my drive to the coast, I had thought of some changes I wanted to make to my film script, so I spent a couple of days revising it. Then I sent it to Cousin Ed, who may or may not have read it before sending it on to his agent. Anyway, we arranged to meet in a few days to discuss it.

Cousin Ed and his agent met me for lunch in a small, beachside restaurant. Ed seemed uncomfortable with his rising stardom, seriously wanting to keep a low profile in his day-to-day life. After a few pleasantries, his agent delivered a verdict that remained my greatest backhanded compliment for many years. He said something like: "I've read your script, and it was not nearly as bad as I thought it would be." Also, he was concerned about the lawsuits and upcoming criminal trials involving many of the people who had been caught up in the Penn Square billion-dollar debt debacle. So, it was "Thanks, but no thanks" on my film script.

In the tradition of the Okies who fled Oklahoma's Dust Bowl during the 1930s depression and headed to California in search of new opportunities, a long, sad story told in John Steinbeck's *Grapes of Wrath*, I decided to stay in California to search for a new job. With Oklahoma's oil industry on its back, and with my creditors on mine, I felt like job hunting in Oklahoma would be like drilling a series of dry holes.

Since I was going to be in California for a while, I checked out of The Beverly Hills Hotel and into a more affordable Holiday Inn near Burbank. I invited Anne and Emily to join me in Los Angeles for a quick summer vacation.

The one thing all three of us best remember about their trip happened when Anne came down with a sore throat and we drove to a walk-in clinic in search of some medicine. Strangely, the nurse at the clinic suggested that Anne gargle a liquid called a surgical scrub. I bought a bottle of it at a drug store and we returned to the motel. My throat had been a little scratchy, so I decided to go into the bathroom and try it first. I was shocked to discover that when I gargled the stuff it immediately bubbled up, sending soapy bubbles into the air and all over my face. I dried my face and told the girls what had happened.

"Do it again . . . Dad!" they exclaimed. "Do it again!"

Never above a little slapstick humor, I created another facial bubble bath and my girls loved it.

After driving the girls to the airport for their flight back to Norman, I realized that, unlike The Mamas & the Papas, my "California dreaming" was not ". . . becoming a reality." I needed to drive back home to face my real life. Back in Oklahoma, the economy was crashing and the employment outlook was still bleak. There was a joke going around that when the McDonald's in Elk City failed they had to lay off a dozen geologists. The economy was so bad in Norman that the Sam's Club closed and the building was converted to a church. Emily observed that the congregation gathered on Sunday mornings to pray for lower prices. I noted that Baker Hughes had discontinued their weekly rig count but would report "rig sightings."

Starting Over

After a year of being self-unemployed, I received a job offer from The RAM Group, the energy consulting firm where I first met Hefner in 1972. The firm was now being headed by Bill Talley and had moved from downtown to Northwest Oklahoma City. I had worked with Bill in 1974 to put together the *Energy in Oklahoma* report to the State Legislature, as previously mentioned. Reluctantly, I accepted the job as a natural gas marketing consultant and resumed the daily commute to Oklahoma City. The demands of my new job spelled the end of my third basketball comeback.

My favorite coworker at RAM was an older, salt-of-the-earth executive named Fred Miller. Fred could spit out self-deprecating observations and politically incorrect sayings faster than I could jot them down. He said he came from a family that was "too poor to paint and too proud to whitewash." Their farm hands "couldn't find their butts with a rake." At times he was "as nervous as a long-tailed cat in a room full of rockers." His friend was "grinning like a cat with a mouthful of canary feathers." Our company had "more opportunities than a mosquito in a nudist colony." An incompetent secretary "couldn't make head waitress at the Girlie Pancake House." And when a long business meeting ended, Fred would observe: "It's like the old girl who got married at the Court House said: 'I guess that's all we can do here.'"

While working at RAM, I was still trying to resolve the personal debts I had run up during the Penn Square days. The value of my oil and gas assets were eroding as production declined and oil and gas prices fell, and the value of our home was declining along with the general Oklahoma economy. While the long-term value of our assets was arguably close to the amount of our debts, our cash flow wasn't flowing fast enough to keep up with our bills. By the summer of 1984, I could see the handwriting on the wall, and knew it wasn't graffiti. Not wanting to declare bankruptcy, I was able to negotiate settlements with our major creditors to exchange our boom house and small interests in more than 300 oil and gas wells for cancellation of a little over one million dollars in debts.

Down but not out, we rented a small house next door to our first Norman home on Hidden Hill Road. Terry's parents had bought that home from us when we moved into our boom house in 1981. Our stay in the rented house only lasted a few months. With a little lobbying help from our girls, Terry and I made a deal with her folks to buy back our original Norman home. After a quick move across the driveway, I realized we had gone full circle.

Unfortunately, the fiber glass swimming pool we had enjoyed during our first stay on Hidden Hill was gradually crushed by ground water. Its sides caved in easily, like an empty beer can. Lacking the funds to repair the pool, we had it buried in the privacy of our own backyard. We did, however, regain our driveway basketball court, where Emily and I wore out a bunch of basketballs, shooting and dribbling them until the black rubber showed through the leather.

Not long after our dog Sugar died, we found a new family pet, a small blonde terrier we called Honey. Even as a puppy, Honey liked to snitch things around the house and hold them for ransom. Once she stole my billfold off a low coffee table and scrambled under a sofa with it. I felt ridiculous, lying on the floor, trying to negotiate with a puppy for my billfold's return. She seemed to have a sense of its value and would not give it back easily. After she turned down a generous offer of doggie biscuits, I grabbed a pool cue and used it to pry loose one of the few possessions I really needed.

On August 7, 1984, after Fritz Mondale defeated John Glenn for the Democratic nomination for President, *The Wall Street Journal* published a satirical article I had submitted for their editorial page entitled "An Oilman Looks Kindly on Mondale." The point of my piece was that since the most likely result of any political act was the opposite of what was intended, I was going to support Mondale, as he was a politician who would truly set out to do me in. To my surprise, my article led to a debate among the board members of a large oil service company in Dallas, some of whom realized I was being satirical while others took me literally. After a long debate, they voted to make a campaign contribution to Mondale.

A little embarrassed by the "unintended consequences" of my first article, I submitted a second one entitled "Let's Get This Show on the Road, Fritz," which *The Wall Street Journal* published on September 27, 1984. Continuing in my satirical mode, I expressed my concern that my candidate's campaign was not going well, even though he was "perhaps the most charismatic presidential contender since Millard Fillmore." To help him turn his campaign around, I offered some new ideas, including a war on divorce, the most divisive social problem facing Americans at that time. Fritz's program "could require couples to pass a Federal Compatibility Test before obtaining a marriage license, set up thousands of Federal Marriage Counseling Bureaus, and require all married people to pass annual relationship maintenance inspections.

"Mr. Reagan can be expected to make a knee-jerk response that the Constitution does not permit the federal government to intrude on such a personal matter," my article continued. "At this point, we'll have the old guy trapped, because clearly the Constitution's Preamble empowers the government to 'ensure domestic tranquility.'"

Penn Square: Gone but Not Forgotten

Three years after its closing, Penn Square was still very much in the news. In April 1985, *The New Yorker* magazine began serializing *Funny Money*, a book "on the Penn Square Bank Collapse." The author, Mark Singer, was a staff writer for the magazine and a Tulsa native, gone coastal. I visited with him several times while he was in Oklahoma City gathering stories and anecdotes from the human comedy known as the Penn Square debacle. I had also sent him a copy of my still unpublished novel, which I thought could give him some worthwhile background, if he could read between the lines. Fortunately, I escaped being described in his book, as his writing seemed to take a bemused, condescending tone toward the local yokels caught up in the boom and bust, as if he were channeling the anthropologist Margaret Mead describing South Sea islanders.

Hefner, of course, plays a leading role in this tale. Singer notes: "In Oklahoma, if you were going to attempt certain stunts it helped enormously to be a Hefner—a genus that, locally, passed for royalty."

Shortly after *Funny Money* was published, along came *Belly Up . . . The Collapse of Penn Square Bank*, a thick, meticulously researched book by Phillip L. Zweig, described on the book jacket as "the man who broke the story on Penn Square" while working as a reporter for *American Banker*. He traces the economic and political circumstances that led to "the tangled and fantastic saga of Penn Square." The book's first chapter, "The Gas Man," focuses on Hefner's lifelong mission to find and develop deep natural gas from the Anadarko Basin. The story soon moves to Hefner's efforts to lobby the Carter Administration and the Congress for "a little help . . . in the form of a special incentive price for deep gas."

Zweig interviewed me in Oklahoma City and quotes me several times, after introducing me as "a baldish, soft-spoken former Oklahoma newspaper man." He reports on my account of Hefner and me meeting with Secretary of Energy James Schlesinger. He also explained: "When Hefner flew to Washington to deliver testimony and to meet with legislators, he did not stalk the halls of Congress making points for deep gas on a day-to-day basis.

That job belonged to GHK aide Bill Dutcher, who camped out at the Washington home (actually, office) of Boots Taliaferro while carrying on the campaign. 'We were more of a guerilla operation. There was no one else in Washington representing explorers of new natural gas.'"

Zweig's chapter 6, perceptively called "Pilot Light for a Boom," quotes me extensively about our lobbying efforts and connects the dots between the deregulation of deep gas, the subsequent deep drilling boom in Western Oklahoma, and the rise of Penn Square Bank.

With these two cautionary tales about Penn Square Bank coming out, I wanted to add my two cents to the discussion, so I submitted an op-ed piece to *The Wall Street Journal* entitled "Confessions of a Penn Square Borrower." To my surprise, they published it on their editorial page on August 15, 1985. (One line from this article lives on, in infamy, today: "I could only tell my banker, you can call my loan, but it won't come." I've heard this line quoted, decades after it first appeared in print. Fortunately, it's not attributed to me.)

After reading my Penn Square confession, *Funny Money* author Mark Singer sent me a letter saying: "I thought: Why did it take me 80,000 words to say what Dutcher has uttered in 400? Then I remembered that *The New Yorker* pays by the word."

Ironically, one of the RAM Group's major clients was the Federal Deposit Insurance Corporation, then the reluctant owner of the oil and gas properties and equipment once owned by Penn Square's best customers. I soon found myself managing some of the same natural gas purchase and sale contracts I had negotiated while I was working at GHK. While GHK's production interests did not end up with the FDIC, the pipeline companies had offered the same contract terms to other working interest owners in many of the GHK wells, and these interests had fallen into the hands of the FDIC. But the pipeline companies were not interested in buying natural gas from the FDIC either. The pipelines' so-called "take or pay" contracts became "no takes so sue us."

One of the natural gas contracts being disputed between the FDIC and Panhandle Eastern Pipeline Company was a twenty-year contract I had negotiated for GHK about six years earlier. Panhandle Eastern was obligated to continue buying natural gas at the high contract prices for the next fourteen years. I negotiated a settlement of this contract dispute that resulted in the pipeline company making large, but discounted, payments to the FDIC to compensate for past failures to take or pay for past contract volumes, and for a release from their future take-or-pay obligations. The RAM Group received a large fee from the FDIC for negotiating the settlement, and I got to continue receiving my paycheck. I was hoping to receive a bonus for my role in negotiating this lucrative deal, but the bonus never came.

During a management meeting about that time, my arrogant boss made a dismissive comment about my career prospects away from his company: "What would you do?" I didn't have an immediate answer, but I decided to explore other opportunities.

— • — • —

PART THREE

"You never count your money
When you're sitting at the table
There'll be time enough for counting
When the dealin's done"

— Kenny Rogers

Welcome to Anadarko Minerals

CHAPTER THIRTEEN

ON MY OWN

M*y work on the FDIC* versus Panhandle Eastern take-or-pay dispute gave me the idea of starting my own natural gas consulting company, initially specializing in take-or-pay negotiations. When I got home that evening, I gathered my family in our kitchen and told them I was considering quitting my job at RAM and starting my own business as a natural gas marketing consultant. With their recent experience with collapsing natural gas markets, they were keenly aware of the risks. But they were all very supportive. Maybe they sensed my confidence that this plan would work, and my excitement about making a new start.

Being in Oklahoma, where business regulations were relatively light, there was no place to go for permission to start a natural gas market consulting company. On April 15, 1987, I simply hung out my shingle and declared myself in business. It cost $500 to register Dutcher & Company, Inc. as an Oklahoma Sub-S Corporation. Of course, at the time, the "& Company" was aspirational. I elected myself as the company's sole director, figuring that would make for quicker board meetings. Then I carved out some workspace in a spare upstairs bedroom filled with racks of Terry's dresses, most of which were elegant and expensive souvenirs from the boom. My first purchase for the company was an IBM personal computer that was nearly too heavy to carry up the stairs.

My enthusiasm for work easily tripled as I realized I was my own boss and responsible for making my business work. Going to work was suddenly something I wanted to do, not something I had to do. In a rare moment of introspection, I realized that I had worked until I was forty-four without ever having a boss I liked. Some were great guys, while others were head cases, but, basically, I did not like the fact that they were my boss. I soon discovered that I do not have a problem with authority, if I am the one who has it. I also learned that exposure to risk is a great motivator.

My initial list of possible clients included independent oil and gas producers confronted with the same natural gas contract problems I had faced at GHK and RAM. In general, the pipeline companies were trying to force the producers into giving up their long-term gas contract rights in exchange for the opportunity to market their gas in an emerging spot market, where short-term sales could be made at much lower prices. Their attorneys had drawn up long lists of real good reasons for terminating the contracts. Some producers, desperately needing the cash flow, agreed to the pipeline's demands, while other producers sued the pipelines to force them to honor their take-or-pay obligations. I asked prospective producer clients not to give up their valuable contract rights without first letting me attempt to negotiate a cash settlement from the pipeline companies for terminating the contracts. If I brought them an acceptable settlement, they could pay me a commission of 15 percent of the settlement amount, then move ahead with finding a new market for their gas. If they did not like the pipeline's settlement offer, then they would not owe me anything. At the time, although there were some take-or-pay lawsuits in progress, it was still an open question as to how the courts would rule on these disputes. With billions of dollars at stake, both sides had at least some interest in settling out of court.

My first client was a small Tulsa company called Falcon Engineering. I had worked with the company's owners, geologist Tex Hartman and engineer John Barrios, during the hectic boom times at GHK. A company joke at the time was that you could gain ten years of experience by working at GHK for five years.

Falcon Engineering owned a 5 percent working interest in a well called the Music 1–2. Their interest was covered by a contract I had negotiated with Southern Natural Gas Company in 1980. At the time, Southern needed natural gas supplies badly enough for me to negotiate a gas contract with very favorable terms for GHK. Seven years later, I flew to Atlanta to negotiate a take-or-pay settlement for Falcon Engineering's interests in this contract. Calculating Falcon's claim required a lot of number crunching, so I retained a former GHK accountant to calculate how much Southern owed for past take-or-pay deficiencies, and Lawson Engineering, a local petroleum engineering firm, to forecast how much Southern would owe during the remaining thirteen-year term of the contract.

Back in Oklahoma City, I met with Tex and John and told them I had made a deal with Southern Natural to settle the contract's past take-or-pay claims and buy out their remaining purchase obligations for $400,000.

"For the whole well?" one of them asked.

"No," I replied, surprised by the question. "For your 5 percent interest."

They were surprised by this sudden windfall and were eager to sign.

"This take-or-pay business may work out," I told myself.

Anne graduated from Norman High School near the top of her class and with impressive ACT scores. She was academically qualified to attend about any college in the country. However, our budget at the time would stretch only as far as OU, where she had a University Scholar Scholarship. That summer, she continued her study of ballet at the Oklahoma Summer Arts Institute at Quartz Mountain, with Ballet Oklahoma in Oklahoma City, and at a ballet program in Aspen, Colorado.

While Anne was dancing, Emily and her friend Sunny Barse played for an Oklahoma City basketball team coached by Ben Hart, who had been an All-American receiver for the OU football team and had played professional football in Canada. By coincidence, he had also been a sophomore starting forward for the Oklahoma City Douglass basketball team that my Bartlesville Wildcats had upset in a semi-final game in the 1961 Oklahoma State Tournament. Ben and his wife Pam had coached a series of Oklahoma City area teams that had regularly beaten Emily's Norman teams in earlier seasons. Under the theory that "if you can't beat them, join them," Emily and Sunny had tried out and made the Hart's basketball team.

Led by future OU and WNBA star Etta Maytubby, Coach Hart's Angels won the State AAU Tournament and qualified for the National AAU Championship Tournament in Shreveport. As a 5' 1" point guard, Emily played well enough in Shreveport to draw some nice comments from the coach of the powerful Louisiana Tech women's team.

One Brick at a Time

After settling a few more take-or-pay claims while working out of my bedroom office in Norman, I decided to open a small office in Oklahoma City. In October 1987, Anne and I went shopping for office space in downtown Oklahoma City. We eventually found some space on the Northwest corner of the twenty-first floor of the Liberty Bank Building, the city's tallest building.

My former boss at RAM, Bill Talley, seemed to base his concept of office space on his service in the Navy as a nuclear submarine officer. Having been crammed into a tiny office during my three years at RAM, I wanted a large office for myself. The space at Liberty included an area that was large enough to double as my office and a conference room. It also included two smaller offices, a storeroom, and a reception area. While there was still no "& Company," I did let some accountants use one of the other offices while they were calculating take-or-pay claims for my clients.

In take-or-pay disputes where the producers had decided to file lawsuits instead of negotiating settlements, I sometimes served as an expert witness for the producers. In one case, I was giving a deposition to a lawyer for El Paso Natural Gas Company, who was being sued over a contract I had negotiated for GHK during the boom. The El Paso attorney had found some records showing I owned some small interests in many of the wells included in the lawsuit. The conversation went something like this: "Isn't it true you have a conflict of interest in this case, since you own interests in many of the wells involved?" the lawyer asked.

"No," I replied.

"We have seen records showing that you do. Why isn't this a conflict of interest?"

"Due to the failure of your clients to honor their take-or-pay obligations, I was unable to make my loan payments, so my bank foreclosed on my interests in these wells. They own them now."

"Oh."

After a moment to contain his embarrassment, he added: "This is why we take depositions."

Working in downtown Oklahoma City, I often ran into people I had known during the boom times. Like me, they were working to adjust to the economic realities of the bust. When I told them I was doing natural gas marketing consulting, I would occasionally get a sympathetic look, followed by the question: "Are you staying busy?" I took this as code for, "Are you doing ok financially?" When I got the "staying busy" question, I would answer, "No." And if they looked concerned, I would add: "I'm making a lot of money, but it doesn't take much time."

In fact, I developed a commitment to the six-hour workday. A slow starter in the mornings, I liked to read the local newspapers at home over a leisurely breakfast. I also liked to avoid the morning and evening rush hour traffic. I would get to work around 10:30 to 11:00 am and head home around 5:30 pm. I bought a new 280 Z for my commute, which was about 30 minutes each way. During the boom, traffic jams were common in downtown Oklahoma City, but during the bust, there was hardly any traffic at all. My favorite commuting song was Bob Segar's "Against the Wind." I sympathized with his line: "Wish I didn't know now, what I didn't know then." I would also rock out to Dire Straights' "Money for Nothing" and "Walk of Life," not to mention Chuck Berry's "Brown-eyed Handsome Man," Johnny Cash's "Folsom Prison Blues," and Willie Nelson's sage advice: "Mamas, Don't Let Your Babies Grow Up to Be Cowboys."

The best thing about being self-employed was that you could set your own work hours, allowing some time for your family and other interests. Time may be money, but time off is life. I did not have the credentials or the patience to work my way up some corporate ladder. Although this may have been a rationalization for keeping down my work hours, my mantra was, "Work smarter, not harder." It seemed to me that keeping your shoulder to the wheel, your eye on the ball, and your nose to the grindstone would be a very difficult position to work from.

One difficulty in running a one-man consulting firm is figuring out where your next project is coming from. I developed a simple Lotus 1–2–3 spreadsheet with monthly forecasts for projects and expected fees in one column and forecast expenditures in another. My forecasts for the current month were usually reliable, while the forecasts for the second months were a little iffy, and the forecasts for the third month were highly speculative.

Another problem was getting paid in a timely manner. I was able to borrow against a bank line of credit secured by my receivables, so I could pay my bills on time, while waiting to be paid by my clients.

My metaphor for my consulting business was that it was like trying to cross a very deep and wide river by jumping from stone to stone. While I could not see the other side of the river, I could see the first stone, and when I jumped to it, I still could not see across the river, but I could see the next stone. After jumping from stone to stone for several months, I still could not see the other side of the river, but I had gone too far to turn back.

In March 1988, Terry and I travelled to Birmingham, Alabama, to watch Billy Tubbs' high-scoring Oklahoma Sooners play an NCAA regional game against a Villanova team coached by Rollie

Massimino. The Sooners trailed at halftime, but late in the second half Stacy King scored on a slam dunk to put OU up by five points.

"Ball game!" I yelled in excitement.

A Villanova fan, seated a couple of rows in front of us, turned around and shouted, "The game isn't over until the Fat Lady sings."

At which point, a heavy-set lady, wearing a Sooner T-shirt, stood up a couple of rows behind us and exclaimed: "Well, what do want to hear?" The Sooners went on to win easily, advancing to the Final Four.

A week later, a friend and I drove to Kansas City to watch the Final Four. Kansas beat Duke and OU beat Arizona. Since OU had already beaten Kansas twice during the regular season, I was confident that the Sooners would beat them again. So confident, I had an OU National Champions T-shirt stuck in my coat pocket, expecting to put it on when the final buzzer sounded. The first half ended with a Finals record score of 50 to 50, as the Kansas players ignored their Coach Larry Brown's slow down game plan and elected to run with the fast-breaking, high-scoring Sooners. It was certainly the best-played half of basketball I had ever seen in an NCAA championship game. The Sooners had three future NBA players in Stacey King, Harvey Grant, and Mookie Blaylock. Kansas had future NBA star Danny Manning and, ironically, two players, Kevin Pritchard and Mike Maddox, who had been high school stars in Oklahoma. Kansas won the game, so my Oklahoma National Champions T-shirt remained in my coat pocket in Kansas City.

As much as I enjoyed Sooner basketball that spring, I loved watching Anne's ballet performances even more. In the Norman Ballet Company's presentation of *The Little Prince*, Anne starred in the title role. Dancing with an effortless grace, and wearing a blond wig, she looked so much like Terry I was shocked. Later that month, she made her professional debut performing in the corps de ballet in Ballet Oklahoma's *Giselle*. Knowing how hard Anne had worked at her craft, it was exciting to see her on stage blending in with the professional ballerinas.

Hiring the ". . . & Company"

While my take-or-pay business was going well, I could see that it would not last forever, as eventually all the disputes would either be settled or tied up in litigation. I decided to begin offering oil and gas property management services. To do that, I needed to hire experienced managers for accounting and petroleum land management. One good thing about starting a business during tough economic times is that some highly skilled people are available. During better times, these people would already have good jobs, and would not be interested in joining a risky oil and gas consulting start-up.

Dutcher & Company hired its first employee when Carol Magness joined the company in May. Carol had graduated from OU a year before me. She had been an accounting executive at GHK during the boom and had also worked for the IRS. Terry and I interviewed her. I found her to be classy and well qualified. Two months later, we hired Mack Ames as our land manager. Mack was another OU graduate and had spent his early career working as a landman for an independent producer in Houston. He had moved back to Oklahoma City after the mid-eighties oil bust hit Texas. His mother, Betty Ames, had been Hefner's administrative assistant at GHK for many years, and his wife, Kim, had worked for Betty while I was still at GHK. We hired another GHK alum, Shirley Burton, as a secretary for the three of us. Finally, there really was an "& Company."

In building my company, I wanted to avoid the "my way or the highway" attitude exhibited by some of my former bosses. While I am not a workaholic myself, I am an enabler. My goal was to hire strongly motivated, self-actualizing, experienced adults, like Carol and Mack, and to give them the authority to go do their jobs without me looking over their shoulder. I told them that working for me was the closest they could come to being self-employed, while still getting a steady paycheck. In keeping with my laissez-faire management approach, we began closing the office at noon on Fridays to give us a jump on the weekend.

That summer and fall, Emily and I played a lot of hoops on a court on the driveway behind our house. In games of one-on-one, we came up with a way to reduce my 8" height advantage while improving our ball handling skills. The defender had to dribble a basketball while still trying to stop the offensive player from scoring. If the offensive player missed a shot, the defender had to keep his or her dribble while chasing down the rebound. Once the defender had both balls under control, it was their turn to play offense.

Emily started as a 5' 2" point guard for Norman High School in her sophomore year. As a great ball handler and passer, but a reluctant shooter, her game was pretty much the opposite of mine. A photo in *The Norman Transcript* that season showed Emily running across the court, with the opponent's 6' 4" center in the background. We joked that, by comparison, Emily looked like a little kid who had run out onto the court during the game.

While attending Emily's home games at Norman High, I would sometimes check out the 1961 Oklahoma State Championship trophy the Norman Tigers had won by defeating my Bartlesville Wildcats in the State Finals that year. But I was only kidding

My girls take the cake

when I told people that we moved to Norman so that I could be close to that trophy.

In what would have been her sophomore year at OU, Anne dropped out of school and moved to an apartment in Oklahoma City, where she had signed up as an apprentice dancer with the professional ballet company, Ballet Oklahoma. While rehearsing for their performance of *The Nutcracker*, Anne became ill and decided to stop her pursuit of a career in ballet.

Our first property management client was a New York investment banker I had done some deals with at GHK. He was a compulsive wheeler/dealer with an insatiable appetite for risk. Although he had just emerged from a personal bankruptcy, he wanted to buy oil-and-gas properties in Oklahoma and Texas while prices were depressed. We bought thirty-five natural gas wells for him from the FDIC at a cost of $2.3 million. Within about eighteen months, we had purchased wells for our client at a total cost of $8 million. He sold them for about $18 million.

By this time, we had collected more than $20 million in negotiated settlements for our take-or-pay clients, but as expected, this business was drying up. On the other hand, our property management client had done so well with us buying and selling producing oil and gas properties for him, we decided to go into this business for ourselves.

One of my favorite highlights from Emily's junior season of high school basketball occurred during a game in Edmond. With only a few seconds left in the game, Emily heaved a desperation shot from half court that swished cleanly through the net. It might still be talked about as one of her team's greatest shots ever if they had not been trailing by twenty points at the time.

Just before the State AAU basketball tournament the following summer, I was asked to coach Ben Hart's team. We called our team the Metro 73ers, since all our players were born in 1973. In a game against players from Northeast Oklahoma, Emily was matched up against a Bartlesville girl who went on to play at Oklahoma State. Emily scored a career high eighteen points to lead our team to an upset win.

In the tournament finals, our opponent's star player was Etta Maytubby, who had been our star player in the previous season. We tried to deny her the ball in the final few seconds of a close game, but she hit a shot at the buzzer to beat us. Emily played well enough to be invited to Blue Star basketball camps at the University of North Carolina and at Clemson University, where college coaches go to scout recruits. Although she was the shortest player at both camps, she held her own against the tougher competition.

— • — • —

CHAPTER FOURTEEN

ANADARKO MINERALS: THE EARLY YEARS

O*n April 12, 1990, I founded a new company* called Anadarko Minerals, Inc. In setting up this company, I once again made myself the sole director. Most of the major decisions I needed to make for this company required a risk versus reward calculation, which led to some long and hard negotiations among me, myself, and I. Finding it difficult to reach a unanimous decision, it was decided that only two votes would be required. This way, a few nagging reservations would not stop AMI from moving ahead with risky ventures.

AMI's initial strategy was to invest in producing wells operated by other companies, but not to operate wells ourselves. Primarily, our targets were so-called non-operated working interests, which require an investor to pay its proportionate share of the well's operating costs and royalty payments. We also sought to buy mineral rights, which could be leased to drillers seeking new production and would generate royalty payments if the new wells were successful.

Our first acquisition consisted of some non-producing mineral rights and non-operated working interests in several natural gas wells within GHK's Elk City Project Area.

Financed by Liberty Bank, this $200,000 acquisition was the first step in a project we called "putting Humpty-Dumpty back together again." Mineral interests, royalty interests, and non-operated working interests formerly owned by GHK and other deep gas producers during the boom had ended up in the hands of the FDIC, banks, trade creditors, and former limited partners. These folks had never intended to own oil and gas producing interests directly, and they were not equipped to manage them. This created a market for oil and gas property managers who could market the oil and gas, pay the royalty owners, and make elections on new well proposals. Dutcher & Company was equipped to manage these interests for clients or buy them for AMI. We relied on consulting geologists and engineers to evaluate potential acquisitions.

Pursuing our Humpty-Dumpty strategy, I knew that Chase Manhattan Bank had acquired some of Hefner's deep gas properties as part of a settlement of loans they had made with one of Hefner's companies. I flew to New York City to meet with the Chase special asset manager responsible for these oil and gas properties. Apparently, the manager was very experienced in real estate deals, but was not burdened with excessive knowledge of the oil and gas business. We reached a deal for AMI to acquire these properties for $2 million.

Now all I needed was to find the $2 million to pay for the properties. This proved to be difficult. The $2 million value of the wells did not include a take-or-pay claim potentially worth about $1 million. The claim was embedded within the same deep gas contract with Southern Natural that I had recently settled for

Falcon Engineering. Unfortunately, I could not find a bank that would give the take-or-pay claim any loan value. Within a few days of the date that AMI was scheduled to close the deal with Chase, I took the deal to Hefner, who by then was busy working on his next fortune. I knew he would understand the value of the take-or-pay claim imbedded in the deal and was familiar with the gas wells themselves.

At the time, AMI's only assets were interests in the minerals and wells acquired in our first deal. I reached an agreement with Hefner calling for him to loan AMI $750,000 in exchange for a 51 percent equity interest in AMI, limited to non-voting shares. With this cash and a new loan from Liberty Bank, we were able to close the $2 million acquisition from Chase in December 1990.

A few months later, I sent Mack Ames to Atlanta to explain to Southern Natural the complicated changes in ownership among the selling parties to their GHK deep gas contact. To our surprise, they immediately offered $1 million to settle AMI's claim. When I countered their offer at $1.1 million, they expressed their concern that new claimants kept coming out of the woodwork. I was confident that AMI's claim would be the last, so I offered to buy the contract from them for $1 as soon as they closed the settlement with us. That way, if any other claimants came forward, it would be our problem, not theirs. They liked that idea, and we settled for the $1.1 million. A few months after AMI received the funds from Southern Natural, I made a deal with Hefner to pay off his loan and buy back his AMI non-voting shares for the original $750,000 he had advanced to us. From this point on, we were able to limit the ownership of AMI shares to our family and three top executives, and to finance AMI's growth with bank debt.

Anne helped me research what little public information was available for analyzing the natural gas market. The American Gas Association put out a monthly publication on natural gas production and consumption in the United States, but the information was at least two months old before it was published, and it was subject to extensive revisions. Baker Hughes published data on the number of rigs drilling for oil and gas in United States. *The Oil & Gas Journal* and other industry trade publications covered various plays in progress. We knew that the oil and gas markets were cyclical. The hard part was determining where we were in the cycles.

A large natural gas surplus, the so-called "gas bubble," hung over the market, often forecast to be eliminated within two or three years. But that turned out to be a rolling period, as the surplus lingered on throughout the 1990s. The major oil companies essentially abandoned drilling in the lower forty-eight states to concentrate their efforts in Alaska, offshore, and overseas. While most natural gas price forecasts called for flat or slowly increasing natural gas wellhead prices, we believed that once the natural gas market shifted from surplus to shortage, there would be a "sea change" movement in natural gas prices. Our strategy was to buy all the natural gas reserves we could afford to finance with bank loans before a major jump in prices hit. Meanwhile, we were able to cover our payroll and other overhead with our consulting and property management fees.

In this environment, AMI began acquiring long-life, slowly declining natural gas reserves.

In our early years, no deal was too small for us. We focused on buying small, non-operated interests in producing natural gas wells located in the Anadarko Basin of Western Oklahoma and the Texas Panhandle. Ironically, one of our early acquisitions consisted of whispering interests in more than three-hundred wells in Western Oklahoma. The seller was a Tulsa independent producer who had purchased them from Utica National Bank a few years earlier.

And, yes, Utica had acquired them from me.

Emily Bounces Back

Emily's basketball season during her senior year at Norman High School was marred by a January battle with chicken pox and ended in a major disappointment. As a pass-first point guard, her best statistic was what we called the SBA (Should've Been Assist). Her teammates would often mishandle her pass or miss an open shot, leaving her with another SBA. Three of her senior friends and longtime teammates had quit the team, and she had difficulty dealing with the intensity of her ambitious young coach. Terry wanted her to quit the team as well, but I encouraged her to stick it out. Although I kept telling her to relax and have fun, she could feel how much I was emotionally invested in her basketball career. I was not trying to relive my glory days through her, but I wanted her to experience the challenge of tough competition and build friendships with teammates that would last a lifetime. Her basketball junkie dad was inadvertently adding to the pressure she was feeling. After her midseason bout with the chicken pox, she saw little playing time as the season wound down. Riding the bench as a senior was an agonizing experience. She stuck it out, but the disappointment hung with her for years to come.

Emily graduated from Norman High School in May. Her graduation speaker was an economics professor who had moved to Oklahoma City from the East Coast and become a successful entrepreneur. He told the graduates something like this: "If you work hard in Oklahoma you can get to the head of the line . . . because it is not a very long line." I thought this was a candid comment and added it to my collection of classic one-liners.

That summer, not wanting Emily's experience with competitive basketball to end on such a sour note, I dropped by the office of my high school assistant basketball coach, Sid Burton. For the past fifteen years, he had been coaching the women's team at Rose State, a junior college in nearby Midwest City. I found that coach Burton was still the upbeat, positive coach I remembered from my Wildcat days and believed that playing for him would be a positive experience for Emily. After hearing my account of her basketball journey, including the interest major college coaches had shown in her during the summer before her ill-fated senior year at Norman High, Coach Burton offered her a basketball scholarship to Rose State. As he put it, "You can coach them up, or you can coach them down."

On August 2, 1991, a headline on the sports page of *The Norman Transcript* read: "Rose State's Burton to coach another Dutcher." In another classic piece of sports reporting, the story quoted me saying that coach Burton "was the best I've ever played for." He described me "as a phenomenal player on his JV team of 1959 which lost only one game." He even recalled my ability "to stand straight still, not move, jump and shoot. You can't find players today that can do that, just jump flat footed and hit." The story also quoted Emily: "I really wanted to play somewhere. I had a bad senior year. It was terrible." She called Coach Burton "a real neat guy. I'm glad I'm getting to play for him. He's the type of person I'd like to play for."

Emily was having a great freshman season, starting as a 5' 2" point guard, racking up assists, scoring on fast breaks, and nailing three-point shots. Unfortunately, during a road game in January,

Emily drives to the basket at Rose State

she met the fate of so many female basketball players, a torn anterior cruciate ligament (ACL) in her right knee. At an awards ceremony after her season ended, Coach Burton called her one of the best point guards he had ever coached at Rose State. Emily transferred to OU, and, after a year of rehabilitating her right knee, she tore the ACL in her left knee while playing indoor soccer. (This second injury ended her basketball playing days, but she has remained my basketball buddy ever since.)

Advice from Attila the Hun

In a letter to AMI stockholders dated January 29, 1992, I declared a dividend of $80 per share and observed that 1991 was an excellent year for AMI, despite the difficult operating conditions being experienced by the entire oil and gas industry. Then, in a take-off on the typical stockholder letter, I added, "The Company was beset by environmental extremists, brainless regulators, greedy politicians, and unscrupulous competitors. However, by a combination of brilliant strategy, cunning tactics, and, most important, by maintaining a sense of humor, we were able to prosper beyond our wildest dreams of avarice."

Selected for the Phi Beta Kappa academic honor society as a junior, Anne graduated from OU in May with a 3.9 grade average and BA in philosophy. Ironically, the first grade on her transcript was a B grade for a one-hour course in ballet she took in the summer before her freshman year. She may have been disappointed with her near perfect grade average, but she took it philosophically.

In July 1992, AMI hired Nick Privett, an experienced reservoir engineer, as our vice president for engineering. We had been using Nick as a consultant for oil and gas reserve evaluations used in take-or-pay negotiations and in oil and gas reserve acquisitions. With Nick working with us full time, we were able to evaluate more deals and bid for more properties at oil and gas auctions in Oklahoma City and Houston. Mack and I would attend the auctions, taking a list of the properties we wanted to buy, and our maximum bid for each property. Realizing that I might get too aggressive during the competitive bidding process, Mack's job was to hold down my bidding arm if the bidding exceeded our predetermined maximum bid.

To determine how much we were willing to pay for oil and gas reserves being sold at auctions or through other marketing channels, our requirement was to maintain a spread of at least 10 percent between our cost of funds and the discount rate used to determine the present value of the reserves. If our bank were charging us an interest rate of 8 percent, we could bid up to the present value, discounted at 18 percent, of the property's forecast net income. For long-life reserves, this rule often allowed us to bid up to four to six years projected net income, while our competitors were bidding based on a quicker payout. As a result, we were often the successful bidders for small deals, and we began building AMI's reserve base, one brick at a time.

The only business management book I had ever read was *The Leadership Secrets of Attila the Hun*. The only advice I recall from the book was to reward the generals. We didn't have any generals, but as an incentive to my three vice presidents, I sold them each twenty-five shares of AMI, for $1 per share, so they each owned nearly five percent of Anadarko Minerals.

While AMI's executives were very good at their jobs, they were generally risk averse. I was the designated risk taker. My tolerance for taking business risks has been enhanced by the fact that I am not all that materialistic. My goal is to build a thriving business, not to accumulate a bunch of stuff. As a business owner, you are faced with a constant flow of buy/sell/hold decisions. In making these decisions, you do not have to be right all the time. You do have to be right more than you are wrong.

Laughing All the Way to the Ruins

That summer, we took a family trip to London and Paris. In London, we stayed at a small hotel near Harrods department store, where Terry had a mission of determining the value of some Meissen china she had purchased from an estate sale in Oklahoma City during the bust. Walking around in downtown London, I made the rookie mistake of checking for traffic and stepping off a curb to cross the street. Luckily, an alert Londoner pulled me back, and as a stream of cars and taxies sped by, I realized I had looked in the wrong direction. I knew they drove on the wrong side of the road in England but hadn't applied this knowledge to my near fatal stroll.

We took a train trip on the Orient Express from London to the city of Bath, where about two thousand years earlier the Romans had built a grand bathing and socializing complex. Fed by natural hot springs, the Roman Baths claims the dubious honor of being one of the best- preserved Roman remains in the world. Riding in a private dining car, we were living it up, drinking champagne, and laughing all the way to the ancient Roman ruins. Terry and I were enjoying the fact our girls were grown, but not gone.

Back in London, Emily and I decided to drop in on the Wimbledon tennis tournament. We had been told by someone that scalping tickets was illegal in London, but we found a young man selling tickets outside the famous tennis complex, and we bought them under the theory that we might never have another chance to attend one of the world's major sporting events. Having been burned by scalpers before, I was pleasantly surprised when our tickets were about four rows up alongside Centre Court. We had a view of the Royal Box, so we got to watch a few of the Royals watching Martina Navratilova play.

On the second leg of this trip, we flew to Paris, where Anne was going to continue her French language and culture studies at the Sorbonne. Before dropping her off, we took a quick tour of the Louvre. I found Leonardo De Vinci's portrait of the Mona Lisa really was "just a cold and lonely lovely work of art," as the Nat King Cole song suggests. We also visited the top deck of the Eiffel Tower, where we enjoyed the view of Paris, but were engulfed by a crowded school of eager Japanese tourists, seemingly joined at the hip.

Life on Hidden Hill II

Before leaving on our trip, Anne had suggested that we buy a newer and larger home, located about two blocks south and across the street, but still on Hidden Hill Road. Unfortunately, we discovered the home was already under a sales contract. Fortunately, when we got home from our trip, we discovered the sale had not gone through, so the home was still available. We toured the home and found that while it was not as nice as our boom house on Grandview, it would be a definite upgrade, featuring a marble entry foyer, a spiral staircase, a much larger kitchen, a play room and four bedrooms upstairs, and a separate office across the driveway.

The builder and his family had been living there since they had completed the construction. Discussing our potential purchase, I told the builder that the home was nice, but that it had a lot more space than we needed. His rejoinder, which quickly became a family joke, was: "You don't neeeeed it, but you waaaaant it." We finally agreed to swap houses, with us kicking in the difference in their value. On Terry's forty-eighth birthday, we moved to Hidden Hill II.

Not long after we moved in, we were visiting with our Persian friends, Said and Maryam, who owned Picasso's restaurant and

Le Visage beauty spa. Their daughter suddenly declared: "You have two dogs."

"No," I responded. "We only have one dog."

"You have two dogs," she repeated, quite confidently for such a little girl.

Rising slowly from my easy chair, I turned to look out on our patio and was surprised to discover that our dog Honey had company, a handsome cocker spaniel named Buffy, who belonged to the previous resident. I returned Buffy to his owners at Hidden Hill I, but he kept finding his way back. Apparently, he was more attached to our new home than to his owners, so they let us have him and, sure enough, we had two dogs.

We ate family dinners at Picasso's very often. At times, Said, who was also the chief chef, would come out of the kitchen to visit with us. Another frequent customer had noticed these visits and concluded that we were the owners and the chef was coming to report on how things were going.

One evening, Terry and I were going to dinner in Oklahoma City with Said and Maryam. Said was driving their van like a bat out of hell, speeding up Interstate 35, weaving in and out of traffic. I was sitting in the front passenger seat, getting more and more concerned. Finally, I asked him to slow down.

"I don't like having people in front of me," Said explained.

"Those people left thirty minutes before we did!" I exclaimed. "You can't pass them all!" He reluctantly slowed down and we survived the trip.

Another of our favorite restaurants in Norman was Othello's, located near the campus corner. A Thai couple, Tinky and Jana Ruangrit, were cooks there and made great Italian pizzas. In 1994, they left Othello's to open their own restaurant, called "Jana's," in a shopping center near our neighborhood. Their menu featured an unusual selection of Italian and Thai cuisine.

My family enjoyed Jana's food and casual atmosphere. The waiters were usually Thai students attending OU and majoring in difficult subjects like meteorology or physics. On most nights there was no problem finding parking near Jana's, but on Tuesday nights the parking area was packed. I asked Jana why the parking area was so full on Tuesday nights.

"The dollar movie is 50 cents only," she replied. I had not realized entertainment in Norman was so price sensitive.

No matter where we ate dinner, we liked to joke around. This was not only fun for us but seemed to entertain the other customers as well. Terry's laugh is so infectious that other customers would find themselves laughing without knowing why. At Tulio's Mexican restaurant, the owner's mother dubbed Terry "the Happy Lady."

Just before her sophomore year began at OU, Emily went through sorority Rush Week and pledged Delta Gamma. As a sophomore, she was able to move into the sorority house as soon as school started. With her open and easygoing personality, Emily enjoyed her sorority life. She decided to major in advertising, which put her in the same School of Journalism I had skated through three decades earlier. Her assignments included working up advertising campaigns for Gatorade and Nike. She also developed an interest in photography that became a big part of her life.

Kobe Was Totally Destroyed, Maybe

In 1993, Dutcher & Company signed up three California limited partnerships as oil and gas property management clients. Although the partnerships had been very successful in the 1970s and early 1980s, they had been struggling with low oil and gas prices since the mid-1980s. Their management fees, a reasonable percentage of their operating profits during better times, had become a multiple of their profits during the downturn. The limited partners revolted against the old managers and hired us to manage their properties at a much lower cost. This required our company to add well operations to our services, since previously we had only managed minerals, royalties, and non-operating working interests.

Later that year, relapsing as a political satirist, I wrote an article that appeared in two politically oriented newspapers, one in Oklahoma City and one in Bartlesville. The story was about the federal government's new Inter-Generational Loan Program, which allowed me to borrow money by simply pledging my children's future income as collateral. When my son was sixteen, he learned his income had been pledged under the IGLP and grew very upset. He said he was going to protest. When I asked him how his protest went, he replied: "I called up my Congressman, and he said, quote: 'I'd like to help you son, but you're too young to vote.'" (I am afraid my article didn't have much impact on federal spending. When I wrote the article, the National Debt was an alarming $4.4 trillion. By March 2021, it had reached $28.1 trillion.)

Anadarko Minerals acquired interests in fifty-one Western Oklahoma oil and gas wells from Snyder Oil Company in early 1994 for $2.6 million. Later that year, we picked up two additional pieces of the GHK puzzle for a total of $700,000. We also made our first oil acquisition, a small, non-operated interest in an old oil field in Montana called Salt Creek.

During the 1990s, Dutcher & Company's consulting and property management fees covered most of our overhead expenses. Unburdened by overhead expenses, AMI was able to reinvest most of its cash flow into additional acquisitions. We slowly built up the company's oil and gas reserves, stacking up small acquisitions, one deal at a time. The interests we were buying were small and widely dispersed. We joked that AMI's properties were spread like a mist across the Anadarko Basin.

In January 1995, Anne was visiting her Japanese friend, Yoshiko, in her home in Kawanishi-Shi, near Kobe, Japan. They had met while studying at the Alliance Francaise in Paris in the Fall of 1993. Anne had been sleeping on a mat when she felt the room shaking from the impact of the devastating Kobe earthquake a few miles away. Yoshiko's home was not badly damaged, and no one was hurt, but Terry and I did not know that when we heard the news about the earthquake, and the phone lines in the area were all down.

We tried contacting the State Department to see if they had any reports on Americans in that area, but they did not have any news. We contacted our friend, Bob Danner, whose company had business partners in Japan, to see if they could give us any news about the situation in Kobe. Later that day, Anne was able to get a call through to let us know she was okay. We were still breathing sighs of relief when we received a fax from Bob Danner's contact in Japan. It read: "Kobe was totally destroyed, maybe." Timing is everything.

Later that year, my dad, at age eighty-four, began experiencing serious heart problems, and my mother, at age eighty-two, began developing short-term memory problems. Del and his wife Dona lived on a ranch a few miles east of Bartlesville, so they caught the duty of first responders as our folks' health issues grew more serious. I started making frequent weekend trips to Bartlesville to see my folks that year. With Dad in the hospital, Mom had moved to an assisted living facility on the east side of town.

Not long before my dad passed away that October, Del, Mom, and I were with him in a private room on the third floor of the Bartlesville hospital. Dad was reclining in his bed, seemingly asleep, having lost interest in a baseball game on a television mounted on the wall across from his bed. Del and I had decided to tell Mom that it was no longer safe for her to drive her car, and that she needed to give us her car keys. Mom, fearing a loss of independence, refused. She argued that she had never been in a car wreck. This was true, if somewhat surprising, given that she tended to creep across town at about ten miles per hour, frequently hitting her brakes for no apparent reason. When we continued to request her keys, Mom, with her flair for the dramatic, stopped crying long enough to announce: "If you take my car keys, I am going to jump out of this window!"

Dad, with perfect, if accidental, comedic timing, shouted at the umpire on television: "That was a strike!"

What a bitter-sweet moment, so sad and funny at once.

After Dad died, I made frequent weekend trips to Bartlesville to visit Mom. She was a skilled *Scrabble* player with a defensive style and command of obscure words good for use in this board game but nowhere else. I didn't worry about her memory problems until I started to win a few *Scrabble* games.

My Fourth Comeback

My fourth basketball comeback was triggered by a phone call one evening during the 1995–96 OU basketball season. I was invited to play in an OU Varsity alumni basketball game after an OU home game. Despite the sparse crowd that stayed to watch the old guys play, I was a little tight and missed a couple of open shots. With one steal to offset one turnover, I was not a factor in the outcome of the game. But it was fun and gave me an incentive to get back on the court. Two years later, I played in my second OU Varsity alumni game. More relaxed and in better shape, I played much better, hitting two three-pointers and making five assists in a fast-paced shoot-out. Most of the players were from the run-and-gun Billy Tubbs era, which was reflected in the final score of something like 135 to 117.

The prospect of playing in more OU Varsity alumni games encouraged me to continue playing noon-time pick-up games at the YMCA. Despite being in my mid-50s, I was determined to keep playing until a knee or ankle injury ended my career. The feared injury bug bit me one day as I was running up the court. Suddenly, for no reason, my left ankle gave out and I went down like I had been shot by a sniper. I was flat on the floor, and my ankle swelled up with a knot the size of a tennis ball. The injury ended my fourth comeback. For the next three years, my basketball playing was limited to shooting hoops in our driveway.

A Titanium Golf Ball

My friend Mike Hewitt invited me to join him and two other high school teammates, Bob Blaker and Stan Ogle, on a golfing vacation in Orlando, Florida. He was nice to invite me since he knew I would be the only non-golfer in the foursome. Beginning with a round of golf at the OU course in the summer of 1965, I had played golf once a decade. I was like the guy in the story who kept hitting new golf balls into a lake. His golf buddy asked him why he didn't use an old ball when trying to drive over a water hazard. He replied: "I've never had an old ball."

My friends showed quite a bit of patience with me as I struggled around the course, spraying balls in all directions with my unpredictable slices and hooks. On the second day of play, while waiting for our turn to tee off, one of my friends handed me what he described as a new titanium golf ball designed to add distance to my drives. I thanked him, realizing my weak drives needed all the help they could get. Unfortunately, while waiting for our turn, I did what I normally would do when standing around with a ball in my hand. I began to dribble it and was shocked when it exploded on the first bounce. I am no Sherlock Holmes, but it did not take me long to deduce that the ball was intended to explode when I hit it with my driver.

My friends shook their heads in dismay, seeming a little upset that I had ruined their practical joke. Apparently, no real golfer would dribble a new ball on a concrete sidewalk.

By the time we reached our early 50s, Terry had several friends who were divorced. She told me that if anything ever happened to her, they would be showing up on my doorstep with a casserole in their hands and a nighty in their purse. I laughed and told her thanks for the warning.

For a Christmas gift in 1996, I wrote Terry a poem called "Your Kiss Is the Truth." And here it is:

In your kiss, I feel the comfort of a shared life,
The little memories, jokes and secrets only you and I know
And can exchange with a wink or a knowing glance.
In your kiss, I feel your trusting, vulnerable, and giving soul
Holding back nothing, an open invitation to an intense intimacy,
If only I am man enough to embrace it, and not back off
From the heat of your passion or the light of your perceptiveness
That sees right through me and still manages to love me.

In your kiss, I feel the depth of your devotion.

A commitment strong enough to build our life on.

A life of shared values, like family and loyalty,

And permission to take risks, knowing our failures will be forgiven,

And our successes will be truly enjoyed.

In your kiss, I find your love,

And that is all I need in the world.

Even after thirty-one years of marriage, I found that a little relationship maintenance, in the form of a song, a love letter, or poem, can go a long way. (The year before, I had given her a crimson Infiniti 1–30, which also went a long way.)

By 1997, the oil and gas production we had been operating for the three California limited partnerships had declined, and most of the remaining value was concentrated in one well, the Hammer 1–19. While this was one of Oklahoma's most prolific natural gas wells, having produced more than fifty billion cubic feet of gas from the Hunton formation, its remaining reserves didn't justify the expenses required to keep up the limited partnership structure. AMI purchased the partnerships' properties, distributed the cash to the limited partners, and the partnerships were closed. With AMI growing and demanding more and more of the time of our employees, Dutcher & Company withdrew from the business of providing consulting and property management services to clients and began working solely for AMI.

Exploring New Ideas

Watching the news on CNN one evening, I noticed random bits of information popping up on the screen. CNN called them

"Factoids." I had a random thought, which was not unusual for me. What was unusual was that I did something about it. What if I just made up some pointless or nonsensical bits of information and called them "Fictoids"?

For example, one of my first fictoids, jotted down on a napkin or possibly on the back of an envelope, was: "German generals urged Japan to attack Pearl Harbor in 1941 because they needed a secure supply of coconuts for German chocolate cake." Another early fictoid observed: "Anchovy fishermen casting their nets off the coast of Peru were often featured in arty Italian pizza documentaries during the early 1970s." Jotting down fictoids, whenever one popped into my head, became a habit, or quirk.

In early 1998, Emily came up with the idea of creating a computer program that allowed users to rotate their personal photos and video clips in place of a stationary screensaver. I agreed to back her in this venture. We found a small firm in Rhode Island that created humorous screensavers and hired them to write the program, which we called Pics 'n' Flicks. As we began our marketing efforts, *The Journal Record*, an Oklahoma business newspaper, ran a front-page picture of Emily, holding a computer with a photo of our dogs, Honey and Buffy, as the screensaver. The caption read: "Emily Dutcher: The University of Oklahoma graduate's company, ECD Productions, is going full steam ahead in the software market with the release of its first product, Pics 'n' Flicks." The program worked great. It offered a wide array of photo frames and mattings, while videos could be displayed inside a television screen, a movie theater screen, or even a drive-in screen. I loaded highlights from NBA games to serve as the screensaver for my office computer. But marketing Pics 'n' Flicks proved to be a challenge. Although our sales were disappointing in volume, they were great in terms of wide distribution. Thanks to the World Wide Web, we had sales in fourteen countries.

We tried get to Mark Cuban, as owner of the Dallas Mavericks NBA team, to use Pics 'n' Flicks as a promotional item for his team. He responded with an arrogant email suggesting that we pay him to use our product, so that we could benefit with our association with his team. We replied that we did not like his deal, but that we would trade the rights to Pics 'n' Flicks for the Mavericks' 7' 6" center Shawn Bradley and two future draft picks. Unsurprisingly, we never heard back on our final offer.

The growth of AMI hit an air pocket in November 1998, when the price of crude oil dropped from over $40 per barrel to $17.25 per barrel. Although most of our reserves were natural gas, the oil price drop caused enough of a dent in our cash flow that I had to lay off three of our eight employees.

Although I wanted our company to keep growing, I was not interested in growth for growth's sake, and I was unwilling to give up any equity in our company. This meant we were limiting ourselves to low-cost bank financing. Providing working capital to independent oil and gas producers was a cottage industry in Houston and Dallas, but the risk to the producer was that the cost of the capital was so high the producer could end up working for his capital providers. In a meeting in Dallas, I explained our financial dilemma to Ken Hersh, a well-known investment banker with Natural Gas Partners, and he gave me some excellent advice: "Just keep doing what you're doing."

After graduating from OU, Anne continued graduate studies in French and economics, including additional studies at the Alliance Francaise in Paris. She also taught French at OU for a while. Even though the OU law school offered to pay her to attend their school,

Anne had wider ambitions. In the summer of 1998, she began her studies in international relations at The John Hopkins University School of Advanced International Studies (SAIS) in Washington, DC. That fall, she journeyed to Bologna, Italy, for her first year of studies in this program.

The Millionaire Next Door

On a cold winter afternoon in January 1999, I noticed a car pulling into the circle driveway of our new up-the-hill, next-door neighbors. I ambled over to introduce myself and welcome them to the neighborhood. My timing was less than ideal. Bob Stoops, recently hired as OU's new head football coach, and his wife Carol were returning to their new home from the Norman hospital toting their twin baby boys, Drake and Isaac, bundled up in basinets.

Not wanting to come across as some type of OU football groupie, I told them I was more of a basketball fan than football fan, but if there were anything we could help them with, they should feel free to ask. On the other hand, I wanted to respect their privacy.

"Good," Carol said, apparently referring to the part about respecting their privacy. In football crazy Oklahoma, they had each achieved rock star status long before Coach Stoops had coached his first OU game.

Prior to Coach Stoops's arrival, OU football had fallen on hard times. Heading to a game in the fall of 1998, I noticed that in the Campus Corner area, across Boyd Street from the OU campus, people were trying to sell game tickets for $20 each. As I walked past the student union, the ticket prices had come down to $10. When I reached the armory building near the stadium, people were giving away tickets. When I reached the stadium entrance, a man was pleading: "Free tickets . . . and I will buy your lunch."

It did not take my next-door neighbor long to turn around OU's football fortunes.

— • — • —

CHAPTER FIFTEEN

A NEW
MILLENNIUM

B*y the turn of the century,* I had compiled a full shoebox of fictoid notes and ideas, so I decided to write them up and market them over the internet. A new company called Fatbrain was offering to publish what it called "eMatter" for a small fee and 50 percent of the sales proceeds.

Wanting to maintain a low profile as the author of this dubious undertaking, I submitted *Fictoid* as: "Bytes of humor in fictional history" and described the author as follows.

"Anonymous Jones is temporarily employed as an Itinerate Professor of Fictional History at Ripley University in King George, Rhode Island, where he is perhaps best known for his observation, 'People who do not know history are free to make it up.' Mr. Jones received his master's degree in fictional history in 1992 from Timbuktu U."

To promote my new e-book, I sent out a news release attributed to Professor Anonymous Jones, but the media would not publish stories attributed to a fictional source. Despite the lack of publicity, I sold several copies of *Fictoids* during my first month on the Fatbrain website. The kind folks at Fatbrain sent me a check for $35 and I never heard from them again. Apparently, their business model did not work.

In the spring of 2000, Anne graduated from SAIS with a master's degree in international relations. By coincidence, Michael Hewitt, the son of my lifelong friends Mike and Patty Mac Hewitt, was in Anne's graduating class. United Nations Secretary General Kofi Anan gave the commencement speech.

That summer, Anne moved to Houston to work for an energy consulting firm. Not wanting to fight the horrific Houston traffic, she rented an apartment in a Four Seasons complex downtown. This worked out well for me, as I got to see Anne while I was in Houston seeking financing for AMI from investment bankers. After she left the consulting firm, she remained in Houston to help AMI keep up with developments in the oil and gas industry and look for investment opportunities.

My Fifth Comeback

In Coach Stoops's second season at OU, his Sooner team beat Florida State in the 2001 Orange Bowl, giving OU its seventh national championship and conferring hero status on my next-door neighbor.

A few days later, I was attending an OU basketball home game against Texas A & M. I was surprised to hear my name being called as the fan selected as the Security Bank half-time shooter. For many years, as I entered Lloyd Noble Arena for an OU home game, I had faithfully written my name on a slip of paper and dropped it into a box to enter this half-time shooting contest. The selected contestant was given thirty seconds to make a layup, a free throw, and a three-point shot. If he made all three shots, and still had time on the clock, he could take a half-court shot for a cash prize of $25,000. The bank's money was relatively safe. In all the years I had been attending OU games, I had only seen the $25,000 prize won once, and that was by an athletic OU football defensive back. Being an optimist, I had practiced for this contest at the YMCA gym and knew I could only miss one shot and still have time to make the four shots required to win.

As the first half of the OU game progressed, I was getting a little nervous about taking these shots in front of more than 10,000 fans. Emily didn't help much when she told me, "Just don't miss the layup." Layup? I was worried about the half-court shot.

When the first half ended, I was escorted to the south basket, introduced to the crowd, and given a basketball. I quickly made the layup but took too much time on my first free throw and missed it. As I grabbed the rebound, I knew I had to hurry. I made my second free throw, quickly dribbled the ball out to the three-point line and shot a turning jumper that hit nothing but net. As I retrieved the ball, I glanced at the time clock and saw that I only had four seconds left. I raced to half court, turned and fired, but with my momentum going in the wrong direction, my shot was painfully short.

A few days later, a friend who worked at the university surprised me with a video tape of my half-time performance, which had been recorded by Sooner Vision, a part of the OU athletic department's media group. I was shooting baskets in our driveway a few weeks later when Coach Stoops came by. I asked him to wait a minute while I ran inside and retrieved the video tape of my half-time shooting efforts. (I wanted to show off my turning three-pointer swishing through the net.)

"This tape has the highlight of the OU basketball season," I said as I handed it to him, without explaining what it was. He looked a little puzzled but accepted the tape. I didn't see him again for a while. Then one morning I was taking our new dog Broono for a walk when Coach Stoops came running down the street, on his way home from an early morning jog.

"Hey Bill, you need to work on that half-court shot," he shouted, living up to his reputation as a hard-working, no-excuses coach.

A Life-changing Event

March 7, 2001, is a date that will live in infamy within our household. I took Terry to the hospital, where the doctors determined that a sinus infection had caused a lesion in her brain stem, affecting her vision and leaving her partially paralyzed on her left side. Although her paralysis and vision gradually improved, this was a life-changing event. She could no longer drive or fly in airplanes. Terry's health problems required me to stop my daily commute to my Oklahoma City office and work more from my home office, going to Oklahoma City for meetings when necessary. Fortunately, my three vice presidents were able to run the company's daily business without me being there in person.

A Company-making Event

Oil and natural gas prices remained low in 2002, giving Anadarko Minerals an opportunity to make its biggest acquisition of Oklahoma producing properties. Southwestern Energy Company, an oil and gas producer, had decided to withdraw from Oklahoma to focus on the development of a huge natural gas resource in Arkansas called the Fayetteville Shale. They had retained Albrecht and Associates, a divestiture company in Houston, to handle the sale. The sales package included 153 oil and gas wells operated by Southwestern and non-operated interests in another 108 wells in central Oklahoma, as well as non-operated interests in two large oil fields in Southern Oklahoma. Unlike most divestiture companies, Albrecht would give bidders an idea of what they expected the properties to sell for. In this case, the expected sales price was around $26 million, which meant that the deal would be a stretch for us but was within reach.

During a management meeting to discuss this deal, I pulled out a clipping of a cartoon that had recently appeared in *The Wall Street Journal*. The cartoon showed a group of managers gathered around a conference table like ours, with the top executive sitting at the end of the table, like I do. All of the managers were shown with their hair standing on end. The caption read: "Very well, the 'yikes' have it." This cartoon really captured our management's feelings about pursuing such a big acquisition.

As we evaluated the properties, we learned that Chesapeake Energy was not bidding on this deal, probably because they were busy on other acquisitions. Chesapeake, a relatively young but rapidly growing public company, was led by its bold and charismatic CEO, Aubrey McClendon. At that time in Oklahoma's oil and gas industry, McClendon, like Hefner in the early 1980s, was "the straw that stirred the drink." Chesapeake bid so aggressively to fuel their rapid growth that they were often the high bidder on any deal they pursued. The fact that they were sitting this one out gave me an incentive to bid more than our usual formula allowed.

We did not have the formal approval of our bank when we submitted our bid, but when we were selected as the high bidder, we went ahead and made a down payment on the deal. Mack worked with the seller to iron out a purchase and sale agreement while Carol, Nick, and I worked with the Bank of Oklahoma to secure the financing. AMI's borrowing capacity under its existing BOK loan agreement, plus the amount they would loan secured by the reserves we were buying from Southwestern, fell about $5 million short of the amount we needed to close the deal. However, we were able to arrange a six-month "mezzanine" loan for that amount, at a higher interest rate, to bring the total loan amount to the $26.5 million we needed to complete the acquisition.

Unfortunately, while negotiating the final purchase and sale agreement, we hit a snag over environmental issues. At that point in our company history, we owned hundreds of small, non-operating working interests, as well as royalty and mineral interests in Anadarko Basin natural gas wells. This purchase from Southwestern would put us directly in the oil business, owning interests in both operated and non-operated oil wells. During our due-diligence inspections of the properties, we discovered a buried oil tank on one of their leases. This discovery made me worry more than usual about the risk of buying into a collection of hidden environmental liabilities.

Mack, our attorney, and I flew to Southwestern's headquarters near Houston to meet with their management to resolve the environmental issues. We were willing to accept liability for any environmental problems, such as oil spills, that occurred after we had taken ownership of their properties, but we insisted that they would have to remain liable for environmental problems, such as buried oil tanks, that had occurred prior to our assuming ownership. The longer we argued about this issue, the more worried I was becoming about what we were getting into. Finally, I said I wouldn't do the deal on their terms. Feeling both disappointed and relieved, but not bluffing, I packed up my briefcase and stood up to leave the room. At this point, their lead negotiator asked us to wait while he went "upstairs" to talk with their senior management about our impasse. We waited awhile without conversation. Their negotiator returned and said their management would agree to our terms.

Their decision triggered a mild panic attack in my head. For an agonizing moment, I still wanted to kill this deal. I felt overwhelmed, as if I were just then realizing the amount of risk and debt I would be taking on. On the other hand, how could I not take "yes" for an answer? Not willing to renege on my word, I agreed to take the deal, fear and doubt be damned.

My appetite for risk taking carried the day. If someone holds a consistently bearish market view, they will be right part of the time, as markets, by their nature, move up and down. But they will also miss opportunities. I would rather lose money on the downside than miss opportunities on the upside. As you build equity in a rising market, you may become more risk-adverse to protect your gains. But remember, if you had not taken a risk to begin with, there would be no gains to worry about losing.

We closed the Southwest Energy deal on November 15, 2002. Going into well operations in such a big way required us to add new employees in our production department. Steve Reynolds joined us a production manager and quickly built a production department that could handle our expanded well operations. Still concerned with the environmental risk posed by the old oil wells, we put the newly acquired properties into a separate company called Dutch Petroleum.

Not A Very Long Line

After closing the Southwestern Energy deal, our debt to BOK totaled nearly $36 million, which made us one of their larger

Oklahoma City business customers. As such, I was invited to join a group of BOK bank executives and some of their top customers for a mid-January limousine trip to Stillwater to watch a "bedlam" basketball game between OU and OSU. The bank customers on this trip included a diverse collection of Oklahoma City's leading tycoons, moguls, and magnates. While waiting at our designated departure spot along Interstate 35 for Aubrey McClendon, the Chesapeake Energy CEO, to join us, we learned he was driving back to Oklahoma City from Tulsa and wanted to meet us at a McDonald's near the Wellston exit on the Turner Turnpike. After a long wait at the McDonald's, it was getting dark by the time Aubrey arrived. It was decided that the quickest way to get to Stillwater from Wellston was to head north on a series of two-lane state highways.

Unfortunately, our driver's familiarity with Oklahoma roads seemed to be limited to the Interstate Highway system. We appeared to be headed in the general direction of Stillwater when the road we were on abruptly ended. With a limo full of men with take-charge personalities, our perplexed driver had his choice of conflicting instructions. He could turn right, turn left, or turn around. Arguments ensued.

Observing this chaotic comedy, I managed to insult the majority of Oklahoma City's business leadership by quoting Emily's high school graduation speaker.

Addressing no one in particular, I said, loud enough to be heard, "This trip reminds me of the quote that if you come to Oklahoma and work hard, you can get to the head of the line, because it is not a very long line." (Implying, of course, that the entire line would fit into a stretch limo.) Our limo eventually found its way Stillwater in time for the game, a two-point win for OSU.

To help comply with the terms of AMI's mezzanine loan from BOK, in February 2003 we packaged up most of our smallest interests in Anadarko Basin gas wells for sale at an auction in Oklahoma City. During this era, auctions of oil and gas properties were held often in Oklahoma City and were normally attended by a few hundred buyers and sellers. On the night before this auction, however, an ice storm had struck Oklahoma City. The auction was scheduled to begin at 9 am. A little before then, I pulled into the ice-covered parking lot of the events center where the auction was being held and was shocked to find only about a dozen vehicles parked in front. I had a sinking feeling that with only a few bidders, this auction was going to be a financial disaster. I had an urge to pull our properties out of the auction before it began but felt that would not be fair to the auction company.

Luckily, despite a small number of bidders, the ones who braved the ice to attend were aggressive. Chesapeake seemed to want every oil and gas interest it could buy, no matter how small. AMI sold its interests in 365 wells for $3 million and used the proceeds to pay down its mezzanine loan. An increase in oil and gas prices that spring allowed AMI to roll the balance of its mezzanine loan into its regular loan. During my first fifteen years of running my companies, I felt we had been running against the wind. In 2002, the wind turned, and with the wind at our backs, our fortunes soared.

Terry and I launched a major home improvement project in the backyard of our home on Hidden Hill. Using the contractor who had built our house, we built a high brick fence on the south and west sides of our property. Then we added a lap pool, a kids' pool, and a hot tub, all connected so that the flowing water could circulate without freezing in the winter. Finally, we built an outdoor kitchen and a fireplace with a tall chimney. (This quality of life investment has paid dividends every year, especially from May through October.)

In March 2003, I drove to Bartlesville to visit my mother on her ninetieth birthday. Mom was still staying at the same assisted living place she had moved into after my dad died. We played our traditional game of *Scrabble*, and she won, as expected. After the game, we skipped out to have lunch at a restaurant at a country inn about halfway between Bartlesville and Tulsa.

During lunch, I told mom that I did not think she looked like she was ninety, and I didn't believe I looked like I was sixty. I suggested that we give each other thirty years. That way, she could be sixty and I would be thirty.

She smiled and said in the nicest possible way: "Or vice versa."

Like her favorite song, she was still "young at heart." She liked to quote from its lyrics: "And if you should survive to a hundred and five, look at all you'll derive out of bein' alive."

— · — · —

CHAPTER SIXTEEN

SEEKING BASKETBALL'S NIRVANA

Trying to stay young at heart that summer, I asked myself what would make a fun vacation. I searched the internet for basketball fantasy camps and was excited to discover that Michael Jordan was hosting a camp called "Senior Flight School" for men over thirty-five in Las Vegas that August.

The camp seemed very expensive: $15,000 for a four-day basketball experience. But the brochure promised not only the chance to play basketball with Michael Jordan, but also the opportunity to be coached by a list of famous coaches too good to believe. The coaches for the upcoming camp would include Chuck Daly, Tubby Smith, George Karl, Bob Huggins, Jim Boeheim, Lute Olson, John Thompson, Mike Krzyzewski, Doug Moe, Jim Calhoun, P. J. Carlisimo, Hubie Brown, Jack Ramsay, Bill Guthridge, Lenny Wilkins, Mike Fratello, and Mike Montgomery. To a basketball fan like me, this list read like an All-Star team of college and professional coaches. Sign me up. At this point in my life, I was more interested in collecting experiences than in compiling more stuff.

To prepare for the Michael Jordan camp, I launched my fifth comeback by playing in noon pick-up games at the Norman YMCA on Mondays, Wednesdays, and Fridays. Knowing I needed to improve my game before showing up at the Michael Jordan camp, I asked OU coach Kelvin Sampson if I could work out at the OU basketball practice gym.

"The gap between playing basketball at the Norman YMCA and playing at a Michael Jordan camp in Las Vegas is just too wide," I explained. He gave me permission to work out at OU for the rest of the summer, noting that he sure would like to join the coaching staff at the Jordan camp. The OU practice gym includes one full-length court with glass backboards at each end and two shorter cross courts with their own set of glass backboards. The walls are decorated with banners marking OU's basketball history, including the Sooners' Big Eight and Big Twelve championship seasons and the team's appearances in the NCAA tournament regionals and Final Fours. For a lifelong Sooner basketball fan, it's an inspiring place to play.

Working out there early on summer mornings, I usually had the OU gym to myself. To warm up, I often started with a shooting game I invented called "Miss Five." Like the name implies, I would shoot mid-range jumpers to see how many I could hit before missing five shots. Shooting is easy, of course, when no one is guarding you, so I could normally hit around thirty-two jump shots before my fifth miss. My record for this game is fifty-four.

I also liked to play one-on-none, full-court games, North versus South. In one game, I would dribble the length of the court and shoot a pull-up jumper from the free-throw line. Then dribble back to the other end and shoot the same shot. I repeated these trips, back and forth, until I made the winning tenth basket on the North or South goal. Then I would play against myself in the same game, only this time I would pull up to shoot from the three-point line. At the end of my workout, I would shoot free throws. (My personal best, eighty-four makes in a row, has stood for several years. I could normally hit more than 90 percent of my free throws in practice.)

At times, an OU coach or trainer would ask why I was working so hard. I would tell them that this wasn't work, it was fun. Work was trying to decipher oil and gas markets at an office computer. To me, the idea of working on my game was an oxymoron.

The Jordan camp required a letter from a doctor stating that I was in good enough condition to play basketball at the camp. I went to see my cardiologist, Charles Bethea, a friend and former high school football teammate, who had been seeing me for several years for my irregular heartbeat and an atrial fibrillation, a racing heartbeat that sometimes kicked in during exercise.

Dr. Bethea asked me how I had been doing, and I said I was fine, except at times I had been getting a sharp pain between my shoulder blades that felt like I had been stabbed with a knife. After some lab work and x-rays, I met with the good doctor again, and he smiled and said he had great news: "The x-ray didn't show any knife."

Emily Takes Me to Camp

Emily, my longtime basketball buddy, was my guest, duty photographer, and evening event planner for the Seventh Annual Michael Jordan Senior Flight School. Checking in at the Mirage, I felt like a little kid on the lookout for basketball celebrities.

We introduced ourselves to Michael Jordan at a "photo-op" session prior to a reception and dinner on the first evening of the camp. Photo-op etiquette allows for some brief conversation while the photo is being taken, so I took that opportunity to tell Michael that Kelvin Sampson would like to be on the camp's coaching staff. He responded favorably, saying Coach Sampson "is a North Carolina guy."

During the reception, I mentioned to the camp director, former USC coach George Raveling, that Coach Sampson would like to be on the camp's coaching staff. "Him and about a hundred other guys," he replied, with more than a hint of sarcasm.

"Well, Michael Jordan liked the idea," I countered. "He said Coach Sampson was a North Carolina guy."

Making a remarkably quick attitude adjustment, the camp director responded, "Oh, yes, I know Coach Sampson. He's a great guy."

(Coach Sampson was on the camp coaching staff the following summer.)

The famous coaches at the Jordan camp, whether college or pro, maintained a good-natured competitiveness, as if to say to their rivals: "I can take my ten rich yahoos and beat your ten rich yahoos any day." While the coaches may well have been joking among themselves about their players' basketball skills, in social situations away from the court there seemed to be a mutual respect, based on a shared love of basketball and a recognition of some measure of success. In real life, the players were corporate executives, investment bankers, doctors, lawyers, and entrepreneurs, generally alpha males when in their own domains.

On the first afternoon of camp, the players were divided up into teams to play in evaluation games. The coaches watched these games, then attended a draft session to pick their teams. I suspected that in the first few rounds, the top centers and point guards were selected, probably guys in their late thirties or early forties with some college or pro basketball experience. In the mid-rounds, I bet that guys who played in high school and have stayed active in church or recreational leagues, or at least regular pick-up games, were chosen. By the late rounds, the selections were down to old players like me, or young guys who had hardly played at all. In summary, the draft process resulted in competitive teams with a wide range of talent and experience.

To keep the competition fair and possibly in recognition that the players had paid a lot of money to attend the camp, substitutions were based on a numbering system designed to equal out the playing time. However, in the last few minutes of a game, the coaches were free to play any of their players and substitute whenever they liked.

The Jordan camp games were played in a huge convention hall in the sprawling Mirage Hotel and Casino. Five college basketball courts had been set up in the hall, which featured plush carpet, chandeliers, and life-size posters of MJ in action. The courts, brought in from UNLV and other nearby colleges, seemed twice as long as the YMCA court I had been playing on at home. They seemed to add a twenty-yard wind sprint to each change of possession.

The camp's program included brief sessions for instructions from the famous coaches. Each team would rotate from one station to the next to learn some of the finer points of basketball. In one session, Lenny Wilkins was attempting to teach campers the deceptive pivot move that Jack Sikma would make while playing for the Seattle Sonics. After watching Coach Wilkins demonstrate the move, I tried to do it myself. Apparently, I did it wrong, even if I did make a shot after my awkward attempt.

"Or, you could do that," Coach Wilkins observed wryly.

In another session, NBA legend and TNT analyst Charles Barkley gave a talk to the campers, then answered questions. He was asked what was the most money he had ever made in one year playing basketball. Barkley answered: "Four million . . . and that was at Auburn."

One-on-One with Michael Jordan

The opportunity to play Michael Jordan one-on-one was offered to campers bold enough to take on this challenge. Waiting in line, I watched him scoring easily and swatting away campers' shots, not really cutting them any slack. Only four months had passed since he had played the last game of his epic NBA career, and his game wasn't showing any rust.

When I stepped up for my turn, he gave me a dismissive look and handed me a basketball. He seemed slightly offended at being challenged to a one-on-one game by a bald, 5' 10", sixty-year-old Oklahoma oilman.

"You just want something to tell your employees about," he commented, his deep voice both friendly and intimidating.

With Emily on the baseline with her camera in hand, I was thinking "photo-op."

"I'll give you the first one," he whispered.

I believed him, even though I was too scared to look at him. I just looked to my left and fired up a jump shot from the college three-point line, just above the top of the key. Swish. My shot brought a little murmur from the crowd, which included Duke coach Mike Krzyzewski and many of the other coaches and campers. We were only playing to two baskets, make it, take it, so I was only one basket away from a classic upset.

"I'm going to guard you this time," Jordan warned, as I took the ball, trying to act nonchalant about my first basket. But I had

One-on-one with Michael Jordan

a problem. Under the camp rules, the players were limited to two dribbles in the one-on-one games. There was no way I was going to get open in two dribbles, and I really didn't want to eat the ball. I took two hard dribbles to my right, head faked, and shot a desperation fall-away jumper that went in . . . and rolled out. The crowd groaned in mild disappointment.

Not wanting to get dunked on, I set up in a defensive position about three steps away from Jordan. As he eyed the basket, I realized I was not even in his line of sight. He quickly drained two three-pointers and I was toast. Shortly after our game, John Rogers, a Chicago investment banker and former point guard at Princeton, ignored the two-dribble rule and beat Jordan by driving to the basket and spinning shots high off the glass. (Rogers' victory is described in the February 26, 2008 issue of *Sports Illustrated* in a story by Chris Ballard called "The Happiest Camper," and a video of their game on You Tube has had more than five million hits.)

The morning after our game, I asked Jordan if he would have given me an uncontested shot from behind the NBA three-point line for my second shot. He said he would have. If I had thought of that sooner, I might have been mentioned in *Sports Illustrated*.

My rookie year coaches, Chuck Daly and Gene Keady, were surprisingly intense for a fantasy camp. Coach Daly had coached the Dream Team in the 1992 Olympics, but still managed to take our games seriously. Even though the teams substituted players in five-minute increments, I was checking the clock constantly to see how much longer I had to keep running. "Darn . . . two minutes to go," I said to myself.

My breathing problem was caused by my irregular heartbeat. If my heart started racing, I did not decide to stop running. I stopped running, then realized I had stopped. What I needed was an adjustable pacemaker that could speed up my heart rate during fast breaks and slow it down for free throws. My best play came near the end of camp. I persuaded our point guard to let me bring the ball up the court, blew past my startled defender (who shouted "whoa" as I raced by him), and nailed a wide-open jumper.

"Dad, you would have played a lot better if Father Time wasn't always tugging on your jersey," Emily allowed, providing an epitaph for my first camp as we walked off the court. Based on Emily's apt assessment of my performance, I decided to embark on a quixotic one-on-one battle with Father Time. But rather than tilting at windmills, I would use future fantasy camps as the venue.

Disappointed and a little mad at myself for the way I had played during my first camp, I realized I had underestimated the level of conditioning required to be competitive at a fantasy camp. I didn't play the age card or whine about my heart condition. I just vowed to get in better shape before returning to the next year's camp.

When camp was over, Garry Munson invited me to play on an over-sixty team called the Sag Harbor Whalers. Since it isn't often that a guy from Oklahoma gets to play on a team called the Whalers, I jumped at the chance, just not very high. Garry, a real estate entrepreneur when not playing basketball, has achieved a legendary status on the fantasy camp circuit.

Thanking Mr. Hefner Twice

That October, Robert A. Hefner III invited me to attend a showing of his Chinese art collection at GHK's offices in Oklahoma City. During the reception, I took the opportunity to thank him for the three times in my life that he had helped me in my evolution from being a newspaper reporter to owning my own small oil and gas company. First, he introduced me to the oil and gas industry as my public relations client in 1971. Second, after my deep gas lobbying days were over in 1978, he assigned me to work in natural gas marketing and financing for GHK, both valuable learning experiences. Third, in 1990, he provided temporary financing for Anadarko Minerals' $2 million acquisition of oil and gas properties from Chase Manhattan Bank. Hefner appreciated my thanks and asked his wife MeiLi to join us so that I could repeat what I had just said to her.

A Trip to the Big Apple

A confluence of three events made for an enjoyable trip to New York City in December 2003. Anadarko Minerals had been named as a finalist for a Platt's Global Energy Award in a category for energy companies that had made dramatic progress in the previous year. Our entry into this awards contest was based on our recent acquisition of oil and gas properties from Southwestern Energy, as this "company-making" deal had moved us into operating oil and gas wells on a large scale and had greatly increased our oil and gas reserves.

The awards dinner was held in a giant ballroom in the Plaza Hotel in Uptown Manhattan. Mack, Nick, and I suited up in tuxedoes for the black-tie event. Mack's wife, Kim, and Nick's wife, Tracey, joined us. Terry didn't make the trip for health reasons, but Anne popped up from Washington, DC, where she was studying at SAIS.

After seeing a write-up on the other two finalists in our category, I was confident we would win. Our story was the only one that fit the stated criteria for the award. However, as the program progressed through acceptance speeches from the long list of award winners in other categories, I became increasingly nervous. For many years, I had had a recurring nightmare, known only to me as "The Unprepared Speech." In my dream, I stood frozen before a huge audience, unable to speak. The audience would grow restless as the dead air space persisted. Nearly dying of embarrassment, I would walk off the podium . . . and wake up happy to discover it was only a dream. As the awards presentations worked their way toward our category, I began to fear that when our name was announced, I would find myself living out my nightmare. Could this be the night of "The Unprepared Speech"?

Finally, the award presentations reached our category. I was shocked when we didn't win. But my disappointment was quickly overcome when I realized this meant that I did not have to give an acceptance speech that night.

But Jason White did. In another ceremony in downtown Manhattan, Jason, the strong-armed but weak-kneed quarterback for the OU football team, was named the winner of the coveted Heisman Trophy as the best player in college football that year.

Another black-tie dinner was set for the next evening to honor Jason for winning this award. I had not bought a ticket for this dinner, as I did not know if he would win the award. But there I was in New York City, with a tuxedo, so I tracked down the offices of the Heisman Trophy sponsor, the Downtown Athletic Club, and bought a ticket at the last minute.

Arriving at the Heisman dinner, I discovered I had been thrown in with a group of sports reporters at a table near the podium. When I mentioned that I was from Norman, Oklahoma, one of the reporters asked me if I knew Coach Stoops, who was seated at the podium next to Jason White and a previous Heisman winner, the elusive and effusive OU running back Billy Sims. (Billy seemed to be enjoying the evening, occasionally blurting out "Boomer Sooner" for no apparent reason.)

"Yes, Coach Stoops is my next-door neighbor," I replied. The inquiring reporter, who worked for *USA Today*, seemed skeptical. When the formal part of the evening program was over, I approached the podium and asked Coach Stoops if he would come over to my table and say hello to a group of football reporters. He was kind enough to accommodate my request, which seemed to boost my credibility with my skeptical dinner partners.

The third event of my busy weekend in New York City was possibly the most important. While Anne was pursuing her studies in international relations, she was pursued by young men from Italy, Germany, Iran, and India. She ended up with a young man from Norway, Ole Andreassen. Ole was also working toward a PhD in international relations at the SAIS campus in Washington, DC. When she introduced him to me in New York City, he seemed a little stiff and formal, standing at attention with a posture like a Prussian General. I was tempted to tell him, "At ease." But I was sure he must be intelligent and considerate, if Anne liked him.

Ole's hometown of Narvik is a seaport located in far northern Norway, north of the Arctic Circle. His father had been the town mayor for many years, and his mother was a high school principal. In many ways, their small hometowns of Norman and Narvik had more in common with each other than either did with Washington, DC. We joked about whether Anne or Ole came from farther out in the sticks.

Wedding Bells for Anne and Ole

As it turned out, Anne liked Ole a lot. In April 2004, they were married in a small, private ceremony at the Ritz-Carlton hotel in Arlington, Virginia. Ole's cousin, Pastor Bob, presided over their exchange of vows. Emily doubled as Anne's maid of honor and official wedding photographer, while Ole's friend Jaime, who happened to be the grandson of the Queen of the Netherlands, served as his best man. We rode around DC in a rented Hummer limousine big enough to accommodate all ten members of the wedding party, which also included Pastor Bob's wife Binnie, Ole's parents, Od and Eldbjorg, Terry and me. I wanted to imitate the local diplomats by flying a Norwegian flag and an Oklahoma flag on the front fenders of the limo, but this idea was voted down. When we got stuck in the cherry blossom traffic, throngs of gawking tourists stared at our imposing limo, trying to figure out who was inside.

Anne and Ole at Jefferson Memorial

Emily captured the essence of Anne's wedding day in a classic photo of the newlyweds holding hands as they walked through the Jefferson Memorial. Pastor Bob and Binnie, an actress in local theater, were a lot of fun as we toured the nation's capital after the ceremony. As our tour ended, Pastor Bob admitted he had always wanted to be a limousine liberal.

Not long after the wedding, Terry was back home, talking with her Polish hairdresser, who, reaching for a metaphor for someone in high places, declared: "I don't care if he is the grandson of the Queen of Holland."

Terry responded: "I know him!"

Shortly after their wedding, Ole began working for the World Bank in DC. Anne continued working toward her PhD in Middle Eastern Studies, often providing editing assistance to her professor Fouad Ajami, a well-known Middle Eastern writer and commentator during the aftermath of 9–11.

Cracking Up Jordan

Emily and I ventured to my second Michael Jordan Senior Flight School in August 2004. As a bonus to the fantasy camp's basketball playing experience, the campers could bring two items for Jordan to autograph. I brought two large photos that Emily had taken during my one-on-one game against Jordan during my first camp.

"These are from our one-on-one game at last year's camp," I explained as I handed him the photos to sign.

"That was not a game," he protested.

"Well, I beat the point spread," I countered.

Jordan cracked up at my claim. He slid down in his chair and was still laughing when I added: "You were favored by two baskets, and you didn't cover."

As a would-be humorist as well as a would-like-to-have-been hoopster, I got as big a kick out of making Jordan laugh as I did out of scoring on him. (Sure, he wasn't really guarding me. He may have just assumed that his mere presence would be enough to make me miss. But at least I hadn't let his aura defense stop me from nailing a three-pointer.)

At this camp, Coach Krzyzewski drafted me as a shooting guard. Compared to my first camp, I was breathing better, so I pushed myself to make steals, grab rebounds, and sprint out on fast breaks. Unfortunately, all this hustle caught up with me during the third morning of camp. I suffered what may have been a mild stroke, but I played through it. Standing at mid-court, I mistakenly thought my teammate was about to shoot a free throw at the wrong basket. I started to yell at the ref but noticed that no one else had

Giving advice to Coach K

a problem with where he was shooting, so I didn't say anything. After a few more trips up and down the court, a time-out was called, and as I started to go to our bench I noticed there was no bench, just fans, where I was headed. When I turned around and spied our bench on the opposite side of the court, I realized why I had thought that free throw was being shot at the wrong basket. I was disoriented . . . by 180 degrees. I drank some Gatorade and was fine by the next time I got back into the game. I kept playing hard, but I did not shoot well the rest of the camp.

During the last game of camp, I had a chance to talk with Coach K while I was waiting to be put back into the game. I told him I thought he did the right thing by turning down an offer to coach the Lakers and staying at Duke. "It's about knowing who you are," I told him. Not that he had asked. I just volunteered this unsolicited advice in case he was having any second thoughts.

The last event at the camp each year was a luncheon where Jordan handed out various individual and team awards. I told Coach K I was sorry I left my jump shot in Norman. Not wanting to make excuses, I didn't say that my stroke messed up my stroke.

— • — • —

PART FOUR

"Dear Sir or Madam,
Would you read my book?
It took me years to write,
Will you take a look?"

– THE BEATLES

Reading early fictoids to Anne and Ole

CHAPTER SEVENTEEN

ADVENTURES IN
SELF-PUBLISHING

In *the fall of 2004, I noticed* my collection of fictoids was piling up. Not wanting to be one of those self-made men who knocked off work too early, and wanting to show my girls that my stated ambitions to be a writer were not just talk, I decided to self-publish a book of my favorite fictoids. Over the past four years, my concept of fictoids had evolved from the random, abstract, off-the-wall notes I had published at FatBrain.com near the end of the previous century. My new requirements were that a fictoid had to tell a story in one sentence, it had to be funny, and it had to be original. Fictoids were not meant to be historically accurate. They were meant to be hysterically inaccurate. Going for intellectual humor, many fictoids included historical or cultural references that the reader needed to recognize to get the joke. At times, a fictoid idea I thought was fresh turned out to be well done. For example, I had written a fictoid about a country and western band from Indiana called "Hoosier Daddy?" When I Googled the name, I got two million hits. (Although several of my fictoids are not politically correct, I believe people who cannot take a joke are taking themselves too seriously.)

Emily and I opened the Creative Division of Dutcher & Company, Inc., in a rented loft on Main Street in downtown Norman. As I was working on selecting and editing the fictoids to be included in our book, I realized the book would need a cover, and might even benefit from some illustrations. I discovered that *The New Yorker* magazine had a company called CartoonBank.com that arranged for publishers to custom order new illustrations to be drawn by one of their cartoon contributors. The Cartoon Bank provided us with sample work from several cartoonists, and we selected Jack Ziegler, based on his style and sense of humor. We later learned that he was a well-known, veteran cartoonist who had published several books of his cartoons, most recently a drinking book called *Olive or Twist?*

We selected thirty fictoids that we thought would lend themselves to illustrations. Ziegler sent us five versions of a possible book cover and rough sketches for a dozen fictoids. We were excited when we saw his work. It was expensive, yet priceless.

In December 2004, Emily and I visited the offices of *The New Yorker* magazine in New York City for a meeting with Andy Pillsbury, the head of the Cartoon Bank. He showed us the upcoming issue of the magazine. Each page was hung from a line, like laundry before the invention of clothes driers. He also described his process for selecting the cartoons for the magazine from a continuous flood of submissions from freelance cartoonists around the country.

Jack Ziegler sent us his final drawings for our four-color cover and twelve illustrations in January 2005. Emily designed the book jacket and layout for the text, and I selected and edited the final fictoids to be included in the book. One difficulty with self-publishing is that it is hard to tell when you are done. I had a lingering desire to keep tinkering with our project, making little changes here and there. Eventually, we decided it was time to go to press.

For our printers, we had selected Edwards Brothers in Ann Arbor, Michigan. Emily and I flew up to Ann Arbor to approve our book's final proofs before the printing process was triggered. We went out for a pizza with our contact at the printing company, a young woman named Jacqueline DeFrancesco. Although it was mid-March, Ann Arbor was still buried in snow. Jacqueline was growing tired of their long, cold winter and was longing for warmer weather. As she admitted using extra hair spray in the mornings to help advance global warming, she pantomimed spraying her hair, using the same gesture and "psst" sound Terry had used when trying to buy hair spray in Switzerland.

We had 2,500 copies of *Fictoids* printed by Edwards Brothers. We asked them to ship 500 copies to our Norman office and 2,000 to Aero Corporation, a fulfillment company in nearby Saline, Michigan. The plan was to have Aero store the books and fill large orders.

On May 23, 2005, we officially launched the marketing of *Fictoids* with a news release distributed nationally by PR Newswire. The news release began by asking: "What is a fictoid?" It then explained: "According to author Bill Dutcher, a fictoid is a bit of fictional history, telling a story in one sentence. In other words, a fictiod is just a fictional factoid. His new book, *Fictoids: Short Fiction . . . Very Short,* provides a humorous look at cultural history from 1220 BC to 2004 and is available at www.fictoids.com.

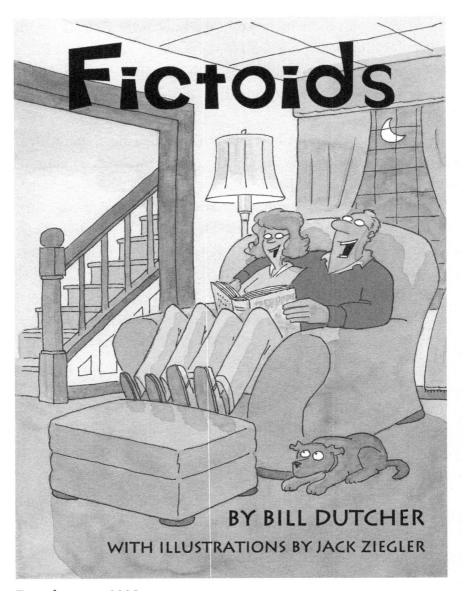

Fictoids cover—2005

"A typical fictoid tells who did what, when, and where," Dutcher explains. "For example, did you know that, after suffering from frequent hangovers, movie star and Las Vegas lounge singer Dean

Martini began an intensive series of acupuncture treatments in 1965, but he had to quit after a dozen sessions, because his friends began to needle him and he could no longer hold his liquor. Of course, you didn't, because it's a fictoid."

The news release added: "Featuring cover art and illustrations by *New Yorker* cartoonist Jack Ziegler, the book includes fictoids about music, movies, plays, books, sports, politics, business, and other topics too random to mention. Its many colorful characters include Sleeping Beauty's sister Lazy Susan, Norwegian film star Harrison Fjord, classical rap artist YoYo MaMa, fashion photographer F. Stop Fitzgerald, sports philosopher Homer Plato, and assistant press secretary Feckless Spinmeister.

"In addition to Dean Martini, the book's illustrations include Leonardo DaVani, who invented both the periodic table and the occasional chair, undefeated shadow boxer Pugnacious Palooka, real estate mogul Donald Trumpet, and Saddam Hussein, playing solitaire in his spider hole.

"Although my book is politically incorrect, none of the humor is off-color or mean-spirited. It's pure fiction and meant to entertain."

Our news release resulted in a favorable book review in the May 29, 2005, issue of *The Oklahoman*, the state's major newspaper. The reviewer, Denny Hall, wrote that there are plenty of fictoids "to be devoured in an Oklahoma City man's funny book . . . which provides a chuckle on almost every page."

In early June, to launch our obviously uneconomic but determined marketing campaign, Emily and I set up a booth at the New York Book Expo, the publishing industry's major annual convention. With me writing the copy and Emily doing the layout and production, we had prepared a ton of promotional material about *Fictoids* to be distributed at the Expo, not to mention a banner for our booth that featured this fictoid: "Literary spam was introduced by Norman E. Mailer in 2002."

As the Expo goers drifted by our booth, I noticed that *Fictoids* seemed to be of more interest to women than to men. I mentioned this to one female visitor and she explained: "That's because most men can't hold two ideas in their head at the same time."

One man who did appreciate *Fictoids* was a book marketer from Australia. We signed a distribution deal with him and shipped him 120 copies to be sold down under.

Our book distributor, Biblio Distribution, arranged for me to sign copies of *Fictoids* during a brief session at one of their booths at the Expo. While I was not exactly overwhelmed by readers seeking signed books, there was a steady flow of people who liked the book well enough to ask me to sign their copy. For a while there, I felt like a real author. Later that summer, we shipped 990 books to Biblio for distribution to books stores around the country.

When we got back to Norman, the local newspaper, *The Norman Transcript*, ran a front-page story about *Fictoids*. This story marked the first time a member of our family had made the front page of the local paper since Emily was featured as a four-year-old angel about twenty-eight years earlier.

That summer, Anne and Ole bought a very tall home on a small, wooded lot in Chevy Chase, Maryland, a historic DC suburb. Surrounded by giant oak trees that could have been planted by George Washington himself, their three-story home featured extremely steep stairs and seemed to be under constant attack by a pesky woodpecker but was otherwise a wonderful place. While Ole's office and Anne's classrooms at SAIS were not far away, their bumper-to-bumper commute to DC proved to be extremely time consuming, and it was not long before they wanted to move back into the city.

— • — • —

CHAPTER EIGHTEEN

LET THE GOOD
TIMES ROLL

To *prepare for my third Jordan camp,* I decided to attend Coach K's fantasy camp at Duke in late July. Modeled after the Jordan camp, the K Academy is also for men over thirty-five, but not quite as expensive. Duke assistant coaches and former star players coach the teams. The K Academy captures the college basketball experience, as compared to the NBA atmosphere at the Jordan camp.

Playing in the venerable Cameron Indoor Stadium, I hit a few shots in the evaluation game and was drafted by a team coached by then Houston Rockets forward Shane Battier and San Antonio Spurs shooting coach Chip Engelland. Chip told me he could tell I was a shooter because I didn't seem excited when I made a basket.

In the championship game, I did manage one career highlight on defense. While I was guarding my man on the right side of the lane, near their basket, an opponent set a solid back pick on me, and my man broke to the opposite wing. By the time I fought around the pick, I was horrified to see my man wide open, about to launch a three-point shot that could have tied the game. In what can only be described as a flash from the past, I ran out to him at twice my normal speed, leaped high in the air, and swatted his shot into the sixth row. A time-out was called, and I had to laugh as I jogged back to our bench for a round of high fives from my teammates. We won the championship, possibly inspired by my blocked shot.

As my team celebrated after the game, Coach K told me I shouldn't have been laughing after blocking that shot. "Act like you've done it before," he said.

"But Coach," I protested, "that was probably just my fourth blocked shot in the past forty years."

"And probably the first in the last thirty-eight," he replied.

Hang Time to Spare

Three weeks later, at my third Jordan camp, I was drafted by Coach K and then Memphis Grizzlies coach Mike Fratello. Even though at sixty-two I was the oldest player there, this camp was by far my best.

A career highlight, or possibly miracle, occurred during an early morning session where campers were playing in three-on-three games with Jordan. The session was being filmed by CBS's *60 Minutes* for an in-depth report Ed Bradley was doing on our host. Jordan kept up a running commentary during the games, apparently for the benefit of the cameras.

After playing one game with Jordan on the other team, I was one of Jordan's teammates in the second game. I was pumped up. (If you can't get excited with Michael Jordan as your teammate in a game being filmed by *60 Minutes*, you may not have a pulse.)

Jordan took the ball at the top of the key and passed it to me on the left wing. I made a quick jab step to my right, faked a return pass to Jordan, then drove past my man along the baseline.

Michael Jordan hand-checks me

Aided by an apparent surge of adrenaline, I elevated to the basket and was shocked to find myself looking at the rim, with hang time to spare. (I had not had such a good look at the rim since college.) I laid the ball on the glass for an easy hoop and heard a murmur from the onlookers, as if they were asking: "Where did that come from?"

We were playing make it, take it, so Jordan got the ball at the top of the key again. Before starting the next play, he paid me my all-time greatest backhanded compliment.

"Don't underestimate my teammates," he called out, loud enough for everyone to hear. "No matter what they look like."

Then he passed me the ball and told me to "hit the winner." I quickly launched a three-pointer that missed. Jordan, not wanting to risk a loss, grabbed the rebound and slam dunked the winner himself.

Each year the campers and coaches received a gift bag when they checked into the camp. The gift bag contained an impressive collection of items endorsed by Michael Jordan. Emily and I had arranged for a copy of *Fictoids* to be included in each gift bag for the campers and coaches at the camp. (I was more interested in who read my book than in how many people bought it.) At breakfast one morning, I met basketball legend Bill Walton. When I introduced myself, he said: "Bill Dutcher . . . the author of *Fictoids*." He added that he hadn't read it yet. For a moment, I was concerned that the subtle humor in my book might be a little over his head. But then I realized that was unlikely, since he was 6' 11" tall.

The games during my third Jordan camp went well for our team, the Heat. We had a pass-first point guard, Carmen Scarpa, who had played at Harvard and did a great job of distributing the ball. When we did screw up, Coach K was there to get us back on track. During a time-out after an ugly series of turnovers, Coach

K told us something like this: "Guys, this is a fantasy camp! Do you screw up in your own fantasies? When you dreamed about playing in this camp, were you dribbling the ball off your foot? I don't think so. But, hey, it's your fantasy."

His remarks seemed to help us regain our composure. We were undefeated as we headed into the championship tournament on the last day of camp.

In the first game of the tournament, I shot four for four, all mid-range jumpers on nice assists from my teammates. In the second game, I was one for one and hadn't hit the rim all morning. Going into the championship game, I felt like I had finally broken the code.

Taking One for the Team

The championship game matched us against the Nuggets, a team coached by NBA coaches Doc Rivers and Doug Moe. We were 6 and 0 and the number-one seed. They were 5 and 1 and the number-two seed. With Bill Walton doing sideline interviews and Michael Jordan watching, the atmosphere was charged with excitement.

With two steals in the first two minutes, I got off to a good start on defense. (I wasn't that quick, just quicker than I looked.) Normally, I don't take charges, a wise policy that has no doubt prolonged my career. But in this championship game, playing for coaches Fratello and Krzyzewski, I made an exception. When I saw an opponent driving to the hoop, I stepped in front of him, my arms raised like I was trying to surrender. He hit me surprisingly hard and knocked me halfway across the paint. One teammate helped me up while another gave the charge signal. But we didn't get the call. Even though it was clearly a charge, the outside ref ruled that my teammate had given his man a little extra shove in the back as he drove toward me. This foul preceded the charge and explained why the charger was moving so fast when he hit me.

Viewing this play on the camp highlight CD a few months later, I could see that my teammate had a hand on the charger's back, but it wasn't clear if he had shoved him into me. The controversial play set off a furor among the coaches, described by announcer Tom Kelly as follows.

"You think these coaches aren't battling for this basketball game? Doc Rivers is up. Doug Moe is up after the officials. And they are going to give the ball out of bounds to the Nuggets. Mike Fratello is up and screaming. Don't think these coaches don't want to win it."

The CD also had an unexpected comment by Kelly as we were setting up an out-of-bounds play before halftime: "Dutcher is an outstanding outside shooter. I've watched more than one of these games and he had a nice touch."

Unfortunately, I didn't live up to his comment in the second half. Trailing by seven points with one minute left, I fired up three much needed shots, but hit only one. We lost the game, costing Coach K his fourth Jordan championship. At least I had achieved one of my ongoing fantasy camp goals: playing when the coaches can substitute freely and the game is on the line.

The camera does not lie. What I called my three-point jumpers look a lot more like a set shot on video. I'm not saying I was tired from playing three games in one morning, but after the awards luncheon, I struggled back to my suite at the Mirage, rescheduled my flight home, and slept for five hours.

An Ill Wind

A few days after I made it back to Oklahoma from Las Vegas, Hurricane Katrina struck the Gulf Coast. This powerful and deadly storm flooded New Orleans and wreaked havoc on the entire coastal area. Katrina impacted my life in two ways, both positive.

The storm damaged the natural gas producing wells and infra-structure in the Gulf area. AMI had a natural gas futures hedge in place that was designed to protect us from increases in transportation costs. This "basis" hedge was based on the difference between the price we received for natural gas delivered to ANR pipeline in Oklahoma and the price of natural gas at Henry Hub, a nexus of natural gas pipeline interconnections near New Orleans. The hurricane caused natural gas prices at Henry Hub to spike to $8 per mmbtu, but it did not impact the delivered price to ANR in Oklahoma. The result was a $2 million hedging gain for AMI, a true windfall.

The second benefit came when New Orleans's NBA basketball team, the Hornets, was flooded out of their home arena. With the NBA season only a few weeks away, they were forced to re-locate for the 2005–2006 season, and decided to move to Oklahoma City.

Oklahoma basketball fans immediately embraced the Hornets team, which was led by NBA 2006 Rookie of the Year Chris Paul, power forward David West, and former Oklahoma State star Desmond Mason. I bought two season tickets, located at mid-court about halfway up the stands. As an NBA fan since the late 1950s, I was excited to have an NBA team in Oklahoma City, even if their stay was only temporary.

Radio Tour

As part of our marketing campaign for *Fictoids*, a New York City public relations firm called Planned Television Arts arranged for a "Morning Drive Radio Tour" on December 6, 2005. The firm booked me for twenty radio interviews on big city stations scattered all over the country, from 6 am to 11:30 am, with an interview every fifteen minutes. I had never been interviewed on the radio before, and I am not an early morning person, so I was a little nervous on the first interview on a Baltimore station, but it seemed to go well. Before long, I was able to relax and enjoy the other nineteen interviews that morning.

Since most of my fictoids were the right length for sound bites, they fit the radio interview format perfectly. Although the interviews had no measurable impact on my book sales, they at least seemed to entertain the radio hosts and their audiences.

Finding the New York public relations firm too expensive, we began taking out our own ads in a publication called the *Radio-TV Interview Report*. Our ads included a few fictoids as examples and quoted some comments from the media. For example, Ron Thulin of KAHL radio in San Antonio, Texas, exclaimed: "It cracked me up. I thought it was hysterical." The ads led to a steady flow of radio interview requests, but no invitations to appear on television. I ended up doing a total of sixty-six radio interviews as part of our marketing efforts.

Unlike the radio interviews, an appearance on *Flash Point*, an Oklahoma City television Sunday morning political talk show, did trigger a spurt of book sales locally. Our discussion mentioned several fictoids with political implications, including Woody Allen's satire about an inexplicably seductive White House intern, "Devil with the Blue Dress On." President Bush's investigation of global warming, known as "Operation: Who Baked Alaska?" also came up.

Burns Hargis, one of the show's hosts, found my little book "Hilarious!" Soon after my appearance on his show, Burns was named President of Oklahoma State University and told me he kept a copy of *Fictoids* on his desk. Luckily, I had refrained from including any Aggie jokes in my book.

Hoping to ride on the name recognition of *Fictoids* illustrator Jack Zeigler, whose cartoons had been appearing in *The New Yorker* for decades, we placed a one-third page ad for *Fictoids* in the magazine's issue dated December 12, 2005. This ad included this fictoid:

"Due to the actions of his predecessor, Henry the Ninth couldn't get a date."

Our ad in the following week's issue of *The New Yorker* featured some of our favorite fictitious characters. Then we splurged on a half-page ad in the magazine's holiday issue dated December 26, 2005 and January 2, 2006. This ad, entitled "Death of a Salesman?" included one of our longer fictoids: "In 1946, Cincinnati salesman Wiley Lomann tried to fake his own death by taking an overdose of placebos so that his family could collect on his life insurance, but the coroner noticed he was still breathing and ruled his ruse a pseudocide."

Although these ads were expensive, they did appear to generate some book sales. By December 26, 2005, my Amazon author ranking had reached its peak at number 3,802. When you consider that hundreds of thousands of new books come out every year, *Fictoids* had at least achieved flash-in-the-pan status. Our first print run of 2,500 books seemed to have sold out. In a surge of misplaced optimism, we had an additional 5,000 copies printed, just as a tailspin in new sales ensued.

Real Estate Ventures

To diversify my investments, while staying invested in real things, I started a real estate venture called William Dutcher Real Estate, LLC. My concept was to buy nice homes in good neighborhoods, fix them up, then rent them to executives or professors expecting to be in Norman for a relatively short period of time. I seemed to always be expecting a wave of inflation right around the corner, so I wanted quality homes that would appreciate against the declining value of the dollar. Even when inflation seems relatively benign, its cumulative effect builds up over time. (A 1960 dollar had the purchasing power of $8.74 in 2020 dollars.) Near the end of the year, my new company made its first investment, a three-bedroom, ranch-style home in west Norman for $185,000.

Emily went into the real estate business that year as well. AMI was doing well enough to buy back $1,000,000 worth of its shares from each of its five minority shareholders. Emily used part of her proceeds from the stock sale to buy some land near the OU campus, tear down an old house that was falling apart, and build two nice homes designed to be rented to OU students. In a meeting with some Bank of Oklahoma investment managers, I noted that Emily and the other minority shareholders had each invested $25 for their shares in AMI in 1990.

"I'm going to write a book about it," Emily joked.

Emily and I flew to San Diego to check out a possible investment in a large residential housing development in an outlying suburb. While touring an area where the developer planned to build several multi-million-dollar homes, we noticed a large apartment complex going up as well. He explained that the apartments were part of an area set aside for low income housing and would cost $340,000 each. I told him that in Oklahoma $340,000 would buy a very nice home with 3,400 square feet.

OKC Hornets Seek Investors

The NBA's 2005–2006 season ended with the transplanted Oklahoma City Hornets team failing to make the playoffs. They finished their season with a record of thirty-eight wins and forty-four losses, placing tenth in the fifteen-team Western Division. Despite their losing record, the team played its Oklahoma City home games in an arena full of loud, enthusiastic fans, getting their first glimpse of big-time basketball.

As the Hornets wrapped up their first season in Oklahoma City, I was contacted by an investment banker from SG Americas Securities, a New York City branch of the French investment banking firm Societe Generale. He was offering limited partnership interests in the New Orleans Hornets NBA Limited Partnership, which was owned by a colorful, controversial entrepreneur named George Shinn.

In a meeting with the Hornets' investment bankers, I admitted that my inner basketball player was excited about the idea of owning an interest in an NBA team, but I warned that my inner businessman was concerned about the team's financial outlook. We agreed that based on the team's warm reception in Oklahoma City, it would be more valuable here than in New Orleans. However, I had heard that the NBA did not want to appear to be abandoning New Orleans in their hour of need, so they wanted the Hornets to return as soon as possible. I also felt the team's excessive debt would still be a problem, which could prevent cash distributions to the limited partners. I asked what the outlook was for a return on investment to the investors.

In a moment of candor, one of the bankers replied, "It's more like return on ego."

As the meeting concluded, they asked what level of investment I might consider making. I told them somewhere in the $3 million to $5 million range, but only if the team moved to Oklahoma City permanently. If nothing else, the meeting got me on their list of potential investors, which turned out to be a good list to be on.

At the time of this meeting, I was aware that a group of wealthy Oklahoma City businessmen, led by Clay Bennett, was negotiating with Mr. Shinn about the possibility of moving the Hornets to Oklahoma City. However, a deal was never reached, as each party wanted control of the franchise. The Oklahoma City group wanted to buy at least a 51-percent interest, while Mr. Shinn would only agree to sell up to 49 percent.

Shortly after the investment meeting, Emily and I attended a Top Hats and High Tops Gala, hosted by The George Shinn Foundation to raise money for its Hoops for Homes charity, which was helping the homeless victims of Hurricane Katrina. We won an auction by making a $17,000 donation to the charity for a trip with the Hornets team to two road games during the 2006–2007 season.

Geezer Hoops

In May 2006, Garry Munson invited me to join his Sag Harbor Whalers to play in the sixty to sixty-five age bracket of the Masters Basketball Tournament in Coral Gables, Florida. Heading to the tournament, I thought the competition in my age group would be easy since I had been playing against men as young as thirty-five at my fantasy camps. As it turned out, the competition was all I could handle. Conditioning and basketball experience proved to be more important than age in determining the level of competition. Several of the Masters tournament teams consisted of players who had been playing together for decades, advancing through the age groups in five-year increments, and staying in good basketball shape over the years. In addition, the games were played on much smaller courts, eliminating a lot of unnecessary running. Most of the players on the Whalers were former college players, including

Flynn Robinson, a 1970 NBA All Star who played with Jerry West for the Los Angeles Lakers during their spectacular 1972 championship season. Two years older than me, Flynn arrived for our first game at the Masters wearing a Lakers jersey and carrying a jump rope to warm up with. In one game, we played a team led by Jim Barnett, a former Boston Celtic forward and longtime broadcaster for the Golden State Warriors.

In our third game of the tournament, I drove to the baseline and, as I planted my right foot to go up for a turning jump shot, heard a popping sound coming from my right knee. A trainer at the tournament examined my knee and said it was most likely just a bad sprain. But I was through playing in the tournament. The Whalers went on without me to win the national championship in the sixty to sixty-five-year-old age bracket, and Garry was kind enough to send me a championship trophy.

Moving On Up

After flying from Florida to Washington, DC, I limped around like a lame duck but managed to attend Ole's graduation ceremony as he received his PhD in international relations from SAIS. Ole was working for the World Bank, while Anne continued pursuing her PhD in Middle Eastern studies.

That summer, Anne and Ole decided to sell their home in Chevy Chase and move to downtown DC. Realizing they would need some financial support to live in the city, I went house hunting with them as they toured various apartments, condos, and co-ops. We finally decided to buy a four-bedroom penthouse at The Residences at the Ritz-Carlton, which we viewed as an excellent joint investment, not to mention a nice place to live. Anne was pregnant as they moved in. Unfortunately, her pregnancy required a long period of bed rest that fall and winter. Fortunately, she could order room service from the Ritz-Carlton hotel kitchen.

Standing in for Ole, I took Anne to a seminar for expecting couples. As the program was ending, I told the group about the time six-month old Anne was standing up in her highchair and took a nosedive. When I caught her by the ankle, her head was about six inches above the kitchen floor. So, mamas, don't let your babies stand up in their highchairs (or grow up to be cowboys.)

Torn ACL Ends Fifth Comeback

After returning home to Norman, I had an MRI exam on my right knee and was surprised to learn that I had completely severed the anterior cruciate ligament. At sixty-three, I felt I was too old for major knee surgery, so I decided to just put my hoops career on hold while I gradually rehabilitated my injured knee through strength training. Alas, the injury ended my fifth comeback, but not my love of basketball. For the next two years, my hoops were limited to playing one-on-none in our driveway.

The Hornets, still recruiting me as a potential limited partner, invited me to observe their team's coaches and management make their selections during the 2006 NBA draft night. With their first-round draft pick, they hoped to select Hilton Armstrong, a 6' 10" center from Connecticut. The tension in the Hornet's draft room built as their number twelve pick approached. When their turn arrived with Hilton still available, the Hornets' drafters celebrated as they made him their pick.

That July, we took out a full-page ad for *Fictoids* in *The Weekly Standard*, a conservative political magazine. Our ad included seven fictoids, including: "Michael Moroni, a scruffy screedwriter and prolific producer of political propaganda films, became the toast of both coasts in 2004 as the far left's leading filmflam artist." Another fictoid in the ad mentioned ". . . a 1992 diagnosis that real estate mogul Donald Trumpet was suffering from an Edifice Complex that led to frequent overbuilding." The ads did not generate any sales for the book, which made me wonder if conservatives had lost their sense of humor.

My favorite review of *Fictoids* appeared that August on a Canadian website called the Serious Comedy site, which offers "reviews for the serious comedy fan."

"*Fictoids* is one of those very rare self-published books that not only looks like it was released by a major publisher but definitely should have been released by a major publisher," the review noted. They cited an example of the "very funny fake factoids hysterian Dutcher has come up with": "Egyptian Pharaoh Amir Ziplock invented self-storage in 850 BC, then marketed his invention through a clever pyramid scheme."

Determined to keep up my efforts to market *Fictoids*, I attended a National Publicity Summit in New York City in September. The three-day event, in the format of literary speed dating, gave a collection of struggling writers and self-publishers, seeking publicity for their stories and books, a chance to "pitch" their projects to skeptical representatives of major media organizations, literary agents, and freelance writers.

My first pitch was made to a producer of the *Regis & Kelly* daytime talk show. I described *Fictoids* as fictional factoids that told a story in one sentence. I added that my book often presented intellectual humor, requiring the reader to catch the cultural reference in order to get the joke. Her response was a sweeping insult to the housewives of America: "We wouldn't want to do anything that would make our viewers think."

I also made a pitch to two producers of a religious television program. Not wanting them to think *Fictoids* would be offensive to their viewers, I told them that the most risqué fictoid in the book was about a hooker in Phoenix who got hooked on phonics and ended up as a libertarian librarian in Las Vegas. They laughed but did not invite me to appear on their show.

My pitch to a producer from CNBC failed to gain me a slot on their channel to talk about business humor, even though I mentioned: "When Pepe Pecadillo, a Peruvian importer, opened Pandora's Boxers in 1997 to compete with Victoria's Secret in an upscale shopping mall in suburban Houston, his shop featured Arabian nighties, which were naughty, and Freudian slips, which were very revealing."

Emily attended a National Geographic photography workshop in Tuscany, Italy, that summer. She got up at the crack of dawn to capture a photo of a classic villa, framed by the morning mist and nestled on a hillside among rows of juniper trees. Printed on a large canvas, the photo hangs in our home and looks like a painting.

Prior to the start of the 2006/2007 season, highly leveraged Hornets owner George Shinn doubled down on his investment in the team by signing shooting guard Peja Stojakovic and center Tyson Chandler to contracts that added nearly $20 million per year to their payroll. My inner basketball player thought strengthening the team was a great move, but my inner businessman thought it was financially reckless. Either way, Mr. Shinn looked to me like the biggest New Orleans river boat gambler since the 1958–59 television character Yancy Derringer.

On October 31, 2006, the Professional Basketball Club LLC, an Oklahoma City group headed by Mr. Bennett, purchased the Seattle Supersonics and agreed to leave the team in Seattle, contingent upon the construction of a new arena for the team. However, Mr. Shinn continued to pursue other Oklahoma City investors, hoping to move his Hornets team to higher ground.

Travelling with the Hornets

Still being recruited as potential Hornets investors, Emily and I were invited to accompany the team on a two-game road trip to the Pacific Northwest. Departing in the late afternoon on Christmas Day, we entered the team's plane, which seemed to be about the size of a commercial 727. Hornets coach Bryon Scott, who had been Magic Johnson's running mate at guard on the championship Los Angeles Lakers teams of the 1980s, sat near the front with the other coaches. Each player had his own seat, with one on each side of the aisle. Their seats were about the size of a barber's chair, allowing them to stretch out their long frames and sleep in comfort. Emily and I made our way to the back of the plane, where we were seated in normal airline seats among the team managers, trainers, and broadcasters.

The next evening, we watched the Hornets play the Sonics, then flew with the team on a late-night hop to Portland. After an evening game versus Portland, we were back on the plane by 10:30 pm and made it to Oklahoma City around 3:30 am. I arrived home exhausted, and I hadn't played two basketball games. It seemed to me that for an NBA rookie, adjusting to the constant travel must be as difficult as adjusting to the higher level of competition.

In February 2007, Anne gave birth to our first granddaughter, Hanna Louise Andreassen. As we brought her back to our Ritz-Carlton penthouse, I joked with her parents about how we could characterize her humble beginnings: "She was born during a snowstorm in inner-city DC. Her father was an immigrant from a remote Norwegian village so far north that he had to travel south to arrive at the Arctic Circle. Her mother was a college student from a small Oklahoma town deep in the heart of fly-over country."

Emily and I took a second two-game road trip with the Hornets team in March. We had won the trip at a Hornets charity auction at the end of their first season in Oklahoma City. The first game was in Phoenix. We were able to watch the team's game day shoot-around and walk-through in the Suns' arena, and to put up a few shots of our own after the team left the court. In Utah, on the second night of back-to-back games, we were interviewed at halftime by a Hornets' television reporter. He embarrassed me a little by reporting how much we had paid for the trip, implying that we were star-struck NBA fans. I replied that, yes, we love NBA basketball and are enjoying our trip, but the money was for a donation to Hurricane Katrina victims.

A Wildcat Goes Wildcatting

In May 2007, oil and gas prices were high, and buying proven reserves was getting very expensive. AMI was flush with cash and had lots of "dry powder" available in our bank loan's borrowing base. Rather than continuing our patient, brick-at-a-time program of buying proven reserves, I felt an itch to do something bolder.

For me, the romance in the oil and gas business was in exploring for new deposits of oil and gas. The hunt could bring the highest rewards when successful, and the risk taking required a bit of devil-may-care macho. (Hefner liked to refer to a GHK well that reached a depth of 31,441 feet in 1983 as: "Man's deepest penetration of the earth.") Advances in three-dimensional seismic had improved the industry's ability to identify structural traps that could contain oil and gas, thus reducing the risk of drilling dry holes. But drilling wells four miles beneath the surface still presented technological challenges due to the extremely high temperatures and pressures encountered at great depth. At an average cost of $9.6 million per completed well, deep drilling remained a very risky business.

Given how much effort I had thrown into lobbying for deep gas deregulation in 1977 and 1978, I felt like diving into an Anadarko Basin deep drilling program would be putting my money where my mouth had been. Participating in a successful exploration program might even fulfill my destiny. Maybe it was meant to be.

Or maybe not. AMI plunged into a high-risk natural gas exploration program in Caddo County, Oklahoma, taking 20 percent of our group's working interests, alongside Marathon Oil and two other Oklahoma independents. AMI participated in drilling fifteen exploration wells over a three-year period. Each well was drilled around four miles deep, searching for natural gas from the Springer formation. Several of these wells came on with high production rates at first but quickly depleted. Others experienced mechanical problems during drilling and in their completion attempts. To make a deep story short, we lost more than $10 million on this exploration program, enough to cure me of seeking future thrills in exploratory drilling. I made a note to myself: "Don't factor in your imagined 'destiny' in making business decisions."

The Hornets returned to New Orleans for the 2007–2008 season, so I withdrew my name as a potential investor in that franchise. I was off the hook, much to the relief of my inner businessman and the disappointment of my inner hoopster. (In December 2010, the NBA purchased the Hornets as Mr. Shinn was not in a financial position to continue owning the team.)

In September 2007, the Greater Oklahoma City Chamber of Commerce included Anadarko Minerals on its Metro 50 list as one of the area's fifty fasting growing privately owned businesses. The award was based on annual revenue growth between 2004 and 2006, a period when increasing production and rising natural gas prices boosted AMI's annual revenues from $24 million to $43 million. During that time, AMI built its oil and gas reserves by investing more than $22 million in drilling seventy-eight oil and gas wells, and more than $20 million to acquire producing properties. I accepted this honor at an awards dinner at the Cox Convention Center but did not have to give a speech. Not wanting to attract competition, AMI seldom sought or received any publicity. It may have seemed to the Oklahoma City business community that we popped up out of nowhere. Out of the fifty fastest growing companies being honored, we ranked fourth, alphabetically.

Emily Goes Around the World in Twenty-two Days

In late October 2007, Emily joined a group of ninety travel enthusiasts for a trip around the world with National Geographic Expeditions. Travelling by chartered jet, their trip covered eleven countries in twenty-two days. As an aspiring photographer, she found endless photo ops as she clicked away alongside some National Geographic professional photographers.

When she returned home, she put together a book featuring her favorite photos from this trip, including this summary:

"Each day somehow managed to top the last, which doesn't seem remotely possible when you consider everything we saw: Machu Picchu in Peru; the Moai Statues at Easter Island; a man-made rainforest in Australia; Angkor Wat in Cambodia; the pandas in Chengdu, China; an orphanage in the Potala Palace in Lhasa, Tibet; the Taj Mahal in India; the wild assortment of animals in the Serengeti Plains; the face of King Tut in Luxor, Egypt; and finally, a Berber Village (via mule) in the Atlas Mountains of Morocco.

"But in the end, each place had its own uniqueness, so that when I try to pick my favorite, it's not an easy task. Machu Picchu was calming; the rainforest challenged me to think environmentally; Tibet raised questions of spirituality; in India, somehow the feelings of happiness of the people seem to prevail over the images of poverty that we witnessed throughout the city; the Serengeti Plains had a nice combination of peacefulness and excitement; and what a historical treasure Egypt was."

She concluded that this experience had changed her life forever.

Ole took Hanna to see a pediatrician for a health check-up that fall. During a discussion about development of her motor skills, the doctor asked if Hanna could stack up three blocks. At that point, Hanna, who was seated on Ole's lap, reached into his coat pocket, pulled out his cell phone, and started playing a Pippi Longstocking video. The doctor observed this behavior and said, "I guess we don't need to worry about the blocks."

Anne, Ole, and Hanna moved to Norman in November 2007. Ole joined Dutcher & Company as our chief financial officer. Anne had completed the course work required for her PhD but put her dissertation on hold to focus on motherhood. The following summer, Hanna, only eighteen months old, made her first trip to Norway to visit her Norwegian grandparents. Anne and Ole had decided to raise her not only to be bilingual, but also to be bicultural. The Andreassens began to summer in Norway, becoming the only people I knew who used "summer" as a verb. Hanna began compiling frequent flyer miles at an early age.

— · — · —

CHAPTER NINETEEN

NO RETIREMENT
FOR ME

Turning sixty-five in January 2008, I had no thoughts about retirement. By then, I had established that working for myself was the only job that worked for me. My business was perking along, much better than expected, and I saw no reason to slow down. I felt I was on a sustainable pace, and that my business and basketball careers would continue to support each other.

In April, Emily met Russ Kaplan, a Norman man who gave her a ride home from the EuroSport automobile shop where he was working. They began dating in May. Russ had worked as a business auditor for General Electric before moving on to the real estate business, but his main interests seemed to be all things automotive. Maybe Emily had been looking for Mr. Goodwrench all along.

My Sixth Comeback

As I headed for my second K Academy at Duke in early June 2008, I was feeling a mixture of low expectations and dread. I feared that at this camp, Father Time wouldn't be tugging on my jersey, he'd be riding on my back. I knew that I would be playing with a severed ACL in my right knee, a tear in my left thigh muscle, and a broken index finger on my shooting hand. I also knew that at my age, you play hurt or you don't play at all. On the other hand, I figured I could go at half speed and no one would notice.

My best moment at the camp came during draft night ceremonies, which mimic the televised NBA draft. The coaches announce their teams, and as each player's name is called, he walks up on the stage and receives a Duke hat from his coach. If the players have been to the camp before, video highlights of their best plays are shown on a big screen as they approach the stage. As I ambled up to the stage, my coach, Quinn Snyder, a former Duke player (now coaching the Utah Jazz) announced to the campers he had picked me on a tip from Coach K that I was a shooter. At that point, Coach K called out from the head table: "He's the Richard Hamilton of Oklahoma." As I walked back to my table, I told Coach K, "Thanks . . . but that's way too much pressure."

Unfortunately, with my right knee not back to full strength, I turned in a lackluster performance. Rounding corners and making other non-basketball-like moves, I probably insulted both Oklahoma basketball and NBA All Star Richard Hamilton. After one game, I told Coach K that he might need to have someone sweep the court because I had left a trail of rust wherever I went.

Crude oil prices peaked at $143.44 per barrel in July 2008. Two months later, Lehman Brothers, the nation's fourth largest investment bank, filed for bankruptcy, an early failure triggered by the subprime mortgage crisis. By December, the oil price had plunged to $53.92 per barrel, and the value of my diversified portfolio of non-oil stocks had crashed as well. During this period, natural gas prices fell from $11.09 per mmbtu in July 2008 to $5.82 per mmbtu in December 2008. Anadarko Minerals felt the financial shock waves from this collapse in prices. Fortunately, due to the high natural gas prices that had prevailed from 2003 through 2008, we were in a strong enough financial position to view the fall in oil and gas prices as a buying opportunity.

On August 22nd, Emily and Russ got engaged and bought a home on Chukkar Court, a few blocks away from us in the Brookhaven neighborhood. The next day, Emily and I headed for my fourth Michael Jordan Senior Flight School.

During the first evening of camp, while Emily and I posed for our photo-op with Michael Jordan, I told him, "We were almost next-door neighbors." He seemed surprised by this news. I explained that we had recently bought a penthouse at The Residences at the Ritz-Carlton in Washington, DC, and that our place shared a common wall with the unit he had lived in while playing with the Washington Wizards. Small world, almost.

Since Coach K was in China coaching the Olympic team, I knew I would be playing for someone else at this year's camp. I was drafted by the Nuggets, coached by Maryland coach Gary Williams and Michigan State coach Tom Izzo.

This Jordan camp offered an evening poker tournament for players and coaches, as an additional entertainment feature. Normally, I am not a poker player, but this sounded like fun, so I signed up. After eight hours on the basketball court, I was playing Texas Hold'em with several other players and Jim Boeheim, the Syracuse coach, just back from assisting Coach K in the Beijing Olympics. I was gradually losing my stack of poker chips when both of my hamstrings suddenly knotted up. Instinctively, I pushed my chair back from the table to try to straighten out my legs. But my chair was on rollers, so I went rolling back fast and was artfully dodged by a waiter carrying a tray full of drinks.

My hamstrings seemed okay when I kept my legs straight, but this left me pushed back from the table, as if I were trying to sneak a peek at the other players' cards. Coach Boeheim was sitting across from me, and I told him, "Don't worry . . . I can play hurt." He seemed too jet-lagged to respond. I soon ran out of chips, so I had to drop out of the poker game.

P. J. Carlesimo, who would soon be moving from Seattle to Oklahoma City as the head coach of the Thunder, had been watching the poker game. I told him that, strangely enough, I had experienced the exact same hamstring problem in late August 1960. I was playing poker with some of my football teammates one evening, after two football practices that day, when both hamstrings knotted up and sent me rolling on the floor in pain.

"What is it about poker, late August, and cramping hamstrings?" I asked.

"If it only happens once every forty-eight years, I wouldn't worry about it," PJ advised.

Led by Coach Carlesimo, the Thunder opened their first NBA season in Oklahoma City in October 2008. As an NBA fan since the mid-1950s, I was excited to have an "in" with our new NBA team. Unfortunately, the team limped out of the gate with a one win, twelve loss record, and my fantasy camp friend PJ was quickly replaced by Scott Brooks. That team included a tall, skinny, sharp-shooting, second-year forward, Kevin Durant, who had torched my Sooners while playing his one-and-done year as a Texas freshman. They also had a point guard from UCLA, Russell Westbrook, whose struggles as a rookie made me fear he might not be NBA material.

The Chair Launch at Cubi Point

During the presidential race that fall, Terry and I gave Senator John McCain's campaign a donation large enough to get me a chance to meet the candidate at a crowded Oklahoma City event. I told him I had been in the Navy at Subic Bay during the time he was flying jets off of carriers in the South China Sea, and I jokingly asked him if he had ever done the chair launch at the Cubi Point Naval Air Station Officers Club. He gave me an expression that implied "Yes, but don't mention it," then thanked me for my service. I thought it was ironic that he had spent his time in the Navy flying dangerous missions as a fighter pilot and surviving brutal treatment as a prisoner of war in North Vietnam, while I spent my Navy years mishandling press relations and playing basketball, yet he was thanking me for my service. Later, during a photo-op with the candidate and his wife, he told her: "Bill, here, served in the Navy." I was surprised he remembered that after meeting hundreds of people that day. My question about the chair launch at the Cubi Point Officers Club must have gotten his attention.

Another donation we made during the 2008 Presidential race got me invited to a quick photo-op with President Bush. I knew the drill. I would have about 30 seconds to say something to the president while a photographer snapped our picture. I thanked him for keeping the country safe from terrorism after 9–11.

" 'preciate it," he responded in his true Texan vernacular. Luckily, he had not read *Fictoids*, where I joked that he was worried that continental drift might bring the country too close to Europe.

Joining the Board of Elgin Energy

An important phone call from Washington, DC, came from my friend and former Bartlesville Wildcat teammate Bob Woody that fall. As a DC attorney, Bob had represented and lobbied for GHK and several other independent oil and gas producers. But I never knew he wanted to be an oilman himself until this call. He told me he had put together an investor group called Elgin Capital Partners, LP, and that they were looking at their first deal. They were considering investing in two Denver affiliated companies, MHA Petroleum Consultants and Bayswater Exploration & Production. He sent me some information on their operations and asked for my opinion of them. After looking over their material, I reported back to Bob that the two companies looked awfully small, by oil and gas industry standards, but that their management looked professional and experienced.

Near the end of the year, the Dow Jones Industrial Average had lost about a third of its value, and my personal investments in the stock market, a diversified portfolio being professionally managed by the Bank of Oklahoma's market experts, had suffered a similar fate. I decided to take my losses and get out of the stock market. Instead, I made a small investment in Elgin Capital Partners, whose operating subsidiary, Elgin Energy, had acquired controlling interests in the two Denver companies that Bob had asked me to comment on. Based on my experience in gradually converting an oil and gas consulting company into an exploration and production company, Bob asked me to join the Elgin Energy Board of Directors, and I accepted.

Elgin Energy's first board meeting was held in February 2009, in the Denver offices of Bayswater. The nine-member board included five from Elgin Capital, including me, and four from the Denver companies. The board was an impressive collection of men with extensive experience in politics, finance, management, geology, and petroleum engineering.

Pastor Bob Performs Another Ceremony

In March 2009, Emily and her fiancé Russ Kaplan were married in the backyard of their new home on Chukkar Court. Emily looked her usual beautiful and happy self as I walked her across the lawn. Pastor Bob performed the ceremony, as he had done for Anne and Ole five years earlier. Russ, a home builder while living in Virginia, joined Emily, Terry, and me in managing Dutcher Investment Properties, which we had formed by merging Emily's and our real estate holdings.

Escorting Emily during her backyard wedding

Playing in a pick-up game at the YMCA in May, a few weeks before my third Duke camp, I managed to get hit in my left eye by an errant pass. Although I shook it off and kept playing at the time, a few days later I noticed that the vision in my left eye was blurred, and I ended up having surgery for a small tear in the retina, a week before camp. The doctor cleared me to go to the camp and play. I may have failed to mention I was still seeing spots in my left eye, especially in bright lights.

Coached by Duke legend Christian Laettner, our team won its opening game, as I hit three out of four shots. After the game, Coach Krzyzewski told me I was moving much better than last year. I thanked him, amazed that he would notice, since all he had done since last year was coach the US Olympic team to victory in China and coach Duke through another season. I was still seeing spots but tried to ignore them. Coach Laettner became the first coach ever to tell me to shoot more.

Hanna, an aspiring ballerina at an early age

During one of the camp's evening receptions, I asked Coach K if he had read the Chip Hilton sports stories as a kid. He said he had read them all and was saving a set of the books to give to his grandson. I told him that, having grown up reading how Chip often led his teams to victory, I always expected to win. (I later learned that former Indiana and Olympic coach Bobby Knight and OU coach Lon Kruger, not to mention fantasy camp legend Garry Munson, had also read Chip Hilton sports stories in their youth. Maybe we should start a book club.)

In the aftermath of the nation's financial crisis, Michael Jordan cancelled his August 2009 Senior Flight School, explaining that the cancellation was for economic reasons: "Your economic reasons, not mine."

That fall, Hanna was still complying innocently with my request that she should call me "Grandfather Dutcher, Sir." (I had jokingly told her parents that she needed to show some respect for the older generation.) She once asked:

"Grandfather Dutcher, Sir, would you like to play some *Candy Land* with me?" How could I have resisted that? (As the years went by, she began calling me "Dutcher, Sir," and eventually, just my preferred nickname, "Dutch.")

— • — • —

CHAPTER TWENTY

FINDING SUCCESS
IN THE EAGLE FORD SHALE

D*espite the ongoing financial crisis,* opportunity knocked in the oil patch. Mack Ames, our vice president and top landman, told me about an opportunity to buy a large block of oil and gas leases, covering 5,000 acres in a huge ranch in McMullen County, located in a sparsely populated, desert area in far Southwest Texas. The acreage was prospective for the Eagle Ford shale formation, and was located within an area where EOG, a large independent producer, was buying three-year leases for $500 per acre. I was aware of some successful natural gas discoveries in the Eagle Ford southwest of this area. I also knew that leases in the Haynesville shale, a prolific natural gas producing area in Northeast Texas and Southwest Louisiana, had recently sold for as much as $20,000 per acre. In addition, I realized buying leases on 5,000 acres in one block was a rare opportunity. Putting together that much acreage in Oklahoma, which was homesteaded on 160-acre tracts in the late 1800s, might require buying leases from more than one hundred mineral owners. Finally, since the industry was at a near standstill due to the national financial crisis, there was not much going on in the market for producing oil and gas properties. Importantly, I also knew that Chesapeake had not entered the Eagle Ford area yet, but if they did, they would barge in aggressively and likely bid up the lease prices. Based on these bits of information, I told Mack to follow up on this opportunity. It might seem that I had decided to pursue this lease acquisition without much planning or analysis, but if I had taken a more studied approach the window of opportunity could have been slammed shut quickly.

Mack learned that the rancher was asking $550 per acre for three-year leases. EOG would not pay this amount since their other leases in this area included favored nation clauses, which would have required them to increase their payments on their existing leases in this area by $50 per acre.

The landman who brought Mack the deal was a longtime friend of his. During the mid-1980s bust, when the chips were down in oil and gas, they had gone into another chip business together. Unfortunately, instead of venturing into computer chips, they had gone into potato chips, and when this did not work out, found their way back into the oil and gas industry.

Anadarko Minerals closed on this lease purchase quickly, paying the $550 per acre and carving out a small overriding royalty interest for Mack's friend for bringing us the deal. During the next six months, we acquired leases on an additional 6,000 acres in the Eagle Ford shale play, bringing our total lease position to 11,000 acres.

Drilling enough wells to fully develop that many acres would have cost hundreds of millions of dollars. As the drilling activity in the area picked up, shortages of drilling rigs and other equipment began to develop. A company our size could not compete with the larger companies in contracting for the rigs, equipment, and other services required for an extensive drilling program.

Another concern about embarking on a horizontal drilling program in an undeveloped shale formation was that the oil and gas production from newly drilled shale wells comes on very strong at first but declines very rapidly in the first one or two years. The rapid decline rates require constantly drilling new wells just to keep production level. My metaphor for this process is running up a down escalator that is gradually gaining speed. To get a feel for this experience, I tried running up the down escalator in our office building. Fortunately, I was in good basketball shape, because my run up wasn't easy. It seemed that I had to run about three times the length of the escalator just to get to the next floor. I got winded, not to mention getting several curious looks from the folks riding on the up escalator.

Realizing AMI's financial and operational limits, I decided we should take a two-track approach. On one track, we began preparing to drill on our initial ranch leases ourselves. We built a lake for a water supply and drilled a test well to allow us to extract core samples of the rocks in the Eagle Ford formation. Meanwhile, on the second track, we kept a close eye on the lease prices in the area. Nick ran a reserve economics forecast to answer my question: "For a typical Eagle Ford well, how much can a company pay for leases before these costs drive down the forecast rate of return to a level that makes drilling the well not worth the risk?" The answer came back that if a company paid $4,000 per acre for leases, their rate of return on the typical Eagle Ford well would drop below 20 percent, which for our company, spending our own money, would not justify the drilling risk.

By April 2010, we had owned our oldest Eagle Ford leases for eight months, and our core sample from the test well indicated that our lease area would be productive, but nothing spectacular. We decided to put our leases on the market before they would begin losing value as their remaining term declined.

We sent out a sales letter to about a dozen E&P companies with interests in the Eagle Ford area. Chesapeake immediately called and asked if they could make a pre-emptive offer. We told them that we would rather let the sales period run its course, so that everyone had an opportunity to bid. Among the more interesting bids was one from Hefner, who proposed a joint venture in which we would retain a healthy amount of the risk but keep some significant upside from future drilling.

Late one afternoon, Mack asked me to come down to his office, where he was on the phone with none other than Aubrey McClendon, the cofounder and CEO of Chesapeake Energy, and known internationally as a frenetic dealmaker. McClendon was calling from Singapore, where he was probably busy flipping Eagle Ford acreage to some Asian investors. Mack had been a year ahead of Aubrey at Heritage High School, one of two private high schools for the scions of Oklahoma City's elite, so they probably knew each other then. I listened in as they negotiated a deal. Mack got him up to a $44 million purchase price for our 11,000 acres by throwing in some drill pipe we already had on the ranch leases in anticipation of drilling our first well there.

By the time of our sale to Chesapeake, we had invested $8 million in our Eagle Ford leases and preliminary operations, resulting in a $36 million gain in nine months. As nice as this gain was, it left us facing a bill for about a $16 million in personal, ordinary income taxes, since we had not held the leases long enough for their sale to qualify as a capital gain. To defer these taxes, we set up what is called a like-kind exchange, which allows a seller to escrow the proceeds from a sale for up to ninety days so that they can be reinvested in similar assets.

The only similar assets we could find on the market in our price range at that time were four oil fields, two in Montana and two in Wyoming, being sold by an independent oil producer from Louisiana. Driven by our tax situation, we were the high bidder and bought these fields for $62.5 million, ushering in a new era for AMI.

— • — • —

CHAPTER TWENTY-ONE

HIGH DOLLAR HOOPS

After making such a large gain on our Eagle Ford assets and reinvesting the funds in the Montana and Wyoming oil fields, I was feeling prosperous but didn't really care about acquiring more stuff. We kept the same house and the same cars. However, I did splurge on three basketball related fronts: Thunder floor seats, fantasy camps, and private jet travel.

The Thunder made the playoffs during their second season in Oklahoma City. As the eighth seed in the Western Conference playoffs, they challenged the top-seeded Los Angeles Lakers in the first round but lost the series two games to four. With Durant, Westbrook, and Serge Ibaka steadily improving and rookie James Harden showing great promise, I said to myself: "These guys are going to be very good. I need to get better tickets."

During the Thunder's first two seasons in Oklahoma City, I had two Club Level seats in Chesapeake Energy Arena, near mid-court, but many rows up. During a ticket renewal session for their third season, I noticed there were two courtside seats available, directly across the court from the Thunder coaches, so I decided to check them out. After recovering from a brief episode of "sticker shock," I bought the tickets, not knowing they were adjacent to Kevin Durant's four seats, used by his family and friends, which made my new seats the best in the house.

My mother passed away on Memorial Day, 2010, at the age of ninety-seven. After a long and gentle decline, outliving my dad by fifteen years, she eventually succumbed to old age. Dad had set up a trust fund for her. She always seemed insecure about money, but took comfort in saying, "I have a trust." Her nursing home expenses gradually rose as she began requiring higher levels of care, and her trust was nearly exhausted when she died. To her final days she was unfailingly polite, as if she had forgotten almost everything but her manners.

On summer nights, I liked to relax on a lawn chair at the end of our lap pool, gazing up at the stars. When I would see The Big Dipper constellation, I would image my dad, fishing from the edge of the lowest star on its handle. After Mom died, I added her to this image, on the star above Dad's, standing by an easel, painting a picture of Dad fishing. Gone but not forgotten, their spirits live in my heart.

My mother's funeral was set for Friday, June 4th, in our hometown of Bartlesville. Showing questionable judgment, I decided to go ahead with my earlier plans to fly to my fourth K Academy on Tuesday. Logistically, the only way I could make it back to Bartlesville for my mother's funeral and only miss the Friday sessions of the five-day Duke camp was to fly out Thursday night and return Friday night by private jet. This got me back to Duke for the Saturday games and the Sunday morning tournament. I didn't want Coach K to think I would bail out on my team during the middle of camp for no reason, so I told him I had flown back to my hometown for my mother's funeral, and he gave me a long sympathy hug.

Playing for Chris Collin's team, I didn't figure too heavily into the game plan. I was able to run the court and had a really good view of the action. Our team went 6 and 1, not losing until the semi-finals of the tournament. I enjoyed the wins but had been hoping for another championship.

Coach Capel's Camp

Three weeks later, back in Norman, I ventured out to OU coach Jeff Capel's fantasy camp. I had advised the OU coaching staff on setting up the camp, based on my experiences at the Jordan and Duke camps. In a briefing for the camp coaches, including NBA star Blake Griffin and former NBA stars Alvin Adams and Harvey Grant, I told them to be sure to keep someone back on defense, because fantasy campers can make open layups. Also, never "ice" a free-throw shooter, because the rest will do them good.

Dishing a no-look bounce pass in traffic

This camp was for men over thirty, and its lower age limit, and lower tuition, made it more competitive than the other two camps. After struggling in the evaluation game, I was drafted by a team coached by Harvey Grant. Later that night, I was at home watching the local sports news and was surprised to see myself on the screen as a sports reporter intoned: "Blake Griffin returns to the University of Oklahoma to coach a sixty-seven-year-old man." He sounded astonished, as if an important archaeological discovery had just been unearthed from beneath the Lloyd Noble Arena in Norman.

Feeling more comfortable on the OU home court, I was able to stay in the thick of the action, hitting a couple of threes, including a "flash from the past" jumper from NBA three-point distance. I also buried a fast-break, pull-up jumper to help preserve a win in the waning seconds of our final tournament game.

My top highlight at the OU Camp was a career-best assist, a no-look, backhanded bounce pass in heavy traffic that drew a murmur from the crowd and prompted legendary OU coach Billy Tubbs to exclaim: "Did you see that pass?"

During a session between games, Coach Tubbs reminisced with the campers about his coaching days at OU. He mentioned he always had a "designated hugger," usually a seldom used walk-on, whom he could hug after a big win, because the star players were always drenched in sweat and he didn't want them ruining his expensive suits. He added that his hugger also helped bring up the team's grade average. I told him later that if I had been at OU while he was coaching, I could have been his hugger.

Old versus Young

Playing in an early morning pick-up game in the OU practice gym, I was matched up against a little kid, who looked to be about twelve years old, maybe 5' 4" and 100 lbs. His dad, a former college star at Texas Tech, was also playing in the game. I was surprised when the kid launched a set shot from NBA three-point range that hit nothing but net. I decided I would have to guard him closer. As he brought up the ball up the court on their next possession, he started veering to his right. Just as I jumped out to block his path, he dribbled behind his back and darted in the opposite direction. By the time I could slam on my brakes, I was on the left side of the court and he was on the other side, at least twelve feet away, firing off another long three-point shot. I had never been burned so badly while challenging a dribbler in my entire basketball career. This was my introduction to future NBA All-Star Trae Young.

As I headed to my fifth Jordan camp in mid-August, I felt I had played my way into the best shape of my over-sixty career. Villanova coach Jay Wright drafted me for his Jordan camp team, apparently in the last round, since I was initially number nine in the substitution rotation on a team with nine players.

By our fourth game, three of our players were injured and out of action, which was a shame as I was our only player on Medicare. Down to six players, we managed to win a close game against North Carolina coach Roy Williams's team. In one play, I was chasing down a loose ball as it rolled out of bounds at Coach Williams's feet.

"How old are you?" he asked as I picked up the ball.

"Sixty-seven," I replied, unsure if I should be talking to the opposing coach.

In the game's final minute, we led by one point, and I was intentionally fouled, probably under their coach's direction to "foul the old guy." I managed to swish two game-clenching free throws.

"That was a fantasy camp classic!" Coach Wright exclaimed when our game ended, as if Villanova had just beaten North

Carolina. Positive and enthusiastic, Coach Wright is the kind of coach I like to play for.

This was the third year I had been the oldest player in a Jordan camp, but the first time I had been older than all the coaches as well. This may have been a factor in the coaches' selecting me for the camp's Inspirational Award. Coach Wright told me he would not have voted for me if I had not made those two last-minute free throws. As the closing ceremony ended, Michael Jordan handed me a nice trophy, the last one presented at the final Michael Jordan fantasy camp.

In another awards ceremony that November, Robert A. Hefner III was inducted into the Oklahoma Hall of Fame, an honor previously earned by his father, Oklahoma oilman Robert A. Hefner Jr. and his grandfather, Oklahoma Supreme Court Judge Robert A. Hefner. Commenting on Hefner's selection, former Oklahoma governor David Walters praised his courage in standing up to the United States Senate, the president of the United States, and the major oil companies during the 1970s to argue that our nation was not running out of the natural gas but in fact held a one-hundred-year supply. During our fight for deregulation of deep natural gas prices, Hefner told me that if the industry ever figured out how to produce the natural gas locked up in shale formations, the nation's natural gas reserves would be measured in quadrillions of cubic feet, not trillions.

Welcome to Montana

The winter of 2010–2011 gave a harsh welcome to AMI's new operating areas. The pump jacks for some of our wells in Montana were completely buried under the snow. We had to dig down through the snow to find them and wait for a thawing out period before we could put our wells back into production. Our Montana fields were located on the Fort Peck Indian Reservation, not far from where General Custer had made his last stand.

Cheering for the Thunder from our new floor seats

In early 2011, oil and natural gas prices were relatively high and interest rates were relatively low. AMI's management decided that it would be a good time to reduce our bank debt by selling a financial instrument known as a volumetric production payment (VPP). Under the terms of the VPP, we sold 735,910 barrels of oil to JPMorgan Chase for a $34 million initial payment and an $11.6 million deferred payment. AMI then paid down its debt to Bank of Oklahoma by $32.8 million, and the bank reduced AMI's borrowing base from $80 million to $50 million. Although complicated to set up and administer, the VPP provided AMI with a long-term hedge of oil prices and reduced our financial leverage. Our obligation to JPMorgan was owed in barrels of oil, not dollars.

Best Seats in the House

The Thunder's first home game in the 2010–2011 season found Emily and me in our courtside seats for the first time. Immediately after the player introductions, Kevin Durant sprinted over to give a hug to his mother, Wanda Pratt, and three other members of his inner circle, seated to my immediate left. He towered over me after his fourth hug, easily avoiding eye contact since he is about a foot taller than me, before darting back to the Thunder bench.

Emily and I met Kevin later that season at an event for sponsors and courtside season ticket holders. I told him I sat just a hug away from his friends and family. He started to give me a hug, but I awkwardly backed away, uncomfortable with our height difference.

During that same event I told Thunder coach Scott Brooks: "I feel like I need to apologize to you. Sometimes during the games my inner coach takes over and I start yelling at the players: 'Block out . . . block out!' or 'Get back . . . Get back!'"

"That's exactly what I am yelling at them," he replied.

Sitting in our floor seats made me appreciate the extraordinary strength, endurance, speed, quickness, toughness, and skill required to compete in the NBA. A player must be strong enough or quick enough to get where he wants to go. A soft pass will be intercepted, but bullet passes are hard to catch. The collisions between pick setters and defenders are bone-jarring. The crash landings after a driver attacks the rim in traffic can be terrifying. A defender who turns his head for a second and loses sight of his man will get burned. Any weakness will be exposed and exploited. (The only mystery to me is why some of these great athletes cannot consistently make a free throw, the athletic equivalent of a two-foot putt.)

During a playoff game against the Dallas Mavericks later that season, Emily, who often sits to my right, had a narrow escape.

Dallas point guard Jason Kidd dove for a loose ball that was rolling toward us. His dive ended with a summersault, with his right foot nearly kicking Emily in the stomach. This could have been bad, as Emily was pregnant with her daughter-to-be, Millie. Fortunately, I was able to grab Kidd's ankle before he kicked her kid. I held onto his ankle for a second, not knowing what to do, then just threw his leg back toward the court. Somehow, in one of the most athletic moves I have ever seen as a Thunder fan, he unwound with a backward summersault and, with a couple of quick steps, was sprinting down the court, leaving my right hand drenched in his ankle sweat.

My Best Duke Camp

On draft night at my fifth K Academy, Coach K introduced the players who were attending their fifth camp and were being honored by having their K Academy jerseys retired. For the duration of the camp, my retired jersey was hung from the rafters of the iconic Cameron Indoor Stadium, along with those of other K Academy veterans and former Duke All-Americans.

Jeff Capel, only two months removed from being the head coach at OU, had played for Coach K at Duke and had joined the Duke coaching staff. He knew me from my summer workouts in the OU practice gym during his five years in Norman, but he drafted me anyway. We had a good team, and Coach Capel involved me in the offense. To cherry pick my favorite statistic from the camp: I shot 50 percent from the field, finishing fourth among the eighty campers in field goal percentage for players taking twenty shots or more.

After our last game at camp, a heartbreaking Final Four loss, Coach K told me it was my best camp in six years. For the first time since we won the championship in 2005, I left the K Academy feeling good about how I had played.

It didn't hurt that I was leaving by private jet, headed straight home to Norman. During the camp, I had commented to a camper, who happened to be an executive with a private jet leasing firm, that I was having a hard time justifying the economics of flying private. He explained that flying in private jets was not about economics, it was about lifestyle.

"Either you can afford it, or you can't," he concluded.

During the deep gas drilling boom, Hefner and some other local wildcatters had commanded their own fleets of private jets, helicopters, and other aircraft. This required hiring pilots, renting hangars, and buying insurance. When the bust hit, their fleets vanished into thin air. Realizing the cyclical nature of oil and gas prosperity, I decided to just buy flight time from NetJets in twenty-five-hour increments, so that, if another bust came along, I would not be overcommitted. My first jet card was for a Cessna Citation, which seated six and could reach either coast from Norman in less than four hours.

Dwyane Wade Blocks Half the Court

After Michael Jordan retired from the fantasy camp business, Dwyane Wade picked up where MJ left off and announced his own camp in Miami in August. Former NBA star and original Dream Team player Chris Mullin was my coach at the camp. He not only gave me a green light for shooting, but also ran some plays for me.

The highlight of the camp was a six-minute scrimmage between our team and a team called "Dwyane Wade & Friends." His friends included two NBA players, Mario Chambers and Raja Bell, and two former NBA players, Jay Williams (the Duke All-American) and Tim Legler, both with ESPN. This game was a serious mismatch, with

Escaping Dwyane with a behind-the-back dribble

Dwyane throwing the ball off the glass, getting his own rebound, and throwing down a monster dunk before our token defense could react.

At one point in the game, I was bringing the ball up the court and was confronted by Dwyane, who, with his seven-foot wingspan, seemed to be blocking half the width of the court. Instinctively, I dribbled behind my back to escape Wade, only to find myself facing All NBA defensive player Raja Bell. Wouldn't you think one NBA star would be enough to guard me? Near the end of the game, I got open on a fast break for a sixteen-foot baseline jumper. Swish . . . nothing but net. The crowd went wild as I pulled my team within twenty points of the pros. After the game, Dwyane told me: "Way to hit the open shot."

Coach Kruger's Basketball Reunion

One week later, I found myself on the bench, just prior to the tip-off of an OU Varsity alumni game. New OU coach Lon Kruger had invited all former OU players back to OU for a basketball reunion. More than one hundred alums showed up, and many of them signed up to play in this game. Much to my surprise, a large contingent from the OU student band came marching in, playing Boomer Sooner. They were followed by OU cheerleaders, mascots, and a slam dunk team. I looked up over my shoulder and saw the east side of the arena filling up with fans. I began to wonder what I had gotten myself into.

With eighteen players on our team, I did not expect to play much. I came into the game with five minutes left in the first half. As if to lower expectations, the announcer informed the crowd that I was observing my fiftieth anniversary of walking on at OU. I was matched up against former NBA player Brent Price, who once scored 56 points in an OU game. Luckily for me, he was 0 for 3 from the field while I was guarding him. He did throw a nice between-the-legs bounce pass to Longar Longar, an athletic 7' NBA D-Leaguer, who flew by me for a slam dunk.

Former OU coach Kelvin Sampson, then an assistant coach with the Houston Rockets, was coaching our team. I was surprised when he put me back into the game for another five-minute run. My best play was a no-look pass to my basketball sparring partner, Mike Neal, who was open in the right corner and drained a beautiful three-pointer.

Guarding Brent Price

Our team rallied to send the game to an almost-sudden-death overtime. Brent Price was fouled and made his first free throw, but someone ruled he had to make both to win the game. Coach Sampson called time-out to "ice" the shooter. When Price went back to the line, Coach Sampson called another time-out. Twice iced, Price missed his second free throw, and our team scored to earn the victory. In a post-game interview, Price was asked what happened.

"It's been twenty years since I played at OU," he replied. Twenty? Try fifty.

The Sunday Oklahoman reported that 5,000 fans attended the game. Most of them came to see NBA Rookie of the Year/Slam Dunk Champion Blake Griffin play. Four of them came to see me. Unfortunately for the fans, Blake decided not to play, but did stay after the game to sign autographs. I played, but the only autograph I signed was for my granddaughter Hanna.

Millie Kaplan Joins Our Team

In December 2011, Emily gave birth to our second granddaughter, Millie. When they got home from the hospital, I was tempted to put a small basketball in her crib but decided to leave her sports career up to Emily and Russ.

During the Dutcher & Company annual Christmas lunch that year, I gave my usual "state of the company" talk and, taking advantage of the captive audience, may have rambled on in giving my annual update of my adventures on the basketball court that year. Walking back to the parking garage after lunch with Ole and Hanna, my always candid, four-year-old granddaughter observed:

"That was the longest speech. I thought it would never end."

I made a mental note to make my next Christmas lunch speech briefer.

My First Jayhawk Camp

University of Kansas coach Bill Self joined the fantasy camp circuit, hosting his first camp in mid-April 2012. On the first night of camp, I played in a scrimmage between teams made up of campers and KU players, just back from their loss to Kentucky in the NCAA national championship game. In a mid-court scramble, I managed to steal the ball from 6' 10" KU All-American Thomas Robinson. I don't know which one of us was more surprised. After the game, I jokingly told him not to feel bad about my steal, as I had once stolen the ball from Marques Haynes. He was very gracious, replying that if I could steal the ball from Marques Haynes, I could surely steal it from him.

The next morning, I placed second in a spot shooting contest when my final shot, a turning runner, was ruled released after the buzzer sounded. That evening, the camp staff upgraded my contest trophy to a tie for first, after deciding that without a video replay, the play was too close to call. I was drafted by Team Manning and coached by ProCamp executive Jim Stoll and ESPN's ubiquitous sideline reporter, Holly Rowe.

My best game of the camp came against a team coached by KU assistant Norm Roberts. During the second half, we were trailing by nine points with nine minutes left in the game. I had hit a couple of jump shots, and could hear him calling out from the bench, "You've got to guard The Dutch." I thought he was being facetious.

Later in the game, I was guarding my friend Garry Munson, the tall and talented player-coach of the Sag Harbor Whalers. Luckily for me, he was playing on the perimeter rather than taking me inside. When he attempted a three-pointer, I somehow got high enough in the air to get a couple of fingers on the ball, and it fluttered down like a wounded duck. A teammate picked it up and fired a baseball pass to me sprinting down the court. By the time I caught his pass, my momentum was about to carry me off the end of the court, so I shot a fading, baseline jumper. As the ball swished through the net, I felt another flash from the past.

A few weeks after the KU camp, an article about the camp by our coach Holly Rowe appeared on the ESPN website. She described my play as "clutch" and quoted me saying the fantasy camps "make a really nice venue" for playing out my one-on-one battle with Father Time.

Two Barcelona Friendlies

In June, during my sixth Duke camp, a charity auction was held to support the Emily K Center in Durham, North Carolina. Named after Coach K's mother, the Center provides a high-quality kindergarten through high school education to poor kids who are smart enough, but not rich enough to attend college. Its graduates consistently earn scholarships to some of the nation's top colleges. During the auction, I won a trip for two to accompany a contingent of Duke people to Barcelona, Spain, to watch two pre-Olympics exhibition basketball games with Team USA being led by Coach K. In these so-called "friendlies," our Olympic team would be playing two of its toughest opponents, Spain and Argentina, just a week before the 2012 Olympics opened in London.

Anne dropped down from Norway to join me in Barcelona for these games. I had booked a large suite for me and a smaller one for her in the Hotel Arts Barcelona, overlooking some sandy beaches along the Mediterranean Sea. By coincidence, we also had a view of a four beachside basketball courts where a tournament was being played.

We had dinner one night with a group, including Duke Athletic Director Kevin White. I told him that I was about five years older than Coach K, and that I felt that he should be able to continue coaching Duke for as long as I can play. He agreed, adding: "Then I hope you keep playing a long time."

Another member of the Duke contingent was a 6' 6" fellow camper and architect who had matched my bid for the trip during the auction. Since the US and Spanish Olympic teams were staying at the same hotel, there were a lot of tall young men walking around the immediate area. When our Duke group went out together, we were often asked by curious onlookers if our tall friend was a famous player. Before long, we gave him a new nickname: "Famous Player." During our stay, Anne and I met and chatted briefly with Olympic point guards Russell Westbrook and Chris Paul.

One afternoon, our Duke group ventured out for a tour of a huge vineyard and winery near Barcelona. During a wine tasting session, we learned that the winery was a privately owned, family business with millions of dollars in wine sales every year. I asked one of our hosts how a family business could grow so big. He explained that it helps to have been founded in 1520.

Our Duke group watched from seats near the Team USA bench as they won both exhibition games. Then the team headed to London, Anne popped back up to Norway, and I returned home.

Lunch with Dwyane

Like LeBron James, I decided to "take my talents to Miami," in my case, for my second Dwyane Wade camp. Only half listening, I was surprised to hear my name during Dwyane's introductory remarks to the campers. He said one of the things he liked about hosting his own fantasy camp was that he got to meet so many guys from around the country. For example, when he was in Oklahoma City to play against the Thunder, he could see me in my courtside seat and know there was at least one person in that crowd who was cheering for him. Not wanting to leave the impression I would ever cheer for the Miami Heat, I had to interject: "Yes, Dwyane, I'm cheering for you *personally.*"

Our coach was Indiana University head coach Tom Crean, who had coached Dwyane during his college years at Marquette. Coach

Crean took his fantasy camp coaching job very seriously, installing five different defenses, including a combination zone/man-to-man defense I had never seen before, but really liked. During a camp three-point shooting contest, I hit 11 three-pointers in one minute. With Coach Crean feeding me perfect passes, I had a nice hot streak, hitting eight in a row until my shot went flat in the last few seconds, resulting in a second-place finish.

At lunch one day, I was sitting by myself until Dwyane joined me. He mentioned that he was looking forward to September, when his book, *A Father First*, would be coming out. I told him that if he was like me, he would soon be checking his book's sales rating on Amazon.com. As it turned out, all he had to do was check *The New York Times* bestseller list.

Our literary discussion continued later, when I mentioned I had done a lot of radio interviews about my book, but that these interviews did not generate many sales. He suggested that I should have done television interviews, like he did. I told him that for an unknown author, television interviews were not really an option.

Dwyane didn't play in the "Dwyane and Friends" exhibition game, as he was still recovering from the off-season surgery that had kept him off the Olympic team. But his "friends," consisting of a group of current and former NBA players, once again dominated a team of volunteer campers.

In this game, I was guarding NBA Hall of Famer Rick Barry, who is one year younger than me and is still known for shooting his free throws underhanded. He brought the ball up the court and tried to go by me with a cross-over dribble. I knocked the ball away, dove on the court to retrieve it, and tossed it to a teammate. This brought a roar from the small crowd, mostly friends and families of the campers. For me, it was déjà vu. I made almost the exact same steal nearly fifty years earlier, as I have already mentioned twice, from former Harlem Globetrotter star Marques Haynes.

For the second year in a row, my hoops season ended with an appearance in the OU Varsity Alumni Game, playing for former OU coach Billy Tubbs. We had another big crowd, estimated at over 3,000 fans. This year I managed to score, picking up a loose ball at the free-throw line and hitting a quick jump shot.

Seventy Years Young

Reaching the age of seventy seemed like an accomplishment. Now I could legitimately call myself a septuagenarian sesquipedalian. Although I was still striving to be "younger next year," possible signs of aging began to show up. I found a note I had left for myself in the kitchen. It read: "Get several." Several what? I had no idea. (My daughters still tease me about that one.) While Terry and I agreed that we seldom drop things, we did notice that things seemed to be jumping out of hands with increasing frequency. Terry likes to keep our house cold. To warm up, I just open the refrigerator and stick my hands in for a while.

If I really want to feel my age, all I need to do is drive past our first Norman home on Hidden Hill Road. In the spring of 1977, I planted two little saplings in our front yard. When I drive past them now, I find these little saplings have grown into huge oak trees that tower above the second floor of the house.

Rock Chalk Jayhawk

When I began my fantasy camp journey at sixty, I never expected to still be playing when I was seventy, twice the age of the youngest players. In April 2013, heading to my second Bill Self Fantasy Camp at the University of Kansas, I felt that expectations should be so low that it would be like playing with house money. My goal was to relax, have fun, and try to help my team win the camp championship. Our coach was Dino Gaudio, who had coached Chris Paul while he was the head coach at Wake Forest.

At a Saturday night dinner, the tournament brackets were announced, and Coach Self gave out some individual awards for players with the most points, rebounds, assists, and steals during the games on the first two days of camp. He then announced that the "Mr. Jayhawk" award would be shared by my friend and contemporary Garry Munson and me. He said the award was for all-around contributions to the team, but it looked more like a Senior Citizen award.

Having won our first three "regular season" games by large margins, we were the top seed going into the Sunday morning tournament. During our "Final Four" game, the man guarding me decided to stay under the basket on defense, leaving me wide open on the right corner. Left alone, I hit the open jumper. A little later, I was left open on the left wing and buried another jumper.

Jim Stoll, the camp director and my coach at my first KU camp, was calling the game over the loudspeaker. After I swished my second jumper, he announced: "Leaving The Dutch wide open is not a sound defensive strategy." I had to laugh at that one.

Protecting a lead late in the game, Coach Gaudio put me in to shoot free throws. As he expected, I was fouled intentionally to stop the clock, and made both free throws to close out our win.

In the championship game a little later, Coach Gaudio told us to make five passes before taking a shot. We complied with his order, and the five passes approach worked out surprisingly well. Our team managed to win without my taking a shot.

Perhaps taking a cue from my prolonged basketball efforts, Anne began her second ballet comeback, dancing with Norman's Classical Ballet Academy. At forty-four, she was twice the age of many of the dancers but was easily the most graceful. I supported Anne's prolonging her dancing career, figuring at least it would keep her on her toes.

More Advice for Coach K

That June, at my seventh Duke camp, I visited with Coach K during the draft night reception. I realized he had not announced if he would commit to coaching the US Olympic basketball team for the third consecutive time, so I suggested that he should, because time goes by faster the older you get, and another four years would just fly by.

During an evaluation game, I was playing on a team with a willing passer at point guard who provided the assists as I hit four out of five three-pointers. Duke assistant coach Nate James was watching this game and drafted me "surprisingly high," according to the always candid Coach K.

My Scott Lake Adventure

For many summers, Del, an avid hunter and fisherman, had taken a trip to Scott Lake Lodge in far northern Saskatchewan, Canada, for a week of fishing for northern pike and lake trout. Flying commercial, it took him two days to get there. When he invited me to join him on his trip, I told him we could get there in one day if we flew private. As my NetJet Citation arrived at the Bartlesville airport, I told the pilots it felt cool to be landing where my first summer job as a teenager was spent polishing the Phillips jets.

Del's two older grandsons, Lincoln Dutcher and James Teague, joined us on this trip. At the time, Lincoln was in OU medical school and James was attending the University of Arkansas on a baseball scholarship. The remote lodge was accessible only by sea plane. Our NetJets flight got us as far as Saskatoon, then we squeezed on board a crowded sea plane for a quick trip to the lodge. This flight took us over what seemed to be hundreds of lakes, scattered over a vast, untouched wilderness.

For Del and me, one of the biggest differences in our lives had been the amount of time spent outdoors. Whether working on his ranch, hunting, fishing, or golfing, Del was outside. I worked in an office building and played basketball in a gym. I had not played football or baseball since high school and played golf once a decade. So just being outside for a week was a thrill for me, but normal for Del.

Our foursome split up into two fishing boats, each with an experienced guide. We skipped around the lake, in search of coves teeming with northern pike. We were in competition, not only among ourselves but also against the other guests at the Lodge. The objective was to catch not just the biggest fish, but as many "trophy fish" as possible. To qualify as a trophy fish, the pike had to be at least 48" long. The fishing required more casting skill than patience. The fish seemed to be everywhere, but somehow preferred to be caught by Del and his grandsons. They reeled in dozens. Meanwhile, feeling like a tenderfoot at a dude ranch, I managed to catch a few, including one trophy fish that was about four times as large as anything I had ever caught fishing in Oklahoma ponds and lakes.

A Shoot-out with Kevin Durant

Back home that August, a true career highlight occurred unexpectedly as I was training for my third Dwyane Wade camp. Gregg

Darbyshire, the CEO of ProCamps, invited me to play some hoops after the first day of Kevin Durant's basketball camp for kids, held in Norman at OU's student recreation center. I arrived shortly before the end of the day's activities so I could say hello to Kevin and his friends, who often sit next to me during Oklahoma City Thunder home games.

Kevin's camp was attended by at least 300 kids, plus their parents, grandparents, and siblings. For the last event of the day, everyone had gathered around one court to watch a game called "Five on the Rack." The camp director, Jim Stoll, called out Kevin, his former University of Texas teammate Damion James, and four early teen campers selected by the coaches to compete in this game. Then he announced he was asking me to join in, describing me as "a seventy-year-old man who was the best shooter at our Kansas University fantasy camp this spring."

The players were spread around the three-point line, with Kevin in the right corner and me just to the left of the free-throw circle. Starting with Kevin, each player would shoot, and if he made it, there would be "one on the rack." If he missed, he would be penalized by the number of points that had been built up on the rack by the previous shooters. When a player is penalized by a total of five points, he is eliminated from the game.

Kevin and I missed our first shots, but then found the basket. The other players were gradually eliminated. One camper survived longer than Damion James, but when he was eliminated, the game came down to just Kevin and the seventy-year-old man. I had two points against me, and Kevin had one. All of campers were cheering for Kevin. (Whatever happened to cheering for the underdog?) Our shoot-out went like this:

Bill: Swish. (No reaction from the crowd.)

Announcer: One on the rack.

Kevin: Swish. (Crowd cheers.)

Announcer: Two on the rack.

Bill: Swish. (A murmur from the crowd . . . I am in a nice groove.)

Announcer: Three on the rack.

Kevin: Swish. (The crowd cheers louder . . . Kevin seems focused.)

Announcer: Four on the rack.

At this point, neither one of us has hit the rim, and either one of us would be eliminated if he missed. I have taken the best shooter in basketball to the brink. My seventeen fantasy camps are beginning to pay off.

Bill: Swish. (The crowd may be getting worried . . . I am feeling confident.)

Announcer: Five on the rack.

Kevin: Swish. (The crowd cheers in relief.)

Announcer: Six on the rack.

Bill: My shot goes in . . . around . . . and out. (The crowd goes wild.)

I was shocked when I missed the shot. I thought it was good when it left my hands. But I felt strangely relieved. I wanted to win, but it would have been a shame to disappoint all the kids. Not to mention the fact that Kevin could have continued making that shot all day.

His hard-earned victory in hand, Kevin told me: "Good shooting." In an awkward response, I replied that his $1 million donation to help the Moore tornado victims was very generous and showed a lot of class.

The next day, I sent a letter to Coach K, telling him I knew he liked to keep up with his former players, so I was reporting on a shoot-out between the two extremes of his coaching levels. My letter described the "Five on the Rack" game between Kevin and me. A week later, I received a handwritten note from Coach K, saying: "Wow! I wish I was there to watch. Thanks for letting Kevin off the hook. I need him to be confident for the next four years for the USA."

Teaming Up with a Much Shorter Kevin

One week later, on the first morning of my third Dwyane Wade camp in Miami, I went through a series of drills used by the NBA Combine to evaluate potential draft picks. After confirming that I was slow and cannot jump very high, I found a free-throw station set up with rebounding equipment. As a machine fed me quick passes, I made fourteen free throws in thirty seconds, which turned out to be the top free-throw score in the camp. For an aging basketball player, "hang time" is the first thing to go. Maybe the free throw will be the last.

Sooner Vision, the broadcast group for OU's athletic department, was shooting a short video about my experiences as a seventy-year-old basketball player to promote the Annual OU Varsity Alumni Game coming up at the end of the month. One of their former cameramen was working for the Miami Heat, so they arranged for him to shoot some footage at the Dwyane Wade camp. This resulted in a one-word interview. Dwyane and I were standing side by side, silently waiting for the interview to begin. The cameraman, not being a broadcast journalist, peeked around his camera and said: "Talk."

We rambled on for a while about the fantasy camp. My favorite line was when Dwyane said: "Bill is an author, like me." He also asked me about winning a championship. I told him my first fantasy camp championship was at Duke, playing for his teammate, Shane Battier.

At the draft party that night, I learned I had been selected by Miami Heat coach Eric Spoelstra, fresh off winning his second straight NBA title. Just before our first game, we were in a huddle by our bench when our little point guard asserted, "The refs will give me a break, because I'm famous." Surprised by this boisterous claim, I responded, "Well, you're not that famous. I have never heard of you." He gave me a comedic double-take but didn't say anything else as the game was about to tip off. I learned later that he was the comedian Kevin Hart, but it was not until I got home that I discovered he was starring in what seemed like a new movie every week.

On the second day of camp, after winning our game that morning, Kevin told me he would not be able to play in our game that afternoon.

"I've got to jump on my jet and fly to the Hamptons for a charity event tonight," he explained. "But I will be back tomorrow."

Our team had two players out with injuries and our center had to go to work at his real job. Without our comedic point guard, we were left with just five players, facing the top team in the camp, coached by University of Indiana coach Tom Crean.

On the opening tip, I guessed where their center would tip the ball and stole it from his awaiting teammate. Then, on their next possession, I picked off a lazy cross-court pass. After we scored, Coach Crean called time-out. Walking back to our bench, I heard him yelling at his players: "This game isn't a minute old and Dutcher already has two steals!"

With a big size advantage, their team pulled out to an early lead. We played them even for the rest of the game, but never caught up. I played hard for the entire thirty-five-minute game, ending up with seven points, three steals, one blocked shot, and several rebounds and deflections.

After the game, I visited with Coach Spoelstra about basketball in the Philippines. I mentioned that, as a young Navy officer stationed at Subic Bay, I was the player/coach of the base basketball team, and that we had played 103 games in the two years I was there. We agreed that Filipino players like to make wild drives to the basket and are very much into "degree of difficulty" on their shot attempts. He told me his dad was my age and played basketball in college. As we were leaving, he asked if he could have his picture taken with me.

"That's a switch," I observed, thinking the photo must be for his dad.

The next morning, we lost in the first round of the tournament, ending Coach Spoelstra's chance for another championship. At the awards lunch, Dwyane Wade said something like this: "We are going to give out trophies for the Camp MVP, the top scorer, top rebounder, and assist leader, but there is no doubt that the best athlete in the camp is Bill Dutcher. He is seventy and still playing."

Shocked by Dwyane's too-kind shout-out, I figured by "athlete" he meant "free-throw shooter."

Six days later, I played in my third straight OU Varsity Alumni Game, this year on the same team with Blake Griffin and former Dallas Maverick Eduardo Najera. Before the game, I watched my opponents warming up on the other end of the court and tried to figure out who I could guard. My best bet seemed to be Terry Evans, who led OU in career three-pointers, even though he last played for OU in 1993. Then I realized I might be in trouble. He was my best match up, and I played with his dad.

Dinner with the King

In October, Anne and Ole flew to the Netherlands to attend the wedding of Ole's friend Jaime Bernardo, the Prince of Bardi, who had been Ole's best man at their wedding. A dinner was held that evening at the Het Loo Palace, built in the seventeenth century and still a favorite country-seat of the royal family. Anne and Ole were seated at a table with Jaime's cousin Willem-Alexander, who earlier that year had become the King of the Netherlands. He confided to Anne that since becoming King he had continued to serve as a guest pilot for KLM Royal Dutch Airlines, a fact that was not revealed publicly until 2017. (With the King as one of its pilots, no wonder it's called Royal Dutch Airlines. Surprisingly, in June 2020, "What is KLM Royal Dutch Airlines?" was the answer to a question on *Jeopardy* about which airline King Willem-Alexander had flown for.)

At Dutcher & Company's 2013 Christmas lunch, I presented Mack and Carol with awards recognizing their twenty-five years with our company. They each received a silver medal commemorating the 1988 Olympics, the year they came on board. After presenting their awards, I got a little carried away and, using a chandelier as an imaginary basketball goal, re-enacted my shoot-out with Kevin Durant that summer, since this classic event was not filmed.

During my eighth K Academy, I played for Coach Capel again. In my favorite play of this camp, I dove for a loose ball in the paint, expecting others to pile on, and was surprised to find myself flat on the floor, alone with the ball, as the other players looked on. I could see my point guard's feet at the top of the key, so I rolled the ball to him. Why was the seventy-one-year-old the only one diving for the loose ball?

Kyrie Irving was one of our assistant coaches. I was sitting by him during one of our games and asked him if he was going to play on the Olympic team in 2016. He replied, "If Coach K picks me I will." Since he was the MVP in the World Cup later that summer, I liked his chances.

In an exhibition game against former Duke players, there was one play I will remember as a personal classic. Each of the eight fantasy camp teams played five-minute games against a Duke alumni team loaded with current NBA players. Before our game, I looked down the court where our opposition was warming up, searching for someone I could guard. There was Kyrie Irving, the MVP of that year's NBA All Star game, so that didn't look like a good match for me. There was Austin Rivers, then a point guard for the New Orleans Pelicans, so that didn't look too promising either. I had to settle for Seth Curry, who at least wasn't in the NBA yet.

Our game was very up-tempo, featuring a lot of slam dunks and long-range bombs by the Duke stars. On my big play, I chased down a long rebound from a missed three-point shot and began dribbling up the court. I was being chased by Shavlik Randolph, a seven-foot-tall NBA journeyman center. He tried to reach in and steal the ball from behind me, but I made a little cut to escape as I crossed the half-court line. I couldn't pull up for a jump shot, because Shavlik would block it from behind. I didn't like my chances of driving to the basket either. I launched a running three-point shot that swished cleanly through the net, shocking not just me, but dozens of fans in the iconic Cameron Indoor Stadium.

— • — • —

CHAPTER TWENTY-TWO

SURVIVING
ANOTHER BUST

The *investments I had been making* in the stocks of oil and gas exploration and production companies since December of 2009 had been performing well, but by the spring of 2014, I was becoming concerned that these stocks were overpriced. It seemed like they were going up just because they were going up. I decided to put into place what I called a "virtual stop loss." While I did not put any formal stop losses in place with my broker, I made a bargain with myself to sell any stock that declined in value by 10 percent of its price on June 20, 2014. Oil prices were around $105 per barrel at that time, but soon began to fall. Oil and gas stocks started falling alongside the decline in oil prices, and by the end of the summer I was out of the stock market. Stocks I had purchased over a four-year period for $5.8 million were sold for $8.8 million, locking in a $3 million gain. If I had continued to hold these stocks much longer, those gains would have turned into losses. Unfortunately, I failed to realize that the stock market was predicting hard times ahead for all oil and gas producing companies, whether public, or private like mine.

Feeling flush after our stock market gains, Terry and I decided to buy a new home on the northwest edge of Norman for $1.8 million. The home sits on six acres and is quaintly zoned as agricultural, even though we have nineteen backyard neighbors nestled up along three sides of our property. The purchase allowed us to recapture the western view of Ten Mile Flats that we had enjoyed on Grand View during the deep gas boom of the late 1970s and early 1980s. The home was only six years old and was designed for senior living by a couple who intended to retire here. Unlike our home on Hidden Hill Rd., the new place features a downstairs master bedroom and an elevator to the upstairs bedrooms.

Right Between the Eyes!

Playing in my fourth consecutive OU Varsity Alumni game that September, I was on defense, running side by side with 6' 8" power forward Jozef Szendrei, a former European pro, who was out on a one-man fast break. I couldn't get ahead of him, so as he approached the basket, I tried to go behind him to flip away his dribble. I missed, and he threw down a powerful dunk. The announcer called out: "Szendrei dunks on Bill Dutcher!"

I brought the ball back up the court, and as I approached the three-point line, I noticed the defense looked a little confused, so I veered over to the right wing and found myself alone. I put up a soft jumper, and the crowd went wild as the ball dropped gently through the net. The announcer exclaimed: "And Dutcher answers, right between the eyes!" That was the type of moment I had long wished I had experienced playing for the Sooners in the early 1960s. Too bad I had to wait half a century for it to come.

The Tide Goes Out

In early December 2014, I was sitting at my desk in my Oklahoma City office when Mack came in and sat down in a visitor's chair in front of my desk. Normally pleasant and upbeat, he looked stressed and got right to the point. He had been diagnosed with stomach cancer that had reached stage four before it was discovered. Shocked by this terrible news, I was fighting back tears as he explained there were new treatments to try, so there was still hope, but, realistically, the prognosis wasn't good. He said he wanted to keep working as long as he could, and I said he should do whatever was best for him and his family. Trying to offer encouragement, I told him that my brother Del had fought off cancer five or six times during the past twenty years, and that he was seventy-five and still going strong.

At the time, oil prices had fallen from $113.80 per barrel to $58.38 per barrel in just the past six months. Meanwhile, natural gas had dropped from $4.74 per mmbtu to $3.44 per mmbtu. It is well known that oil and natural gas prices are cyclical. The hard part is figuring out where you are in these cycles. This was why hedging our oil and natural prices was one job I kept for myself, rather than delegating it to a manager. In fact, this task has consumed more of my time than any other part of our business. The swings in oil and gas prices can be daunting, if not overwhelming. I tried not to panic or overreact. I remained optimistic that prices would bounce back soon. I refused to admit that we were in a new, low-price environment for oil and natural gas prices that would require major changes in our company's size and structure.

At our annual Christmas lunch that year, I repeated Warren Buffet's famous quote, "When the tide goes out, you can see who has been swimming naked." Then I assured our employees and guests that we still had our trunks on. But to add a note of caution,

I also quoted an amended version of a line from Rudyard Kipling's poem *If*. "If you can keep your head while all those around you are losing theirs, you may not understand the situation."

Carol Magness, Dutcher & Company's first employee, retired on December 31st after twenty-six years as an integral part of our company's success. Carol occasionally mentioned that when she started with us, she only expected to help us out for a few months. But she stayed, and as our vice president for accounting, she brought credibility to our consulting and banking relationships that allowed us to build a going concern. Carol timed her exit well. Oil prices had been cut in half during the second half of 2014 and were still falling. The next two years were not much fun.

Shortly before tip-off at a Thunder home game in early 2015, I noticed Thunder guard Reggie Jackson lying down on the court along the north baseline. Two of his Thunder teammates raced over to help him up, as players normally do when a teammate goes down. But when they reached him, he tried to fight them off. They persisted in trying to help him up, until a buzzer buzzed, and they had to go to the Thunder bench. Jackson looked a little angry as he got up by himself. I concluded his teammates had inadvertently ruined his intended "die-in," a symbolic act being used nationwide as a Black Lives Matter protest.

Two months later, during a Thunder home game versus the Miami Heat, Emily and I were sitting in our courtside seats, directly across the court from the Thunder coaches. A Heat player fired an errant bullet pass from across the court, apparently aimed at no one, but heading directly over Emily's head. Emily ducked, and I reached back over her head, stretched out like a first baseman trying to catch a high throw, and tipped the ball with my right hand. I couldn't see the ball and thought I had missed it, but before lowering my hand I felt the ball on my fingertips again. I juggled the ball a few times, finally got it under control, and fired a one-handed pass back to the ref. Dwyane Wade, who had witnessed my juggling catch from a few feet away, commented:

"You still got it, Bill."

This was one of my all-time greatest catches, in any sport, on or off the court, and marked the first time an NBA player had spoken to me during a game.

Stanley Ogle, my high school teammate in basketball and baseball, passed away suddenly in April 2015. Stan was a real people person. I remember walking down a hallway with Stan, in between classes at College High, early in our sophomore year. Stan had only been in Bartlesville for a few months, but he already seemed to know more of our classmates than I did. Appropriately, he spent most of his career as a human resources executive.

Mack continued to come to work while attempting to fight off his cancer, but his health continued to decline. In recognition of his loyalty and hard work in building our two companies, I gave Mack a substantial lifetime achievement bonus. I wanted him to know how much he was appreciated. A few days later, in May 2015, he died, at the much-too-young age of fifty-eight. Although he was fourteen years younger than me, we were friends away from work, sharing conservative political views, and attending OU and Thunder basketball games together.

Stan and Mack were two of the best men I have known. Shaken by their loss, I had to wonder: "Why is God taking the good ones first?"

There had been times in the history of our two little companies that natural gas prices had been low, and other times when oil prices had been low. With oil prices sinking, it was a bad time for natural gas prices to collapse as well, thanks to soaring production of shale gas and an extremely mild 2014/2015 winter. (Natural gas is heavily used to heat homes and businesses in the winter, so mild winter weather reduces demand, causing gas prices to fall.) This simultaneous collapse of oil and natural gas prices caught the nation's oil and gas exploration and production companies off guard, touching off a wave of bankruptcies. The public oil and gas producers that avoided bankruptcy saw the price of their stock plunge to new lows.

Anadarko Minerals and Dutcher & Company managed to survive this brutal downturn, but not without some serious belt-tightening to cut overhead expenses and the owners taking some big financial hits. Since we had bootstrapped our growth using only bank debt, we did not have any outside investors to worry about. We had a long working relationship with the Bank of Oklahoma's energy lenders, but they were understandably concerned about our remaining a going concern, while bigger independent producers were driving off financial cliffs like Thelma and Louise.

Anadarko Minerals had followed two basic principles in bidding for oil and gas reserves over a twenty-five-year period. The first, as mentioned earlier, was to keep a spread of at least 10 percent between our cost of funds and the discount rate being used to determine the present value of the reserves. We also kept a close watch on the metrics prevailing in the acquisition market at the time, such as the price per barrel of reserves and the price per daily barrel being produced, but our bid would be determined by the present value calculation.

The second principle we followed when making acquisitions was "don't pay twice." By this, we meant don't pay for future production from wells that had not been drilled yet. The term "proven reserves" includes non-producing categories such as proved undeveloped, probable, and possible. Some aggressive sellers seem to stretch these hypothetical reserves estimates to include "conceivable" and "imaginable." The problem with paying for this so-called "upside" is that you still have to pay for the cost of drilling the wells needed to produce these reserves, thus running the risk of "paying twice." Also, if oil and gas prices crash, the value of undrilled leases and undeveloped reserves doesn't just decline, it disappears, often leaving bankruptcy as the only way out.

Maintaining these two conservative principles meant that Anadarko Minerals had little success in bidding for oil and gas reserves from 2011 to 2013, when most of the industry was paying aggressively for upside, not only for production but also for leases. However, our discipline during boom times helped us survive the 2014–2016 crash in oil and gas prices.

Avoiding bad deals is as important as making good ones. Industry people will congratulate you when you close an acquisition, but their congratulations may prove to be premature. At times, AMI bid too high on certain properties but did not get them because someone else bid even higher. As Garth Brooks sings, "Sometimes I thank God for unanswered prayers."

When these prices started dropping during the second half of 2014, my initial reaction was the downturn would be brief and that prices would bounce back within twelve to eighteen months. I resolved not to panic. I had told my employees that I appreciated their loyalty and that I believed loyalty should run both ways, so I would do all I could to avoid the layoffs already being seen in other oil and gas companies. Our little company was being tossed around in rough seas, and we were forced to become more seaworthy to survive. I did not want to be the boss who asks: "What have you done for me lately?" However, in my efforts to avoid layoffs, I did cut salaries by 10 per cent across the board and the company stopped contributing to their retirement accounts. We did continue paying for the employees' health insurance.

Unfortunately, these cuts in our overhead expenses did not make much of dent in our company's cash flow problems. As the downturn dragged on, I had to begin laying off employees and adding the work they had been doing to the workloads of those that stayed. The layoffs were painful, both to the employees and me, as some of the people asked to leave had been with the company for many years and had done nothing to deserve losing their jobs. But the layoffs were needed to reduce our overhead to a sustainable level in a new low-price era that was showing no sign of improving. Sudden and violent price swings are the reason that working in the oil and gas industry is often compared to a riding a roller coaster. In cutting overhead, I gave ground grudgingly, not wanting to overreact to a temporary drop in prices. However, I had been around long enough to know that at times oil and gas prices have remained depressed for a decade or longer.

In what must have been a rare mother/daughter ballet event, Anne and eight-year-old Hanna appeared in the Classical Ballet Academy's presentation of "Swan Lake." Although they were not on the stage at the same time, Terry and I enjoyed seeing them dancing in the same performance.

On June 12, 2015, *The Wall Street Journal* published my comment on their recent article about federal subsidies for ethanol. I wrote: "The corporate-welfare program for ethanol grows out of Iowa's enhanced political power attained by hosting the first voting in the presidential primaries. If the first primary were held in Florida, we would all be driving cars fueled by orange juice. At least we would have a choice: pulp or no pulp." (Actually, I borrowed the last line from Emily.)

The Hoops Roll On

My 2015 basketball season got started later that month when I arrived at the Dwyane Wade camp in Miami. Our team, the Warriors, was coached by former St. John's coach and fellow septuagenarian Mike Jarvis. Our best player was NFL cornerback Darrelle Revis. In another "Kevin Hart moment," I told Darrelle that I had heard he was a football player, but I did not know who he was. I asked him what team he played for, and he said the New York Jets. Then I asked what position he played, and he said cornerback. I told him I had played cornerback in high school, but, in my day, we played both offense and defense, so I played halfback as well.

"There was none of that two-platoon stuff for us," I explained. "Our quarterback played middle linebacker." He seemed impressed by that combination.

Later, I learned Darrelle had played for the New England Patriots in the most recent Super Bowl. But it was not until three weeks after camp, when he appeared on the cover of *Sports Illustrated,* that I realized the All-Pro cornerback was truly an NFL star.

Our team was good about sharing the ball, which helped me score ten points, on five of eight shooting, as we won our first tournament game Sunday morning. In the second game, I was one for one from the field, but on the bench with our team trailing in the fourth quarter. Jay Williams (the Duke All-American, ESPN basketball analyst and Dwyane Wade Fantasy Camp Commissioner) was commenting over a portable mike on the two games in progress. I was surprised, and a little embarrassed, when he told the crowd: "The Warriors need to put in Bill Dutcher . . .

and give him the ball!" Unfortunately, our coach did not take his advice, and we lost the game, mainly because we had no answer for the opposing team's big center. Jay continued his kind comments at the awards dinner, saying I should have been the camp MVP. The response from some of the campers seemed positive, in a going-along-with-the-joke sort of way.

That August, OU coach Lon Kruger drafted me for his team at the USA Basketball fantasy camp, being held in conjunction with the summer training camp for Team USA, in Las Vegas. After our evaluation game Wednesday morning, I had a seat along the baseline, between the two courts of the UNLV basketball practice facility, to watch a practice session for the assembled Olympic hopefuls. After they completed their drills, a horde of sports reporters and commentators flooded in to conduct interviews with the NBA stars competing for slots on Team USA. I took advantage of the chaos to visit with ESPN basketball analyst Sage Steele. I mentioned that I was a seventy-two-year-old basketball player myself, but she seemed skeptical, asking if I had any film. I told her I had a highlight film of my over-sixty career and suggested she ask Jay Williams and Shane Battier about me when she got back to ESPN. Then Blake Griffin came up and told her I was his shooting guard in the OU Varsity alumni games, which must have helped my credibility.

After talking with Blake and Sage, I noticed Kevin Durant having his picture taken with the young son of the ProCamp CEO Gregg Darbyshire, so I ambled down the court to say hello. Kevin, who often seems somewhat reserved, was surprisingly friendly, asking me if I was playing in the fantasy camp. When I said yes, he suggested he might come back to watch the game that afternoon. That would have been quite a switch, since I had watched hundreds of his.

Before our game Thursday morning, I visited on the bench with our best player, Dred Irving, who is Kyrie Irving's dad and a former pro player in Europe. I told him it seemed strange that he was my teammate, because just a year earlier his son Kyrie had been my assistant coach at Duke. He said I should feel blessed for still playing basketball at seventy-two. I replied that I felt blessed already.

Early in the game, Dred passed me the ball in the right corner and cut to the basket. I hit him with a quick "touch pass," and he scored a driving layup. Unfortunately, I had awakened that morning with a dull headache and played most of that morning's game in a fog.

However, I did have one exciting defensive play. With what seemed to me to be a burst of speed, I ran down an opponent who was out on a one-man fast break. I dove in front of him just as he angled in to shoot a layup and got my right hand on the ball. But he clipped my legs as I flew by, sending me into a twisting, backward somersault along the base line. Fortunately, there were no photographers to collide with, so I was able to roll out of my dive and back onto my feet. As I was coming up, I saw the opposing coach, Mike Fratello, observing my tumble with a look of absolute horror on his face, as if he had just seen a train wreck. The ref ruled it a clean block, and I told him "good no call."

In the Friday morning tournament, with about ten seconds left in the game, we led by three points as their top player dribbled past the three-point line, driving toward our basket with a full head of steam. I slid off my man to cut off the driver's path to the basket, expecting him to pull up for a shot. Instead, he charged toward me, but I got a hand on the ball. As I tried to retrieve the loose ball, he gave me a big shove in the back, sending me flying into a face-first landing in the paint. I was a little shaken up by the play and felt a small cut on my right cheek, so I lay there awhile to make sure I wasn't hurt. The ref called a foul on my assailant, giving me a one-and-one free-throw opportunity. Coach Kruger asked me if I was okay to shoot the free throws, and I told him I was fine, even if I wasn't quite sure what had just happened. I realized that if I missed the first free throw, they would have a chance to tie the game with a three-point shot and send it into overtime. Relaxed and in my element at the free-throw line, I clenched our victory by swishing both free throws. They did hit a three-pointer at the buzzer, but it was too little, too late. We won by two points and advanced to the camp's "final four."

Returning home, I gave Coach Kruger and his son Kevin a ride back to Norman in my rented private jet. I apologized to Coach Kruger for how badly I had played during the games on Thursday but told him I had an excuse I bet he had never heard before. I blamed my poor performance on the barometric pressure, which had given me a headache all day. Thursday evening, a major thunderstorm drenched Las Vegas. When the storm finally passed through, my headache cleared up right away. Coach Kruger allowed that he had never heard that excuse before. (Of course, he hadn't coached many seventy-two-year-old players before.)

My performance may have been affected by another type of pressure. I call this type the "barrel-metric pressure," which is inversely proportionate to the price of a barrel of crude oil. During the past year, the price of crude oil had dropped from $104 per barrel to $53 per barrel. The lower the oil price, the higher the barrel-metric pressure, which is felt primarily in the wallet, possibly causing a pain in the butt that could have affected my jump shot.

Later that month, while warming up for my fifth consecutive OU Varsity Alumni Game, I noticed we had only ten players on our team. Coached by former NBA star Alvin Adams, I played nearly half the forty-minute game. After the game, I was interviewed by Ryan Aber, a sportswriter for Oklahoma City's *Oklahoman* newspaper. The next morning, an article about my basketball career appeared on page two of the sports section, along with a picture from the previous year's alumni game. The story was written for their "Collected Wisdom" feature, which the week before had been about Coach K's fabled basketball career. In what must have been a serious drop-off in wisdom collecting, I told about my heartbreaking loss in the 1961 State Basketball finals and my walk-on years at OU, then skipped ahead to my first Michael Jordan camp at age sixty.

Terry and I celebrated our fiftieth wedding anniversary on August 25, 2015. We had been together through early marriage poverty, middle-class normalcy, deep gas boom prosperity, unemployment anxiety, and back to middle-class mediocrity. By building our own companies, we had bootstrapped our way back to prosperity. The thought of going back to Go, fifty years later, was stressful. But, having been there before, we knew we could handle it.

The Thunder invited Emily and me to sit with the owners during their 2015–2016 season's opening game versus the San Antonio Spurs, in exchange for giving up our floor seats for use by Kevin Durant's mom and dad. Before the tip-off, I visited with legendary oilman Aubrey McClendon, who was very friendly, but clearly puzzled about who I was. I reminded him of the $44 million Eagle Ford lease deal my company had made with him while he was CEO of Chesapeake. Spurs shooting coach Chip Engelland came over to say hello to us both. Chip had been Aubrey's roommate at Duke, and my coach at Duke's K Academy. I also met one of the

Gaylord sisters, who was surprised when I told her that my first job out of the Navy was as a reporter for *The Oklahoman*, when the newspaper was owned by her family.

Meanwhile, Back in the Oil Patch

As the oil and gas markets remained depressed during 2016, it became increasingly difficult for AMI's cash flow to service both its debt to Bank of Oklahoma and its volumetric production payments to JPMorgan. This forced AMI to make some asset sales. By selling its two Wyoming oil fields and other assets, AMI was able to raise about $16 million to pay down its debt to BOK and buy back its two VPPs from JP Morgan. Our VPPs had worked out well, since we sold them when oil and gas prices were relatively high and bought them back when prices were much lower.

To keep the companies afloat while AMI worked on these asset sales, Terry and I made capital contributions to Dutcher & Company and loans to AMI. Thanks to dividends paid by AMI since 2003, Terry and I had built up about $23 million in personal financial and real estate investments outside the company. AMI was the goose that had laid these golden eggs, and we were determined to keep this goose alive. In 2015, we began liquidating our personal financial and real estate investments, including our most valuable rental properties in Norman, and pouring the funds back into our oil and gas companies.

A combination of expense cuts, asset sales, and nearly $11 million in capital infusions from Terry and me kept the doors open while we struggled through the industry's downturn. After twenty-five years of smooth sailing, AMI found itself in rough seas. Luckily for me, we never quite reached the point where I had to decide if the captain would go down with his ship. We did have some contentious discussions with the Bank of Oklahoma. Even though we never missed a required principal or interest payment, the bankers pointed out that AMI was not in full compliance with some of the covenants in its loan agreement. This made our loan seem riskier and made our bankers a little seasick. I told them I had no interest in negotiating some type of "cents on the dollar" repayment deal. I would pay them back every penny I owed them. The bankers seemed a little skeptical.

AMI hired Andrew Rische, a young landman from Houston, to be our manager for land and business development. What Andrew lacked in experience, he made up for in enthusiasm. In dealing with the Bank of Oklahoma to work through the price crash, AMI's asset base was receiving no credit for the value of its oil and gas leases being held by production from its old, vertical gas wells in Western Oklahoma. By 2016, the industry's interest in drilling horizontal wells to develop shale and other formations in this area was perking up. Established oil and gas producers began drilling more wells, and new oil and gas companies backed by private equity investors were swooping into the Anadarko Basin, hoping to buy distressed oil and gas assets at bargain prices. Andrew was tasked with raising funds by making three- to five-year term assignments of AMI's drilling rights on these leases. He hit the ground running, and within fourteen months he had sold about $11.4 million of these drilling rights to six independent oil and gas companies.

In his 1998 novel *A Man in Full*, Tom Wolfe describes the declining status of a bank's "valued customers" who had taken out large loans, referred to as "sales" by the bank's "marketing department," during prosperous economic times. As market conditions decline, the "customer" becomes a "borrower" and eventually a "debtor." If conditions continue downhill, the loans are turned over to a special assets department for foreclosure, and the once-valued customer becomes a "shithead." We were able to get our debt back to an acceptable level without anything hitting the fan.

It might seem that avoiding bankruptcy is a pretty low bar to be called an achievement. But during the first two years of the price crash, 113 public and private independent oil and gas producers declared bankruptcy, involving nearly $75 billion in debt.

After whistling through this financial graveyard, AMI entered a rebuilding mode, older, and hopefully wiser. During the past decade, the oil and gas industry has been in a sweeping transition, moving from a "looking" industry, where exploring for and finding new fields was the key to success, to a "mining" industry, where the location of oil and gas trapped in shale formations is widely known, and the key to success is mining these resources economically. Adjusting to this new reality proved to be a challenging task.

Failing a Stress Test

On a Saturday morning in February 2016, I had been struggling with another round of layoffs in my home office. The price of oil that month had dropped to $33.75 per barrel, so the barrel-metric pressure was extremely high. I walked into our bedroom and turned the TV to an OU basketball game. As I sat down on the edge of my bed, I noticed something very strange. The wooden blinds on our bedroom windows were moving horizontally, as if they were scrolling across a computer screen. Lying down on my bed, I noticed the ceiling fan seemed to be moving, but it was not turned on. Then I looked at the ballgame on TV, and it seemed normal. I thought I must have just had a dizzy spell, so I watched the ball game for a while. But as soon as I sat up on the edge of my bed, the blinds were scrolling by again. I began to fear I was having a stroke and asked Terry to call 911.

An ambulance arrived quickly. The emergency guys had me lie down on a stretcher and deposited me into the back of the ambulance. After a five-minute race down Robinson Street, we pulled into the emergency entrance of Norman Regional Hospital, and I was carted to the emergency room. After I described what I had experienced, the emergency room doctor invited me to spend the night in the hospital. That afternoon, I was seen by a cardiologist and a neurologist. Sunday morning, I went through a series of tests, including an echo cardiogram, a brain MRI, and a carotid artery ultra-sound. After the test results were in, the attending cardiologist concluded that I had experienced a transient ischemic attack (TIA), also known as a mini-stroke or a warning stroke. And then he sent me home.

My cardiologist, Dr. Charles Bethea, had often warned of the risk that with my irregular heartbeat and atrial fibrillation, my heart might throw off a blood clot that could travel to my brain and cause a stroke. Luckily, I got off with a warning. He told me to rest for two months before I resumed playing basketball. He said I was better off playing basketball than not playing, apparently realizing that the love of hoops had gotten me to age seventy-three in pretty good shape.

Dr. Curtis Williams, my primary care doctor, put me on Eliquis, an anticoagulant. Until then, when nurses would ask me for a list of my medications, I could tell them I wasn't taking any. On a visit to his office, I was on a crowded elevator, mostly filled with people of my generation. On the elevator's first stop, an energetic young man bolted out the door, shouting, "You all have a great day!" As the door closed behind him, I observed, "Must be a visitor." My fellow riders laughed in agreement.

— • — • —

CHAPTER TWENTY-THREE

HOOP DREAMS
DIE HARD

Having survived twin setbacks, one fiscal and one physical, I decided to press on with my challenging hoop endeavors. Working out in mid-April at the OU basketball practice gym, I noticed Buddy Hield shooting around at the other end of the court. After leading OU's basketball team to the Final Four, Buddy was preparing for his upcoming NBA basketball career. Having read recently that Buddy was a huge Kobe Bryant fan, I invited him to join me for the Thunder's home game versus the Los Angeles Lakers. The game would be the last NBA road game in Kobe's twenty-year NBA career. At first, Buddy jumped at the chance to see his hero, but then seemed disappointed when he realized he had a conflict that night. He had to attend an awards banquet in Oklahoma City to receive the Oscar Robertson Trophy as the nation's best college basketball player. Both events started at 7 pm on the following Monday.

"Can I come at half?" he asked.

"Sure," I replied, but worried that by the time he got there the game would be nearly over.

According to news reports the next morning, Buddy accepted his award, gave a very short acceptance speech, said he had to go see Kobe play against the Thunder, and bolted out the door. I was surprised when Buddy joined me early in the second half. Kobe had scored 13 points in the first quarter and was playing when Buddy walked in. Standing in the corner a few feet away from us, Kobe acknowledged his arrival and Buddy advised him to put up a quick three-point shot. They kept up some friendly banter during the game. Kobe seemed relaxed and unconcerned that the Lakers were trailing by 30 points. He must have been resting up for his historic 60-point scoring binge in the final game of his career, two nights later in Los Angeles.

The next time I saw Buddy, a few days later, he was finishing a workout at the OU practice gym. Buddy couldn't thank me enough for inviting him to see Kobe at the Thunder game. Finally, on his fourth "thank you," I replied, "If you really want to thank me, play me a game of 'No-dunk Horse.'" He looked surprised. "I'll beat you," he warned. I said that would be ok, and we set up a game for noon the next day.

I arrived at the gym at eleven the next morning, knowing I would need a good warm-up before our game. Buddy, known for his strong work ethic, had been there all morning. I warmed up awhile, but not long enough, and Buddy, shooting a bunch of runners off the wrong foot, skunked me in the first game. I had planned to "hold serve" with a steady diet of mid-range jumpers, but I was a little too pumped up and was shooting long. He agreed to play me one more game. To take advantage of my extra adrenaline, I moved out to NBA three-point range and hit three in a row, shocking the small crowd that had drifted in and stayed to watch us play. Buddy matched my first two three-pointers, but missed the third, receiving an "H."

Not wanting to take any chances of an upset, Buddy resorted to a collection of "Horse shots." I matched a couple of his very deep corner shots, launched from a few feet out of bounds. But when he started hitting high-arching shots from directly behind the glass backboard, he found a shot I couldn't make and quickly finished me off. It was fun, though. (When Buddy won the three-point shooting contest during the 2020 NBA All Star weekend, the value of the "H" I put on him during our Horse game went up dramatically.)

Early in the second half of the infamous game six of the Thunder versus Warriors 2016 Western Conference Finals, I was shocked to see a swarm of players, led by Stephen Curry, pursing the basketball and headed right toward me. I extended both hands in self-defense, and Curry veered off to my right, a step away from landing on Emily. I planted my right hand on Curry's chest, right on the Warrior logo on his jersey, and slowed his momentum as he fell toward us. He quickly bounced off my hand and returned to the fray on the court. Emily, a former point guard herself, told me she could have caught him, implying that she might have enjoyed taking the charge. I told her I realized he is cute, but my dad impulse to protect my daughter had taken over.

On the Fourth of July, 2016, Kevin Durant declared his independence from the Oklahoma City Thunder and became a free agent. Dribbling a red-white-and-blue basketball and following my granddaughter Millie during a neighborhood Independence Day parade that morning, I had been confident he would re-sign with the Thunder. I was shocked and disappointed when I learned he had decided to leave, after the Thunder had come so close to defeating the Golden State Warriors in the Western Conference Finals a few weeks earlier.

Prior to the Thunder's classic "cupcake" game, which marked Kevin Durant's first game in Oklahoma City since joining the Golden State Warriors, I saw his mom, Wanda Pratt, standing at mid-court. I waved to her, and as my former courtside seat neighbor for the past five seasons, she came over to my seat and gave me a big hug. As the game went on, I was a little shocked by the level of sheer hostility directed toward Kevin by the vast majority of the jilted Thunder fans. Apparently, some fans had confused signing a contract to play for the Thunder with checking into the Hotel California, where "you can check out any time you want, but you can never leave."

Fan Charging

Attending a Thunder home game versus the Memphis Grizzlies in January 2017, I had another close encounter with an NBA player. Shortly after tip-off, the Thunder fans were still standing, awaiting our team's first basket, when the Grizzlies' Tony Allen, a veteran 6' 2" guard from Oklahoma State, made an airborne attempt to block a three-point shot by Russell Westbrook. Allen failed to block the shot, but his momentum carried him on a path straight toward me. He extended both arms and pushed off my chest with both hands, the quicker to get back into the play. His push-off sent me flying backward, my feet in the air, and my back crashing into my courtside seat. Fortunately, in the Thunder's home arena, the courtside seats are well-padded and connected to each other in a long row. I ricocheted off my seat and back onto my feet, as if I had done a seat drop on a trampoline. I immediately put my right hand on the back of my neck, making a referee's signal for a charging foul. Some of the fans nearby got my point.

Honoring a Fallen Brother

A moving event occurred during a midseason basketball "Bedlam" clash between OU and OSU in Norman. A local car dealer sponsored a brief "Patriot of the Game" ceremony during the first media time-out of each Sooner home game to honor a member of the military, often for service in Iraq or Afghanistan. At this game, a fraternity brother of mine, Mike Thomas, was honored posthumously. A Marine lieutenant, Mike was killed in Vietnam in 1967 after saving the lives of several men in his unit. He was awarded a Navy Cross for his heroism. As a Sigma Chi at OU, Mike was a popular, care-free guy who played forward on our fraternity basketball team. If you had known him then, you would never have expected him to join the Marine Corps. But most of us who graduated from OU in the mid-1960s were destined to be in the military one way or another, due to the buildup of forces for the Vietnam War. Nearly all of Mike's fraternity brothers were in their seventies, retired, veterans, on Social Security, and on social media. When the word got out about Mike being honored at the game, Sigs from all over the country started asking for tickets. The on-court ceremony included members of Mike's family and his Marine squad, including one of the men whose life he had saved. Looking on from the area behind the south basket were about thirty-five Sigma Chi's, along with their wives and grown kids, gathered in his honor. After a moving excerpt from his Navy Cross citation was read to the crowd, they erupted in a standing ovation.

Since Coach Krzyzewski is a West Point graduate and served there as an assistant to Coach Bob Knight, I thought he would be interested in Mike's ceremony, so I mentioned it in a post K Academy letter. (We had exchanged letters and note cards from time to time since I was on his team during my second Michael

Jordan camp in 2004.) His note cards were usually handwritten, but this time he responded by email, saying: "All of us should be forever grateful for the many, many men and women who have given their lives to protect our freedoms. The Sigma Chi's came out strong that night to honor Mike and the principles and values he died for. I am standing now as I give an ovation to all of you!"

After a Thunder home game that spring, I looked down the courtside toward the ABC Sports broadcast area and saw Sage Steele, the basketball commentator I had met at the Team USA fantasy camp in Las Vegas in 2015. I waved to her and was a little surprised when she waved back, as if she remembered me. As I walked down the court to say hello, I noticed I was being eyed suspiciously by a uniformed security guard apparently assigned to protect her. Being in Oklahoma, where people tend to be inclusive, I explained to the security guard that I had met Ms. Steele in Las Vegas, at a Team USA basketball fantasy camp, and that she had been skeptical of my claim to be a seventy-two-year-old basketball player, until Blake Griffin came up and said I was his shooting guard at OU. The security guard seemed a little perplexed, as if he had not expected to be included in the conversation. Sage said she remembered me.

"You're the guy who won the game," she added, probably referring to my hitting two free throws in the waning seconds of a close game in the Team USA camp tournament.

A Quick Business Update
Terry and I sold our Washington, DC, Ritz-Carlton penthouse in June and reinvested the money in our family businesses. For eleven years, our Norman and Narvik families had enjoyed the condo's convenient location, halfway between Norman and Norway.

Anadarko Minerals launched its first comeback during the summer of 2017. We bought a package of interests in producing wells and leases in Garfield County, Oklahoma, for $2.3 million. This was quickly followed by a winning four lots being sold on an online auction for $3.96 million. The lots included interests in a total of seventy-two wells scattered around Western Oklahoma. We were back in the hunt.

Your Jumper Still Works!

As my ninth K Academy approached in June 2017, I felt behind the curve in my conditioning for the camp, set back that spring by some crankiness in my right knee, the one missing its ACL for the past eleven years. I was drafted by former Duke star Chris Carraway, an assistant coach at Marquette. During the first game of camp, I made the mistake of crashing the boards for a rebound. I bounced off one of the bigger guys and landed on my neck and shoulders, under the basket. My neck was stiff and sore that evening. I told Coach Carraway I should be able to play the next day, but I might be making a lot of no-look passes if I still couldn't turn my head.

Shortly after the camp, I received a note from Coach K commenting: "Your jumper still works!" In an email later that summer, he added: "I actually think you are better in your seventies than you were in your sixties." (Actually, I was better in *the* 60s.)

That August, my seventh consecutive OU Varsity Alumni game found me playing point guard on a team with just eight players. In a play destined for my memory bank of highlights, I stole the ball from former OU great Daryle "Choo" Kennedy as he attempted to blow by me with an exposed cross-dribble. (This steal was nearly identical to the one I had made from Marques Haynes in 1963, not to mention the one from Rick Barry nearly fifty years later.) Having always felt you should get to shoot what you steal, I scooped up the loose ball, dribbled full speed toward our basket, and pulled up for a three-point shot. My shot went in, and crawled back out, triggering a loud and heartfelt groan from the crowd. It seemed a growing number of the OU alumni game fans had done the math and figured out that if I last played at OU in 1962, I must be seriously old.

At seventy-four, but not feeling my age, I headed to Kevin Durant's fantasy camp, held in the Golden State Warriors' practice facility in Oakland, California. Unlike many Thunder fans, I was not still mad about Kevin's bailing out on the Thunder. Emily, Russ, and Millie joined me for a quick trip via NetJets. I was drafted by former NBA coach and longtime television analyst Mike Fratella. He had been a head coach in the NBA for seventeen seasons, with stints at Atlanta, Cleveland, and Memphis. He knew me from various fantasy camps over the past fourteen years. In a triumph of hope over reason, I contributed to Kevin's charitable foundation to enter a game of On the Rack. Since the game included Kevin and Chris Mullin, two of the best shooters in basketball, my chance of winning was slim. Unlike in my surprising performance in the On the Rack shoot-out with Kevin at OU four years earlier, my shooting in this game was off and I was quickly eliminated. But Kevin and Chris put on an awesome shooting display, each burying countless NBA three-pointers until Kevin finally missed one, giving Chris the win.

In mid-January 2018, my first basketball season over seventy-five got off to a surprisingly good start. I was facing a passive zone defense in a pick-up game at a local church. Shooting barely challenged jump shots from the baselines and wings, I hit nine in a row, scoring 19 of our team's 21 points in a quick victory. I had hoped to keep playing at seventy-five, but this was ridiculous.

Millie, taking photos at Kevin Durant camp

Elevator Pitch!

Emily and I attended a reception for NBA Commissioner Adam Silver in the Thunder's corporate headquarters, located in the southwest corner of Chesapeake Energy Arena, prior to a home game late that season. The commissioner gave a talk and answered questions about the NBA from Thunder fans who happened to be corporate sponsors or courtside ticket buyers.

After his talk, Emily and I found ourselves on a crowded elevator with Commissioner Silver, Thunder chairman Clay Bennett and members of their respective entourages and staffs. Standing behind the appropriately tall commissioner, I reached up and tapped him on the shoulder. As he turned around, I raised my hand and said, loud enough for everyone on board to hear, "Elevator pitch!" He gave me a curious look and I announced, "I would like to play in the celebrity game during next year's All-Star weekend."

Surprisingly, he said, "OK . . . the game is in Charlotte."

Always willing to take "yes" for an answer, I responded: "I'll be there."

At that point, Clay Bennett chimed in with an endorsement: "He's really good."

(I didn't know where he got that idea. I didn't even know they were scouting me.)

Just then, the fifteen-second elevator ride was over, and everyone went their separate ways. Strangely, that incident was a special moment to me, as it brought together three of my major selves: floor seat guy, basketball nut, and humorist. (It was my humor impulse that made my making an elevator pitch on an actual elevator too funny to pass up.)

Later, I began to fear that the Commissioner had responded so quickly he might have thought I was kidding. I sent him an email, via a Thunder executive, explaining that I was serious, as playing in that game would make a great story for the book I was writing about my basketball career.

After giving the concept of fame a lot of thought, I had decided that the only thing better than being rich and famous is being rich and obscure. However, the thought of playing on national TV in the NBA celebrity game seemed like so much fun that I was willing to give up my quiet life in low-profile, low-stress obscurity for the chance to play in that game.

Commissioner Silver responded to my email, noting that I was "obviously passionate about the game." He added that he had forwarded my email to the man on his staff in charge of selecting the rosters for the celebrity game, who later emailed me to suggest that I contact him in the fall to follow up. The guy's contact information said he was an "influencer." Googling what that meant, I figured his job must be to influence people on social media. Since I only have about twenty Twitter followers and haven't tweeted anything in the past few years, I was concerned that my lack of influence might be a problem.

During the four months leading up to my tenth K Academy in June 2018, I played full-court pick-up ball for about an hour and a half, three days a week, at the church. I was getting in pretty good condition when, in mid-May, I pulled some muscles in my groin and abdominal areas. Although these injuries were not painful at rest, I looked like a penguin trying to run.

My drill for determining if I am in camp shape was as follows: Dribbling full speed from one basket to the other and back, I shot layups on the first trip, runners on the second, pull-up jumpers on the third, and college three-pointers on the fourth. After these eight full-court sprints, if I can hit the final three-point shot comfortably, then I can declare myself ready for camp. In mid-May, I was still injured and nowhere close to being in "camp shape," so I dropped out of that year's K Academy.

When the OU Varsity Alumni Game rolled around in August, my injuries had still not healed. I could jog gingerly, but I couldn't even stride, let alone sprint. I had to opt out of the game, no doubt disappointing my nascent fan base.

In September, always the optimist, I contacted the NBA influencer to follow up on my quest to play in the NBA celebrity game, alongside rappers who I had never heard of, but probably had millions of followers on social media. In social climbing, I had always subscribed to the theory that success is not based on who you know. It's based on who knows you. While I was obviously not a celebrity, I was known in certain basketball circles by people like Mike Krzyzewski, Dwyane Wade, Kevin Durant, Mike Fratello, and Jay Williams, not to mention my OU friends like Lon Kruger, Blake Griffin, Buddy Hield, and Trae Young. Apparently, my basketball credentials were not strong enough to influence the influencer, who emailed me that I was going to be invited to the NBA All-Star Weekend but did not mention anything about playing in the celebrity game.

I found myself in a "Catch 22" situation. I thought that playing in the celebrity game would make a great story for my book, which in turn would make me a celebrity. But if I had to become a famous writer to get into the game, it would be too late to put my nationally televised celebrity game experience into my book.

My groin and abdominal injuries healed at a snail's pace, keeping me off the basketball court until the following January. When I turned seventy-six, I realized I had reached the fiftieth anniversary of my athletic peak, as I was twenty-six in the previously reported game when I scored thirty-nine points against a Marine Corps team. To celebrate, I went to the YMCA, where I did manage to make fifty-two consecutive free throws, confirming that the free throw is the last thing to go. My health had improved enough that I could jog and stride, but I was still afraid to try to sprint. Meanwhile, the NBA influencer had gone silent, so I emailed him to say that due to my injuries, I would not be able to play in the NBA celebrity game coming up in February. I watched the game on TV, and concluded that, if I had been in camp shape, I could have raised the level of play, while contributing to the NBA's exercise in defining "celebrity" down.

A Rare Condition and a Wounded Knee

In mid-May 2019, with the Duke camp rapidly approaching, I had to notify them once again that my injuries would prevent me from attending. Then, to make matters worse, I had another health setback on the Fourth of July. I woke up that morning experiencing a strange condition: swelling in my ankles, knees, wrists, and hands, and weakness in my calves and quads. These joints were not painful, just swollen and stiff, while these muscles felt rubbery. My primary care doctor said I had a rare condition known as remitting seronegative symmetrical synovitis with pitting edema, or RS3PE syndrome. He said he had seen one case of this syndrome about twelve years ago. It was treated with prednisone and cleared up in about a year. He added, "This condition has a cause, but we don't know what it is." Acquiring such a rare condition seemed like a dubious achievement, like being admitted to an exclusive club. The good news was that the R stood for remitting, so it should gradually go away.

The bad news was that my condition immediately worsened a problem I had been having with my right knee, which would go out suddenly as if I had stepped into a hole, and I would fall to the floor. During the past few years, this would happen once every few months, sometimes after a hard workout. But in my newly acquired condition, it began happening frequently and for no apparent reason, just walking through my home. At the Kevin Durant camp, I had talked about my wounded knee problem with another camper who had been my teammate at a previous K Academy and was a neurological surgeon. He suggested surgery, as had a knee surgeon in Norman. Although my right knee, the one with a severed ACL, was the one collapsing, I felt like it was a nerve problem instead of a ligament or tendon problem. Also, if

I were too old for knee surgery at age sixty-five, I was still too old at seventy-six. Desperate, I called a "Hail Mary" play and went to see Dr. Li, a Norman acupuncturist known for seemingly miracle cures. My injured knee felt better after the first treatment. After six treatments I declared it cured. My RS3PE condition began improving, but at a painfully slow pace. It became clear to me that, after a ten-year run, or possibly jog, I had come to the end of my sixth comeback.

Comic Relief from a Tiny Maltese

Terry always loved our pets, but she had been especially close to Broono, a cocker spaniel who had been her comfort dog for many years while we were living at Hidden Hill II. In recent years, we had often talked about getting another dog, and we ended up adopting a two-year-old Maltese named Dolly. A strong-willed, six-pound bundle of energy, Dolly has proven to be a constant source of entertainment and comic relief. She is not terribly imposing as a watch dog, but she makes a wonderful greeting dog. Whenever someone she knows arrives, she prances around, stands up on her hind legs, and spins around in tiny circles, making our friends and family feel welcome. If she wants to be fed, let outside, or just acknowledged, she is not bashful about barking orders, and if I try to ignore her she will tug on my pant legs to get my attention. Or she will untie my shoelaces, like I untied my dad's when I was her age. When she does something wrong, she is too cute to stay mad at for long. It took her a few months, but she eventually got us trained to respond to her needs and desires.

Playing boardgames with my granddaughter Millie proved to be educational, for me. At age seven, she beat me in *Connect Four*, and blew me away in games of checkers and three-dimensional tic-tac-toe. (Maybe I can lure her into a game of *Scrabble* before her vocabulary gets better than mine, if it's not too late for that.)

A Quick Look Back

Looking back at my quixotic over-sixty basketball career, I must admit that, at first, the little boy in me was a little star struck being around so many famous basketball coaches and players. But now I realize they are nice, normal, highly successful people, with enough natural talent and a strong enough work ethic to climb to the top of a very steep pyramid.

Most of the fantasy campers are highly successful in their day jobs, and their confident and competitive natures show through in their basketball endeavors, irrespective of their basketball skills or experience. As Coach Krzyzewski puts it, the camps give the campers a chance to "just be guys." As a former journalist embedded in the world of fantasy camp basketball, I can report that the camps confirm that "the difference between a man and a boy is the cost of his toys."

My goal in playing fantasy camp basketball has been to play well, not to play well for my age. I have tried to roll back my physiological age, while ignoring my chronological age. I have been playing for the moments, the unexpected flashes from the past. I discovered a strong correlation between how hard I worked out and how well I could play, as if my game had been locked up in my long-term muscle memory, awaiting oxygen.

Based on my experiences playing fantasy camp basketball until age seventy-four, overcoming injuries liked a severed ACL in my right knee, two broken fingers on my shooting hand, a detached ligament in my left biceps, a pulled groin, stretched abdominal muscles, and a detached retina, not to mention an irregular heartbeat, I have concluded that the age factor is overrated. If an NBA player wants to retire at age thirty-six, or even age forty-two, due to injuries or just a desire to move on to another chapter in his life, that's fine. But it is not a player's chronological age that matters. What matters is his physiological age. Although some gradual decline in conditioning due to age is inevitable, most of the decline is due to changes in lifestyle or expectations. With some extra effort, that retirement date can be pushed off for years.

Now that I have been out of action for more than two years, when I resume basketball activities, it will mark the beginning of my seventh comeback. I suspect that the seventh comeback will be the hardest. You may have heard about guys who "hang on too long" and refuse to quit playing. I could be the poster boy for that stubborn demographic.

After seventeen years of going one-on-one with Father Time, I can confirm that the old geezer is a tough opponent. The guy is just relentless. You push him and he pushes back. But don't concede too easily. If you keep playing, you may be able to carve out a decade or more of wonderful experiences that conventional wisdom would have had you leave on the table.

Pressing Ahead

While my basketball career was winding down, my adventures in the oil patch continued to provide daily doses of excitement. Oil and gas prices trended downward during most of 2019, but I viewed these weak markets as a buying opportunity. Our bankers at the Bank of Oklahoma did not share my optimism, and we had no room for additional borrowing under our loan agreement. Nevertheless, when two packages of small, non-operated working interests in wells located in active Anadarko Basin drilling areas came on the market that spring, I decided to evaluate them while looking for new sources of financing.

Although making additional acquisitions when already well leveraged can be risky, I felt that increasing AMI's proved producing reserves during a down market was a better long-term strategy than cutting back on our overhead or debt.

By late August, we were able to close both acquisitions for a total price of about $13 million, even though financing these deals required moving our banking business to Arvest Bank.

Having placed our bets with these two acquisitions and with little "dry powder" to finance additional purchases, I decided it would be a good time for me to step down as chief executive officer of Anadarko Minerals and turn over the responsibility for the company's day-to-day operations to my son-in-law, Ole, who had served as our chief financial officer since joining the company in 2007. My other son-in-law, Russ, continued to work with Emily in managing our Norman real estate business, Dutcher Investment Properties, and in buying investment properties for themselves.

My favorite coach, Sid Burton, was inducted into the Bartlesville Athletic Hall of Fame in October. A two-part feature on Coach Burton in the *Bartlesville Examiner-Enterprise* reported that as head coach of the 1966–67 College High basketball team, he led the Wildcats to the AAA state championship, upsetting highly favored Oklahoma City Douglas. The story noted that "Douglas was billed as King Kong in the final, while the Wildcats were mostly consigned to the Fay Wray role." It could have mentioned that Sid was the assistant coach for our Wildcat team that upset top-ranked Douglas in the 1961 state tournament semi-finals.

Sid's story continued: "His journey took him to Rose State College, where he coached women's basketball and taught for seventeen years prior to retiring. One of his biggest thrills at Rose State was coaching Emily Dutcher, the daughter of Bill Dutcher, who he had coached." Emily and I were thrilled that he was thrilled by coaching her. She was afraid he would not even remember her.

In December, Anne flew to Washington, DC, to see a surgeon who had operated on her successfully a few years before. This time, surgery was needed to remove a tumor in her left breast. Lab tests showed that the tumor was cancerous, but the surgeon was confident that its removal had left Anne cancer free. However, as a precaution, Anne was advised to undertake a lengthy program of chemotherapy and radiation treatments, in case the cancer had spread to other parts of her body. The idea that Anne could have cancer was soul piercing. On the night we got the news, I was praying for her health and had an experience I had never felt before. I felt that God was listening. Not that He responded, but that He heard me. Before, whenever I had prayed for someone, it felt like I was just putting a message in a bottle and dropping it in the ocean. Anne had her first chemotherapy session after Christmas and basically put her life on hold for the duration of the treatments. Somehow, she was able to keep her spirits up and stay positive about the outlook for her health.

Ole's role as AMI's CEO started out smoothly enough, allowing him time to deal with Anne's health crisis and support Hanna's budding career in musical theater. In January 2020, twelve-year-old Hanna starred as Mary Poppins in the Sooner Theatre's presentation of *Mary Poppins, Jr.* I was blown away by her performance: acting, singing, dancing, and flying above the stage supported by nothing but an umbrella and a few invisible wires.

The shocking coronavirus pandemic brought the NBA season to an abrupt halt on March 11, 2020. Just before the tip-off of a

Thunder home game versus the Utah Jazz, the discovery that Jazz center Rudy Gobert had tested positive for the virus resulted in the NBA postponing the game and ultimately the season. At the time, the Thunder were ranked fifth in the Western Conference standings, greatly exceeding the low expectations at the beginning of the season.

Ole's job as CEO got a lot more difficult, as the oil and gas industry was slammed on three fronts. First, a mild winter had left a surplus in natural gas supplies that was driving down its price. Then, a battle for world market share led to Saudi Arabia and Russia engaging in a price war that drove down the world oil price. The third blow came on the demand side, when a worldwide shutdown of economic activity to battle the coronavirus pandemic drove already low oil and gas prices to bargain basement levels. The confluence of these three forces threw Anadarko Minerals and most of the nation's other oil and gas companies into a crisis mode, fighting for survival. Still recovering from the 2014 thru 2016 downturn, AMI was forced to make another round of severe cuts in its staff and expenses, while shutting in or shedding uneconomic wells.

At least the summer brought some relief on the health front. Anne completed her chemotherapy and radiation treatments and was able to "ring the bell" signifying she is cancer free. Meanwhile, my episodes that had been previously diagnosed as warning strokes were reevaluated by my doctors and were determined to have been caused by vertigo. Since I would rather deal with an inner ear problem than a heart problem, I took this as good news.

After fighting off cancer for numerous rounds over many years, Del finally lost one and passed away in July, at the age of eighty. After working as a banker for a few years in Tulsa, he moved to Bartlesville and began a long career as a commercial catfish farmer, building twenty lakes and ponds on a ranch east of town. As an athlete, Marine, rancher, hunter, and fisherman, Del was a classic man's man. Del and Dona had three children, fourteen grandchildren and five great-grandchildren. I had always had the feeling that my big brother was running interference for me as we advanced through the years. With him gone, I am feeling more exposed as I move toward whatever fate awaits me.

Given our age and health issues, Terry and I began hiding out from the pandemic in late March, staying at home and relying on Amazon, QVC, UPS, Federal Express and, most importantly, the younger generation to keep us supplied with groceries and other essentials. Since I have been working from home for most of this century, our recusal from normality hasn't been much of change for us. We just pretended to be Bonnie and Clyde, lying low and hoping the virus will not find us. Once we received our Covid-19 vaccinations, I felt free to move about the outside world, resuming my hunting and gathering activities.

My over-sixty basketball career, including twenty-four fantasy camps and seven OU Varsity Alumni games, had become a challenging lifestyle that kept me active, healthy, and looking forward to my next business venture or hoops adventure. However, at seventy-eight, barring a quick economic recovery and a miraculous seventh comeback, those days of competitive hooping are probably behind me. I can still shoot hoops with Emily in the driveway but getting back into fantasy camp condition may be a bridge too far.

Socrates sagaciously observed that, "The unexamined life is not worth living." I would add that the unlived life is not worth examining. While examining my life for this book, I wondered where I would land in history if I subtracted my current age from my birth date, as if, at birth, I had moved back in time instead of forward. I was born in 1943. After living seventy-eight years, but moving back in time, I would be back to 1865, the year marked by the end of the Civil War and the assassination of President Abraham Lincoln. Those momentous events seem like ancient history, but realizing they were within my lifespan makes them seem more immediate. But, as the Prophet writes, "Life goes not backward, nor tarries with yesterday."

Pressing ahead, I am keeping an eye on our family companies, as we wheel and deal in the always volatile, never dull, and now improving real estate and energy businesses. Business aside, where it should be, I recently found myself in the kitchen with all my girls. I was helping Terry reorganize our freezer, while Anne, Emily, Hanna, and Millie were visiting at our kitchen table. I asked Emily if Hanna and Millie had seen her favorite video clips from the *I Love Lucy* television shows. They had not. Before long, all four were gathered around a laptop, laughing hysterically at Lucy stomping grapes in Italy. When they began watching the skit with Lucy and Ethel wrapping chocolates on an assembly line in a candy factory, I knew what was coming and couldn't resist joining in the fun. As the assembly line speeds up, Lucy and Ethel start getting behind and begin stuffing chocolates in their mouths and into their blouses. When they began hiding the chocolates under their hats, the decibel level from the laughter in our kitchen reached levels I last heard during a fourth-quarter rally at a Thunder game. I have found satisfaction with colleagues at work and excitement with teammates in sports, but to find pure joy there is no one like family and no place like home.

— • — • —

EPILOGUE

Now *that you have read the string of anecdotes* that have made up my life, you may (or may not) be wondering what I have learned from these experiences.

Life is how you look at it. As I survey the human comedy, I try not to take myself too seriously. As noted earlier, the autobiography I wrote in the third grade was entitled: "What I have lived through." At age seventy-eight, I feel like I have lived through enough to offer a few specific suggestions. So, listen up, boys and girls. Here are some ideas that might help you become a winner in the game of life.

In high school, learn as much as you can. In the long run, it is what you learned, not what grades you received, that matters. Play at least one team sport. Coaches make strong role models and can teach you the value of teamwork, and teammates often become lifelong friends.

In college, learn something useful, join a fraternity or sorority, have fun, but don't turn your college years into a four-year vacation. If you can't earn a scholarship in a Varsity sport, walk on or play intramurals. Find a part-time job to keep down your student debt.

Staying busy will force you to learn how to manage your time, a useful skill no matter what you do in life.

After college, volunteer for military service. You will be given more responsibility in the military during your early twenties than you would in most civilian pursuits. While the time spent in military service may put you behind your contemporaries in the job market, the experience and maturity gained should allow you to move past them if you stay alert to new opportunities. And you will have served your country.

Enjoying another sunset over Ten Mile Flats

Do not have a career. Have a life in which your work is an important part but does not crowd out time for your family life, your health, or your fun. Do not use working for your family as an excuse for staying away from them. If being devoted to an abstraction called your career requires you to invest too much of yourself in its pursuit, you may end up succeeding in your career but failing in life. Your work allows you to make a living and contribute to society, but it doesn't define who you are. It's just what you do. Find a job or start a business that lets you set your own schedule, then do not work for more than six hours a day, six days a week.

Marry someone you love and stay married. If you have problems, work them out. Guys, if you are frustrated, discontent, or angry with your wife, step back and look at her as the person you fell in love with. Unpack all the baggage of expectations you have loaded her down with, all the things she "should be doing" as your wife. Give her a break. Give her credit for her efforts. Imagine what kind of life she could be living if she had not gotten tied up with you. You may not be the easiest person to live with.

As you stay together, your shared experiences over a lifetime can deepen your love and pay compound interest. Two whole people, each with their own values and integrity intact, can make a solid couple. Going through life as part of a couple is the best way to go. A whole person will be concerned with what he or she can contribute to a relationship, not just what they can get out it. But two half people cannot complete each other.

If you are single and looking, just work on fulfilling your own potential until another whole person comes along. (If you have watched enough Hallmark movies, you may believe the best way to meet your future mate is to literally bump into them.) It is better to be single than in a bad relationship, which is the kind you will have with someone who doesn't know who they are and are depending on you to define them.

Have children and treat them as small adults, respecting their personhood as they grow up, not dismissing them as just kids. Especially in their early years, one of their parents should stay home.

Treat everyone you meet with respect. Make true friendships with people of all races, rather than claiming you like all of them, but not actually knowing anyone outside of your own.

Unfortunately, I cannot tell you how to get rich quick. But I have a few ideas that might help you get rich slowly. And, having been poor, rich, and somewhere in between, I can certify that being rich is more expensive and not worth sacrificing your family relationships for. Here are some suggestions.

Look for opportunities to start your own business. Opportunity knocks, but it does not barge in and drag you out of your comfort zone. Do not jump into a business that has low barriers to entry, as you will likely find too much competition. Find a niche where you can provide a product or service that cannot be easily provided by someone else. When looking for that niche, remember that there is opportunity in complexity.

Going out on my own proved to be one of the best life decisions I have ever made. Overnight, work went from being a burden to be tolerated to an adventure to be pursued with high energy, if not passion. I quickly learned that I did not have any problem with authority when I was the one who had it. When you are building your own business, all your efforts can add value that will continue to contribute to your benefit. By contrast, when you are working for a paycheck, you are gaining experience but not equity, so there may be very little carry over value if you leave the job. It is easier to maintain a stable balance between your home life and work life when you are self-employed, and it is easier to be a team player when you are the one calling the plays.

If you have your own business, hire tough and manage easy. Find mature, self-actualizing adults, and treat them as assets to be developed, not costs to be held down. If they have personal difficulties that interfere with their jobs, cut them some slack and show them that loyalty runs both ways. Treat them with respect, not distain. Treated well, your employees will grow with their jobs and keep pace as the company grows. And your place of business will be a pleasant place to be. While profitable growth should remain the objective, realize that there are times when the hardest thing to do is to do nothing. Don't chase growth for growth's sake or create make-work to keep everyone busy. Bigger isn't necessarily better.

This should be obvious, but I will mention it anyway: keep a positive spread between the cost of your financing and the rate of return your business is generating. You do not need a degree in finance, but you should understand the financial concepts of discounted present worth and the accretion of discount, as both are critical in slowly building wealth. If you work smarter, rather than harder, you can build a company that will run itself on a day-to-day basis, leaving you free to set strategy, allocate resources, take the risks, and still have time for your family and other interests. Just be sure you own the business, rather than letting the business own you.

One general observation I have often quoted comes from the Bible: "I returned, and saw under the sun, that the race is not to the swift, nor the battle to the strong . . . but time and chance happeneth to them all." I happen to agree with this view, so I would not go so far as to say that character is fate. But your character, built day by day through thousands of decisions, large and small, will drive the kind of life you live, and will determine how you handle whatever life throws at you. Your choices not only count, they add up. Life is a decision tree and the decisions you make advance you up the tree and out through the branches. (This may explain why some people end up out on a limb.) As you get older, it gets harder to go back and remake the decisions that got you where you are today.

There are no short cuts to being happy. Never dwell on "if only"—that one person, job, place, or thing, just out of reach, that could make you happy, if only they or it were yours. While there is no magic formula for being happy, I believe the essential ingredient is integrity. I define integrity as a "oneness," measured by the degree to which your actual self lives up to your ideal self. Integrity requires doing the right thing, even if it is difficult or beyond what is expected or required. If you feel scattered, like you are watching yourself in a bad movie, you may be losing your integrity. To be happy, you need to keep your integrity intact.

You must also maintain your integrity to develop and keep self-confidence, which you will need in dealing with life's challenges and opportunities. Self-confidence is not something you just have or don't have. Self-confidence is earned by making good decisions. By giving each decision your best shot, you can build a strong sense of self, one that is worthy not only of your own trust and confidence, but the trust and confidence of others.

The stronger your self-confidence, the less you will worry about what other people think of you. A healthy disregard for what others think of you will allow you to take more risks, because it will reduce your fear of failure, and it will allow you to get up, dust yourself off, and try again if you do fail. You don't have to be right all the time, but it helps to be right more often than you are wrong. Just realize that the only people who do not make mistakes are people who do not do anything. As your risk tolerance increases along with your self-confidence, you can become a force, a person who makes things happen, instead of a person who just reacts as things happen to them.

Another value essential to maintaining your integrity is loyalty. You certainly owe loyalty to your family. If they cannot trust you, who can? You also owe loyalty to your friends and coworkers. Even though you may regard your relationship with your employer as more of an arms-length negotiation, a deal is a deal and you need to keep up your end of it while you are cashing your paycheck. In any relationship where other people are counting on you to perform, to contribute to a team goal, if you give less than your best effort you are chipping away at your own integrity and cheating your own chance for happiness, even if you seem to be getting by with less than your best.

There are some mistakes that you will never quit paying for. You may just have to accept these payments as part of the cost of living. It is better to avoid these mistakes, no matter how strong the pull of immediate gratification or imagined upside. While there may be times when you need to forgive yourself and try to put your bad decisions behind you, don't get too good at this. Feel free to beat yourself up for a while.

You should rein in your self-confidence well short of arrogance. Hubris and pride appear during the boom and are punctured during the bust. The success you enjoy during a boom may be magnified by market forces creating a wind at your back. Moreover, arrogance can cloud your judgment. It is hard to see the downside with your head in the clouds. Yes, things happen for a reason, but not necessarily for a good one. Accept good fortune gratefully and skeptically, because markets can turn down gradually, then crash suddenly. You will need to be resilient when they do.

Ironically, you have a better chance of getting rich if you are not materialistic. People overly concerned with the material things in life are likely to be too afraid of losing something to take the risks required to make any serious money. Our economic system is called capitalism for a reason: it's about risking capital today for the possibility of creating more capital tomorrow. Blessed are the risk-takers, for they create jobs.

Give out of generosity, or a desire to help others, not out of an obligation to "give back." If you have earned your wealth honestly, then you have already provided others with a product or service that was worth more to them than the resources you used to provide it. That difference in value was your well-earned profit, yours to give away as much or as little as you would like. So, give your money, and your time, until it feels good.

Show your love for the people closest to you, the people who love you, your inner circle. There should be a few loved ones in your life who you care more about than yourself. The ones you would storm the beach for. It can be hard to get outside of yourself enough to really love someone. But during the best of times, you will want someone to share the joy, and during the worst of times, you will need someone to share the pain. To have them then, you need to love them during ordinary times, when your own needs are clamoring for attention. Loves grows through shared experiences, easy or hard, exciting or mundane. And, unlike money, the more love you give today, the more you will have tomorrow.

Maintaining your integrity by staying true to your core values can be made easier if you approach your life with realistic expectations. One thing that impresses me about life is its temporary nature. Like Old Man River, it just keeps rolling along. If there is a life after death, I hope my spirit is invited to participate. But I believe this life should be lived as if it is the only one we will know. This approach focuses the mind on what we can do each day to make this life better for ourselves, our loved ones, and those around us.

Don't expect life to be easy. Life is hard, because its unanswered questions are hard. It seems mankind has been given a mind capable of asking difficult questions about life, but unable to find or grasp the answers. At some point, reason must give way to faith. I believe in a God who created the universe. The laws of physics and nature are too eloquent to have been created by chance. Does God care about every living creature? Possibly. Does He care what name we call him by? Probably not. I believe you can be spiritual without being religious, in a going to church on Sunday, organized religion sort of way. If God does judge how we spent our time on earth, I would rather be judged on how I treated other people than on how many hours I spent in church. Surely God can distinguish substance from form. And if you seek to be pure in spirit, love God and life, and are open to God's love and forgiveness, then why do you need intermediaries to relate to God? If you do, fine. Go to church. Participate in the rituals and ceremonies. Sing in the choir. But don't check your spirituality at the door as you leave. Carry it with you in your daily life, in the way you relate to and care about others.

Alexander Pope wrote: "Hope springs eternal in the human breast . . . Man never is, but is always 'to be' blessed." Despite its complexities, even its tragedies, life is good, people can be good, good things happen. Be aware of life's dangers, be open to life's possibilities, and contribute in your way to make life better. Start with your closest relationships, where the way you live your life will have the most impact, and work out from there. Does everyone get what they deserve? Surely not. Some get more, some get less. But there is always that chance, so live your life in a way that if you do get what you deserve, you will be happy with that outcome.

— • — • —

Made in the USA
Coppell, TX
09 May 2022

77605119R00249